SILENT EXODUS

SILENT EXODUS

A first-hand experience and academic exploration of
the complicated challenges of leading a Latino
church in the twenty-first century.

STEVE PINTO

XULON PRESS

Xulon Press
2301 Lucien Way #415
Maitland, FL 32751
407.339.4217
www.xulonpress.com

Unless otherwise indicated, Scripture quotations taken from The Holy Bible, NIV. (1984). Grand Rapids: Zondervan Publishing House. Used by permission. All rights reserved.

Scripture quotations taken from Santa Biblia: Reina-Valera. (1995). Miami, FL: Sociedades Bíblicas Unidas. Used by permission. All rights reserved.

New King James Version. (1982). HarperCollins Publishers. Used by permission. All rights reserved.

Printed in the United States of America.

ISBN-13: 978-1-6628-0500-4

To my beloved wife and children,
to my dedicated parents, to the Pinto Tribe,
and to the pastors, elders, leaders, and volunteers of Faro Church.
Thank you for your continued support, encouragement,
and understanding.

———————

CONTENTS

THE SILENT EXODUS

"The silent exodus is a crisis of infertility and preservation, an inability to retain and reclaim emerging generations due primarily to changing demographics, an increase of influence of post-modernistic thought, a void of relevant leadership, and recent challenges with technological advances."

Several years ago, my wife and I went to a Claim Jumper restaurant on a date. When we arrived, we were greeted and given a booth to sit somewhere in the back of the restaurant. After the greeter showed us our table, she left and said that our server would be with us momentarily. As my wife and I sat and talked for a while, we realized that our waiter was taking a long time to take our order. So, I said to my wife, "Let's play a game. Let's sit here and see how long it takes for someone to serve us." She agreed.

As we waited, we just enjoyed each other's company and talked. Every few minutes, we would comment, wondering where the waiter could be, and joked if it was even possible for them to forget about us entirely.

Ten minutes turned into twenty minutes and twenty into thirty minutes. Ultimately, we agreed that we would wait ten more minutes. If they did not acknowledge us by the end of the appointed time, we would leave and eat elsewhere. We waited ten more minutes, a total of

1

forty minutes, and no one realized or acknowledged that we were there. So, we left.

We walked out through the front door, and no one noticed anything. We came in, sat in an air-conditioned room for about forty minutes, and walked out, and nobody saw it or recognized it. That is what you call a *silent exodus*!

After being welcomed and led to our table, none of the Claim Jumper employees realized that we were in their restaurant. No one realized we left, and, in the process, they lost our business and gained some bad publicity from this book.

Recently, we drove by the same Claim Jumper, and my son asked me, "Dad, is the food there good?" I answered, "I do not know; I did not get to try it. Their food may be delicious, but your mom and I never got to experience it."

I have entitled this book *The Silent Exodus* to encourage Latino church leaders to individually and corporately reclaim and retain our present and future generations that are silently leaving our churches and, more specifically, first-generation monolingual churches.

There is a silent exodus happening in America at large and in Latino churches in general. The silent exodus is a crisis of infertility and preservation, an inability to retain and reclaim emerging generations due primarily to changing demographics, an increase of influence of post-modernistic thought, a void of relevant leadership, and recent challenges with technological advances. Unless the church takes Latino teenagers and emerging adults—who are the primary targets of these challenges—more seriously, the future of the Latino church is in doubt.

I write this book amid a worldwide pandemic caused by the coronavirus, a financial crisis due to a national quarantine, a countrywide movement of protests, and during a deep political divide, the likes of which perhaps we have never experienced before. All of our establishments, institutions, organizations, and even churches are being morally questioned, fundamentally challenged, and fiscally strained. People are startled, scared, suffering, and need clear direction and hope in dark times. I hope that this book provides some encouragement and clarity in these complicated and complex times.

Sadly, there is a void of strong, healthy, and relevant spiritual leadership in the church at large, and as this book will explain, specifically among the Latino church. Amid these crises, I have often asked myself where the Latino generational church heroes and influencers are. Where are the Latino church leaders who can provide sound and biblical guidance to the church during these challenging times?

This book is about a generation of US-born Latinos who are leaving the churches founded by their immigrant parents in search of social influencers, spiritual heroes, biblical clarity, and ecclesiastical leadership elsewhere because of a reluctance among foreign-born church leaders to prioritize changing demographics at the expense of cultural tradition and lack of cultural awareness and relevancy.

This book explores, from first-hand experience and academic exploration, the complicated challenges of being part of, serving in, and developing a Latino church in the twenty-first century here in the United States. As first-generation immigrants age out of their leadership, and the Latino church progresses into the second and third generations, how does the Latino church continue to endure? What should a Latino church look like today?

Moreover, this book will critically engage the complexities of Latino culture, theology, and leadership among multigenerational realities. How does the Latino church face the challenge of making space for multigenerational identities and developing the leadership skills to embrace predominantly Latino communities that are increasingly becoming monolingual and multicultural? These questions and more are what I explore in this book.

Historically, this is a considerable undertaking as ministry trends and outreach do not adapt to expected shifts in population, sociological factors, and the growth of English-dominant Latinos. According to Rodríguez (2009), denominational and local churches have used a monolingual model of outreach to Latinos in the United States that is generally unsuccessful. Rodríguez explained, "During the past one hundred and fifty years of mission among Latinos in the United States, most denominational and local church leaders have assumed a 'Spanish-speaking church model'" (Rodríguez, 2009, p. 103). He argued that this model "still dominates the landscape of Latino ministries among evangelicals in the United States" (Rodríguez, 2009, p. 103).

Given considerable changing differences in population, sociological factors, fluency in English, and religious attitudes between foreign-born Latinos and native-born Latinos, there are profound implications for many realms of the mission of Latino churches in America and indeed for anyone seeking to understand the nature of changing demographics in multicultural yet monoethnic churches in the United States.

I hope that this book can equip pastors and emerging leaders for positional and non-positional leadership in Latino ministry settings. Leading strategically in a Latino church context requires critically engaging the complexities of Latino culture, theology, leadership, and multigenerational realities.

Today's Latino churches face the challenge of making space for multigenerational identities and developing the leadership skills to embrace predominantly Latino communities that are increasingly becoming more bilingual or monolingual (English-speaking only) bilingual and multicultural.

In my doctoral research, I researched certain ethnic groups who, similar to the Latino church, are losing their ability to keep their emerging adults due to their inability to communicate and connect with them. The first-generation leadership of pastors, elders, and deacons are unwilling to make cultural recognitions to shepherd their emerging adults effectively. They feel that one of the church's purposes is to be a haven where the ethnic culture and language are kept safe and retained.

I found that these ethnic churches choose between going out of business or developing a new ministry focus. Those ethnic churches that widen their base of relevance see organizational survival as a possibility and begin preventing the silent exodus of emerging generations.

Without question, Latino churches do change in response to the demands of growing second and third generations. I am convinced that the commitment to certain cultural forms far outweighs the obligation to the Gospel's message in too many Latino churches. However, we must remember and accept that churches do not exist to primarily keep the culture and language of a particular country or ethnicity. It exists to preach the gospel and to make disciples.

That is the reason why this book is divided into three subject matters: *Understanding Changing Demographics Among Latinos in America* (Part One), how to *Prepare for the Recruitment and Retention of Emerging Generations of Latinos* (Part Two), and *Leading the Latino Church in the Twenty-First Century* (Part Three). Each requires careful study and appreciation and must be studied in context. None of these topics stand alone, but in conjunction, contribute to the silent exodus of US-born Latinos.

Additionally, this book encompasses the significance of implementing bilingual and monolingual English church services to reduce the silent exodus of second-and third-plus generation Latinos and intermarried Latinos to meet the changing demographics described in this book.

The Silent Exodus in General Terms

I have been teaching youth ministry courses for over fifteen years. I have continuously kept my finger on the pulse of youth ministry across the country and in the Latino community. I have found that the Latino church is not exempt from the exodus of emerging generations; it is just not as equally documented due to the lack of scholarship in this area. Therefore, identifying the silent exodus begins in general terms.

Much has been written about both the biblical illiteracy of the emerging generation of believers and the silent exodus of young people from the church in general. Many have documented this drift, and I have witnessed it anecdotally as a youth pastor and pastor for about twenty years.

There is a silent exodus happening in America and, by de facto, in Latino churches in general. The growing statistics should alarm us enough to do something about the dilemma. Larry Barnett's 2016 NextGen research revealed that Christianity's decline in the United States spans every population segment—young and old, male and female, within every race, at all income and educational levels, and in every geographic region. He explains that adults (and teens) who are younger, highly educated, knowledgeable, high achieving, technologically engaged individuals who may have religiously diverse friends are the most likely to leave the faith.

Generally speaking, most prominent surveys today find that about 70 percent of teenagers involved in church youth groups stop attending church within two years of their high school graduation. This is true across denominations. For example, Kingsriter reported that between 50 percent and 66.7 percent of Assemblies of God young people who attend a non-Christian public or private university would have left the faith four years after entering college. Also, data from the Southern Baptist Convention indicates that they are currently losing 70–88 percent of their youth after their freshman year in college.

Moreover, a recent study conducted in 2019 by the American Enterprise Institute found that younger Americans report much more disaffiliation than older Americans. Seventy percent of young adults who had left their childhood religion to become unaffiliated report that they stopped identifying with their childhood religion when they were younger than eighteen.

Another recent survey conducted in 2019 by the Pew Research Center found that 65 percent of American adults describe themselves as Christians when asked about their religion, down twelve percentage points over the past decade. The survey found that, currently, 43 percent of US adults identify with Protestantism, down from 51 percent in 2009. One-in-five adults (20 percent) are Catholic, down from 23 percent in 2009. Over the last decade, the share of Americans who say they attend religious services at least once or twice a month dropped by seven percentage points, while the stock who say they attend religious services less often (if at all) has risen by the same degree.

The silent exodus is exhibited with the raw numbers of emerging adults leaving the church and sometimes even the Christian faith, but it is also highlighted with an increased lack of sound biblical orthodoxy.

For many years, I have used Christian Smith's classic text, *Soul Searching: The Religious and Spiritual Lives of American Teenagers,* as our leading textbook for our youth ministry courses. Smith's research discovered that most teenagers in America are incredibly inarticulate about their faith, religious beliefs, and practices. Unfortunately, this reality includes Latino emerging adults. The Barna Group reminds us that, "The kindergartners who started school in 2016 were the first American class in which minority ethnicities made up a majority of students, and whites are the minority," with Hispanics composing the largest minority among Gen Z, making up 21% of the entire generation (The Barna Group, 2019, p. 30).

Smith explained that the dominant religion among contemporary US teenagers is what he calls "Moralistic Therapeutic Deism," which he summarizes in a creed of five tenants: (1) A God exists who created and orders the world and watches over human life on earth; (2) God wants people to be good, nice, and fair to each other, as taught in the Bible and by most world religions; (3) the central goal of life is to be happy and to feel good about oneself; and (4) God does not need to be particularly involved in one's life except when He is needed to resolve a problem; and (5) good people go to heaven when they die.

In the end, Smith's study indicates that American teenagers are heavily influenced by postmodern philosophical thought and the ideology of individualism that profoundly shapes the broader culture. This is reflected in a non-judgmentalism and a reluctance to suggest that anyone might be wrong in matters of morality, faith, and belief. Sadly, even within Christian circles, it seems that emerging generations live in a sphere of relativism and have strayed away from the tenant of Christian orthodoxy.

Although Smith's research concluded in 2005, his findings are still relevant among Gen Z, as verified by a more recent study. In 2018, in their book, *Gen Z: The Culture, Beliefs, and Motivations Shaping the Next Generation*, The Barna Group explained that Gen Z's worldview (and, in turn, their moral code) is highly inclusive and individualistic. They directly quote Moralistic Therapeutic Deism as the primary tenant of belief among Gen Z (The Barna Group, 2018, p. 81).

Emerging adults continue to be an open-minded group of people who are sensitive to others' feelings and experiences and wary of exerting any one point of view as right or wrong. In fact, the percentage of people with a biblical worldview has declined in each generation: Boomers, 10 percent, Gen X, 7 percent, Millennials, 6 percent, and Gen Z, 4 percent (The Barna Group, 2018, p. 25).

More specifically, The Barna Group found a notable lack of faith engagement among Hispanic Christians in both teens and adults (The Barna Group, 2018, p. 74). They specify that the Hispanic population "make up more than 13 percent of the U.S. population but represent only 7 percent of engaged Christians among teens and 10 percent among adults (The Barna Group, 2018, p. 74).

Why is this happening? Well, primarily, The Barna Group explained that American churches lack the racial and ethnic diversity necessary to meet these challenges. But that is not all. I think that leading researcher David Kinnaman provides some additional insight. In his book, *You Lost Me: Why Young Christians Are Leaving Church… and Rethinking Faith*, he identified some critical factors for reluctance among emerging generations.

First, in his research, he indicated that nearly 25 percent of eighteen-to twenty-nine-year-olds said that "Christians demonize everything outside of the church" most of the time. He also recorded that 22 percent said the church ignores real-world problems, and 18 percent said that their church was too concerned about the negative impact of movies, music, and video games.

Second, Kinnaman also found that 33 percent of survey participants felt that "church is boring." Twenty percent of those who attended
church as a teenager said that God appeared to be missing from their
church, and 17 percent of young Christians said they had "made mis-
takes and feel judged in church because of them."

Third, his research found that many young adults do not like how
churches appear to be against science. Over 33 percent of young adults
said that "Christians are too confident they know all the answers," and
25 percent of them said that "Christianity is anti-science." Over 33
percent of young adults said they feel like they cannot ask life's most
pressing questions in church, and 23 percent said they had "significant
intellectual doubts" about their faith.

To compound the issue, a view from the periphery shows that men
and women have been entering the ministry at older ages in the past
few decades. For example, a 2001 report by the U.S. Bureau of Labor
Statistics stipulated that the median age of full-time, graduate-educated
ministers was forty-five (Carroll, 2006). However, I have discovered that
according to annual reports of a denomination which shall go unnamed
demonstrates a gradual increase in age across gender and ethnicity. The
average age of a pastor continues to increase gradually. The average age
of pastors in this denomination was fifty in 2003, fifty-two in 2008, and
fifty-four in 2013.

Here is the point, ultimately, the silent exodus must be bridged.
If we cannot produce disciples, we will never reproduce leaders; if we
cannot reproduce leaders, we cannot reproduce pastors; if we cannot
reproduce pastors, we cannot produce churches; and if we cannot reproduce churches, communities are left without the foundational tool of
God's kingdom to reach and disciple the lost.

The Silent Exodus from Personal Experience

Having briefly explored the silent exodus in general terms, this book
will also report more specifically on the nature of the implementation

of a monolingual English service at a bilingual church with the purpose of targeting and retaining second and third-plus-generation Latinos, including intermarried couples.

In doing so, this book explores and challenges the reluctance of Spanish-speaking dominant churches to accommodate changing demographics and researched whether a commitment by first-generation Latino church leaders to evangelize and disciple second and third-plus-generation Latinos primarily through a monolingual English church service model can be successful in their recruitment and retention.

The Context of Faro Church

Changes in the general composition of the Latino population have severe consequences for first-generation Latino churches hoping to recruit and retain second- and third-generation Latinos. Such was the challenge and opportunity for Faro Church, a bilingual, multicultural, and mostly monoethnic church in Southern California.

Faro Church was founded in 2002, primarily by a Spanish-speaking immigrant Christian community with a vision to reach second- and third-generation Latinos by bridging the generational and cultural gaps through relevant bilingual (English/Spanish) biblical teaching. While the bilingual church model has provided opportunities for retention of some of its second-generation Latino congregants, it has also become a hindrance in the retention of several second-generation Latinos and most third-plus-generation Latinos.

As highlighted by *The Orange County Register,* Faro Church reflects a unique Latino demographic and is one of a handful of Latino churches that provides weekly services that are entirely bilingual interchangeably between Spanish and English (Jelden, 2015). Everything spoken, printed, sung, or produced during a worship service is translated consecutively or with subtitles (for videos).

Before the implementation of the research, the church provided two identical bilingual services on Sundays (9 a.m. and 11 a.m.). The senior pastor of the church is Joshua Pinto, a bilingual speaker, who linguistically and culturally manages an understanding of the first-generation Latino immigrant. Alternatively, the church is also led by this author (Steve Pinto), his biological brother and associate pastor who is a bilingual speaker, who linguistically and culturally manages an understanding of the second- and third-generation Latinos.

Both immigrated from Bogota, Colombia, in 1987, and their partnership has proven to be essential in the forming of the identity and distinctive of Faro Church. This providentially formed balance has given Faro Church a clear vision and provides the leadership necessary to fulfill the church's mission.

With little variation throughout its seventeen-year history, the church's vision and mission have revolved around the founding premise to reach the second- and third-generation Latinos. The church's mission reads:

> To attract a multicultural base of unsaved, un-churched, disconnected, and disillusioned people through bilingual relevant teaching, creative presentations, and a genuine heart of service. To intentionally attend to their spiritual and physical needs through acts of love and healthy relationships. To attach them to Christ, our church, and our community through careful discipleship. (Faro Church, 2015)

Faro Church functions under an Episcopalian church polity where the senior pastor and associate pastor are in direct accountability to an elder board and together govern the church's mission. The elder board is composed of nine members, six of whom are founding elders and first-generation Latinos. In the process of time, the church has added three more elders to reflect the church's numeric growth and ethnic and generational diversity.

A ministry staff composed of a pastoral team of twelve pastors and nineteen deacons carry out the day-to-day ministerial load. Through their leadership and guidance, Faro Church provides twenty-three community ministries and ten operational ministries. Faro Church specifies ministries to children, youth, young adults, men, women, couples, the elderly, and missions along with other ministries of emotional and grief support.

The Demographics of Faro Church

Faro Church is located in Lake Forest, California. At just over sixteen square miles, the city is located at the heart of Orange County with a growing population of nearly 85,000 (City of Lake Forest, 2017). Latinos make up 26.7 percent of the total population, making them the second largest group after Whites (65.6 percent) and before Asians (16.1 percent).

Faro Church is a Pentecostal church of the Assemblies of God denomination. The congregation averages a Sunday worship attendance of approximately 425 people. Sixty-eight percent of the congregants are first-generation Latinos, 29 percent second-generation Latinos, and 6 percent third-plus-generation Latinos (2018 Faro Church Demographic Survey). Spanish is the primary language used by 48 percent of the congregants while 34 percent identify as bilingual (English and Spanish dominant), and 18 percent as English-only speakers (2018 Faro Church Demographic Survey).

Although Mexicans are the dominant sociocultural group in Southern California, the current membership of Faro Church reflects the broader Latino diversity of its community as it is comprised of individuals from over seventeen different nations, thirteen of which are Spanish-speaking countries in the Caribbean, North America, Central America, and South America. (Argentina, Bolivia, Colombia, Costa Rica, El Salvador, Guatemala, Honduras, Mexico, Nicaragua, Panama, Peru, Puerto Rico, and Venezuela).

Sigmoid Curve

Malphurs's (2013) analysis of the problems affecting many churches relates to the crisis facing Latino churches in America today. The "life cycle" of many churches is reflected in what is called a sigmoid curve, or an S-curve, in which a church is planted (1), births (2), grows (3), trends up to maturity (3), but it eventually plateaus (4), and if nothing interrupts the cycle, it will ultimately decline and die (5) (Malphurs, 2013, p. 9).

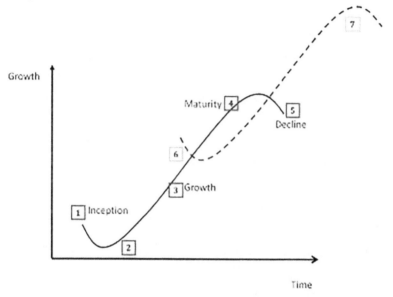

Figure 1. Sigmoid curve. Adapted from a variety of graphs in *The Life Cycle of a Church* by A. Malphurs, 2013, pp. 9–16.

Malphurs warned churches and organizations with these words:

> All good things (and even some bad things) end. In a world of constant, turbulent change, many relationships and most organizations do not last. The pattern is that they wax and eventually wane. Even brand-new institutions and organizations such as a church will, in time, plateau and then die. No matter

what institution it is, organizational "dry rot" sets in. The institution becomes brittle, ceases to function, and expires. (pp. 10–11)

This is why it is vital for churches to identify organizational plateau or decline and implement a strategic planning process to avoid organizational death by setting the organization for a second S-curve.

Although difficult to accurately target specific origination points, Faro Church had experienced two previous plateaus and is currently in a plateau. The church was planted in November of 2002, with a core group filled with great anticipation and excitement but with little experience. The early years were filled with much internal organizational growth but little numerical growth.

The first plateau happened around 2006/2007; after finally experiencing attendance growth from fifteen to about 200, Faro Church had exhausted its existing meeting room, and the bivocational pastors and church volunteers were experiencing signs of ministry burnout.

Unknowingly, yet providentially, the church leaders strategically planned for the leasing of a more significant building to accommodate for growth, a ministry strategy that emphasized "Doing Church as a Team" (DCAT), and the hiring of a full-time pastor to better serve the church. They realized that a common mistake in church growth is allowing too much time before a full-time pastor is placed in service.

In addition, the leaders also learned that churches that overcome growth barriers plan to overcome the barrier by establishing growing organizational structures and have a strong pastoral body that accomplishes the work through a strong lay ministry. By the grace of God, a new S-curve was birthed in 2009 with the hiring of the first full-time pastor, the implementation of DCAT, and the leasing of a new building. These changes led to a renewed evangelistic focus and excitement for ministry. The strategic planning led to attendance growth from 200 to about 300 congregants.

In 2012, after averaging about 300 congregants in Sunday attendance for about two years, Faro Church began to experience signs of ministry weariness and lack of numerical growth as it experienced the second plateau. Again, the leadership team strategically planned a similar process of looking for a stable, large meeting space, emphasizing a robust contemporary worship setting, and hiring two more full-time pastors to accommodate and prepare for future growth.

As a leadership team, they learned that the 250–300 attendees barrier is the most critical of all church sizes (George & Bird, 1993, p. 129). It can decline, or it can grow, but it will not remain the same. Ninety-four percent of the churches in the United States today have an attendance of 350 participants or less (George & Bird, 1993, p. 145).

As the church moved past the 250–300 attendees barrier, it needed to make particular organizational moves to continue growing. Overcoming the barrier represented moving from a small, stagnant congregation to a fast-growing church. Eventually, in 2013, Faro Church was able to lock-in a long-term lease in a prime church meeting space that allowed for potential growth, a modern worship setting, and the hiring of two more full-time pastors. These moves revitalized the church again and led to subsequent numerical growth. Faro Church is now averaging an attendance of about 425 congregants on Sundays.

The Issue at Hand

Faro Church is a tightly networked community where parishioners are described as a family; most have multiple connections to other church members through familial relations, intermarriage, and friendship. Thus, Faro Church create a natural linguistic and cultural community. It offers its parishioners a place where their native culture and language are valued while providing a context in which a bilingual and multicultural identity has a high status and clear purpose in the religious domain.

However, the continued commitment to bilingual services had become a challenge in the retention of some second- and third-plus-generation Latinos. These factors made Faro Church a favorable environment for the study of cultural and linguistic identity in a theological and church community.

Since the beginning of 2018, the church had been experiencing a new plateau in the church's life cycle. Although the bilingual model served as a tool to retain some second-and third-generation Latinos, I wanted to more clearly understand the changing demographics among Latinos to prepare for their recruitment and retention.

This book is the result of a journey to understand the emerging generation of Latinos. In the first five chapters of this book, I provide relevant research findings that led to the continuation of bilingual services and the implementation a monolingual English service at Faro Church. This was done to reduce the "silent exodus" of second-and third-plus-generation Latinos and including intermarried Latinos.

More specifically, the Epilogue provides the research findings from this implementation, including several surveys among Latino emerging adults and ministry leaders. I pray you find the data useful and helpful to your ministry.

Also, I believe that there is wisdom found in both the theoretical and in the experiential; therefore, in chapters six through eight, I provided appropriate leadership tools birthed from first-hand experience for contextual leadership to achieve a more relevant ministry in Latino Churches. These leadership tools can help you define and navigate the challenges of post modernity and technology.

Although many challenges and opportunities still lie ahead for Faro Church, I hope that this research helps you as it has helped Faro Church to begin a process by which we can recruit and retain the next generation of Latinos for the glory of God.

Terminology

Before we get started, I want to define some terms and ideas that will help you better understand my terminology.

Multiculturalism among Latino churches in America can be observed differently compared to mainstream American English-speaking churches often described as multicultural or multiethnic.

While Latino churches may be Spanish-speaking or bilingual (Spanish and English), they can reflect a wide array of nationalities and cultures. The majority of congregants may represent the Latino ethnicity while reflecting different nationalities from the Caribbean, North America, Central America, and South America. Each of these countries have unique cultural manifestations and linguistic variations of the Spanish language.

Therefore, the terminology *multicultural yet monoethnic* can be used as a reference to the vast array of people from possible Spanish-speaking countries and cultures congregating at any given Latino church in America.

Latino and Hispanic will be used interchangeably throughout this book to refer to all individuals of Latin American ancestry who reside either legally or illegally within the borders of the United States of America. Also, US-born and native-born Hispanic/Latino will be used synonymously in this book to refer to Latinos including second- and third-generation Latinos who were born in the United States of America. Similarly, the terms foreign-born and immigrant will be used to refer to first-generation Latinos who reside in the United States either legally or illegally.

The *silent exodus* refers to the identified trend of second- and third-plus-generation Latinos who are slowly and respectfully disconnecting from regular church attendance at Latino churches in America that hold to a Spanish only or bilingual (English and Spanish) ministry model.

A better understanding of the silent exodus requires a clear delineation of generations in order to more effectively identify each group along with a comprehensive etymological picture of the changing demographics and linguistic realities among second- and third-plus-generation Latinos. Helpful in understanding dissections of generations, Suro and Passel (2003) provided these definitions of generations:

> *First Generation*: Born outside the United States, its territories or possessions. Can be naturalized U.S. citizens, legal immigrants or undocumented immigrants.

> *Second Generation*: Born in the United States with at least one foreign-born parent. U.S. citizens by birth.

> *Third-plus Generations*: Born in the United States with both parents also born in the United States. U.S. citizens by birth.

These definitions are adopted and used throughout this study to provide a clear foundational understanding of the use of first-, second-, and third-plus Latino generations.

Additionally, the term *emerging adults* will be used as a generic description of people between the ages of eighteen to twenty-five, which encompasses an important demographic that includes many second- and third-plus-generation Latinos. Arnett (2000) explained, "Emerging adulthood is proposed as a new conception of development for the period from the late teens through the twenties, with a focus on ages 18–25" (p. 469).

Immigrant churches refers to first-generation churches planted with a monolingual Spanish (or native language) ministry model in the United States (Kwon, Kim, & Warner, 2001, p. 128; Rodríguez, 2009, p. 103). *Intermarried* refers to marriage between people of different races, ethnicities, or languages (Rodríguez, 2009, p. 103; Suro & Passel, 2003, p. 9).

Finally, *race and ethnicity* are used in this book to refer to a person's shared cultural practices, perspectives, and distinctions that set apart one group of people from another. That is, race or ethnicity is a shared biological or cultural heritage. Although the terms can be used synonymously, it is my preference to use the term *ethnicity* rather than race to stress the fact that human beings are described biblically as one race with different ethnicities (Acts 17:24–28).

Ok, let us get started...

PART ONE:

UNDERSTANDING CHANGING DEMOGRAPHICS AMONG LATINOS

CHAPTER 2:

GENERATIONAL CHARACTERISTICS CONTRIBUTING TO THE SILENT EXODUS

"It is possible for a second- or third-plus-generation Latino to lose the Spanish language yet still desire and be attracted to the Latino culture."

Much is still to be determined about the emerging generations from immigrant families and churches. It is uncertain, for example, how they will respond to the current newfound pressures of Latino identity driven by political attitudes, polarity, racism, and confusion about the immigration policy in America. However, recent research provides five critical areas of generational change. The primary generational characteristics impacting the retention of second- and third-plus-generation Latinos in the church and the potential for change or improvement are language patterns, retention of identity, education and income variance, population increases, and intermarriage.

Language: The Three-Generation Pattern

An immigrant's native language has a high probability of being lost in just a generation or two. Immigration patterns over the past half-century demonstrate an increase in Spanish-speakers due to immigration from Latin American countries. From 1965 to 2015, roughly half of all immigration came from Latin American countries and added 30 million people, most of whom came speaking Spanish (Pew Research Center, 2015).

However, while new immigrants are Spanish monolinguals, research shows that their children tend to become bilinguals who overwhelmingly prefer English (Krogstad, 2016b). As a result, the immigrants' grandchildren are likely to be English monolinguals. Linguists call this phenomenon "the three-generation pattern" (Ortman & Stevens, 2008, p. 3). In essence, it means that non-English languages in the US are lost by or during the third generation.

Surveys show that in 2000, 48 percent of Latino adults aged fifty to sixty-eight spoke "only English" or "English very well," and 73 percent of Latino children aged five to seventeen also spoke only English as noted in Figure 2 (Krogstad, 2016a). By 2014, those numbers had jumped to 52 percent and 88 percent, respectively (Krogstad, 2016a). In other words, the shift from Spanish to English is happening nationwide, both over time and between generations (Krogstad & Lopez, 2017).

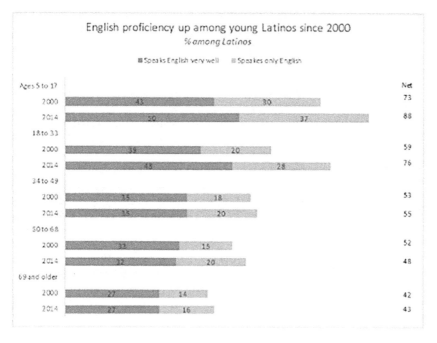

Figure 2. English proficiency up among young Latinos since 2000. Adapted from
Rise in English Proficiency among U.S. Hispanics is Driven by the Young
by J. M. Krogstad, 2016a.

Note: Latinos who speak English proficiently are those who speak only English at home, or
if they speak a non-English language at home, indicate they can speak English "very well."
Figures may not add to net due to rounding.

Figure 3 demonstrates that 73 percent of Latinos spoke Spanish at home in 2015, down from 78 percent in 2006. In a similar finding, according to the 2002 National Survey of Latinos, conducted jointly by the Pew Hispanic Center and the Kaiser Family Foundation (Figure 4), Spanish speakers make up most of the first-generation (Suro & Passel, 2003, p. 8). The second generation is substantially bilingual, and the third-plus generations are primarily English speakers (Suro & Passel, 2003, p. 8).

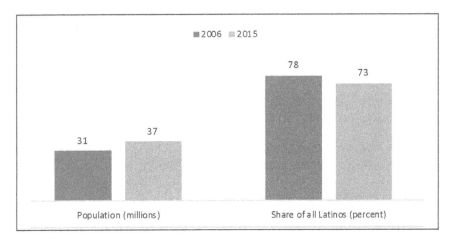

Figure 3. Latinos who speak Spanish at home. Adapted from *Spanish Speaking Declines for Hispanics in U.S. Metro Areas* by J. M. Krogstad & M. H. Lopez, 2017.

Note: Only those Latinos who are ages 5 and older.

As noted in Figure 4, one of the primary differences between Latino generations is primary language use. Seventy-two percent of first-generation Latinos are Spanish-dominant, whereas, only 7 percent of second-generation and 0 percent of third-generation Latinos are (Suro & Passel, 2003, p. 8). Conversely, 78 percent of third-generation Latinos are English-dominant, and 22 percent are bilingual, whereas, 46 percent of second-generation Latinos are English-dominant, and 57 percent are bilingual (Suro & Passel, 2003, p. 8). In comparison, only 4 percent of first-generation Latinos are English-dominant, and 24 percent are bilingual (Suro & Passel, 2003, p. 8).

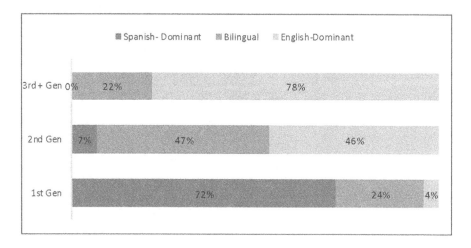

Figure 4. Primary language among Latinos. Adapted from *The Rise of the Second Generation: Changing Patterns in Hispanic Population Growth* by R. Suro & J. S. Passel, 2003, p. 8.

Guglani's (2016) research also found that while some Hispanics are monolingual Spanish speakers or Spanish/English bilinguals, others are monolingual English speakers. She cited other researchers to illustrate that "immigrant families typically lose their native language within two to three generations of arrival" (Guglani, 2016, p. 345). Hence, she explained, "Their children tend to show a stronger proficiency in an increasing preference for English, becoming English dominant or monolingual" (Guglani, 2016, p. 345).

Moreover, there is the reality of linguistic identities and a complex array of language dialects. Guglani (2016) explained:

> These dialects mirror the full range of ethnic identities, encompassing features of the Spanish varieties spoken in the land of origin and U.S. Spanish varieties, which reflect features of the particular Hispanic group(s) living in a given community, together with borrowings and adaptations from English. (p. 345)

Additionally, it is not strange to find Spanish/English bilinguals typically engaging in code-switching, alternating between languages according to situation and speaker. Hence, "As in the case of ethnic identities, linguistic identities are not fixed, and Hispanics may choose to adopt more than one, according to their linguistic resources" (Guglani, 2016, p. 345).

Retention of Ethnic Identity

An underlying challenge for the retention of second- and third-plus-generation Latinos is the question of ethnic identity. A significant function of a church community is to provide for the religious and spiritual needs of its members (Rom. 12:5; 14:19; 1 Cor. 12:7; Eph. 4:11–13). However, in the Latino church in America, there is an added dimension where the church and its activities can also maintain its members' ethnic identity. In other words, "the heritage of an ethnic minority or immigrant can lead an individual to join a particular church, and the structure of the church" (Choi & Berhó, 2016, p. 91). However, as specified in the "Three-Generation Pattern", an immigrant's native language has a high probability of being lost in just a generation or two.

Language does not seem to transcend ethnic and cultural appropriation. In a recent study completed in 2016, Guglani (2016) reported that older, first-generation immigrants viewed language and culture as inextricably linked and believed that passing the Spanish language to their children is an essential parenting responsibility. However, he made a substantially significant distinction. He found that younger, US-born, second-generation Latinos, along with those who immigrated at a young age, prioritized Latino culture over the Spanish language (Guglani, 2016, p. 345).

This is an important distinction as it points to a unique factor among second- and third-plus-generation Latinos. It is possible for a second- or third-plus-generation Latino to lose the Spanish language yet still desire and be attracted to the Latino culture.

Moreover, since the majority of second- and third-plus-generation Latinos in America usually prefer to speak English and have an affinity for the American culture, they are not fully accepted by foreign-born Latinos. Rodríguez (2009) pointed out that "many second and later-generation Hispanics nonetheless 'perceive' that they are treated as second-class citizens in the country of their birth and often treated as 'outsiders' in the churches of the dominant group" (p. 113). Hence, Latino English-speaking churches play a vital role in the evangelization and retention of second-generation and US-born Latinos.

Furthermore, Rodriguez's (2009) evidence supports the idea that traditionally White, English-dominant churches have failed to attract the growing number of second- and third-plus-generation Latinos due to cultural variances. Rodríguez explained:

> Unfortunately, many church leaders fail to recognize that even though the linguistic and cultural distance between U.S.-born Hispanics and the dominant group has been minimized due to a preference for English and higher levels of acculturation, the legacy of 150 years of cultural conflict, marginalization, and discrimination has not only alienated many U.S.-born Hispanics from many institutions of the dominant group, including the church, they have also reinforced ethnic identity. (p. 113)

This ethnic alienation can be traced back as early as 1981. In his research, Arce (1981) discovered several factors that reinforce Latino identity among second- and third-plus-generation Latinos. Arce pointed to continued immigration from Latin America, the strength of familial ties, and discriminatory treatment in the US as contributing factors, among others, to the strengthening of Latino identity into the second and third generation.

To summarize, Arce (1981) further explained that the discriminatory treatment of Latinos spawns concentrated ethnic dependence while obstructing sociocultural interaction and contact with non-Latino groups. Consequently, this has the involuntary consequence of reinforcing Latino ethnic identity (Arce, 1981).

Educational and Income Variance

Research has also found that US-born Latinos have distinctly higher levels of education than their first-generation parents (Figure 5). For example, "in 2000 more than half of the first generation lacked a high school diploma compared to a quarter or less of the native-born generations, and, similarly, there are significantly higher levels of college attendance among the native born" (Suro & Passel, 2003, p. 8).

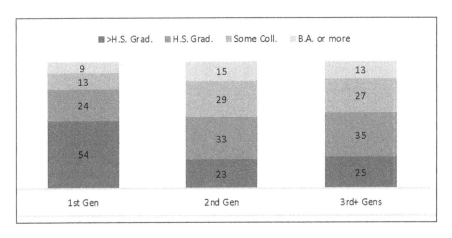

Figure 5. Educational attainment for Latinos aged 25–64 by generation. Adapted from *The Rise of the Second Generation: Changing Patterns in Hispanic Population Growth* by R. Suro & J. S. Passel, 2003, p. 8.

Additionally, Latinos are increasing in college enrollment (Figure 6). Pew Research reported that "35% of Hispanics ages 18 to 24 were enrolled in a two- or four-year college, up from 22% in 1993—a 13-percentage-point increase" (Krogstad, 2016b).

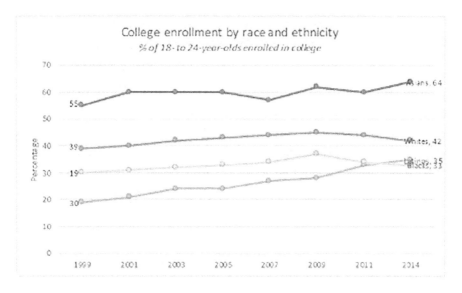

Figure 6. College enrollment by race and ethnicity. Adapted from *5 Facts About Latinos and Education* by J. M. Krogstad, 2016b.

Notes: Blacks and Asians include Hispanic portions of those groups. Whites include only non-Hispanics. Hispanics are of any race.

Not surprisingly given the differences in language and education, native-born Latinos have been earning more than the first generation. According to Current Population Survey data for the second quarter of 2003, first-generation Latinos had mean weekly earnings of $457, the second generation was earning $535 per week, and the third $550 (Suro & Passel, 2003, p. 9). This economic variance continued to make strides in 2013. Along similar lines, second-generation Latinos were doing better than the first-generation in median household income ($58,000 versus $46,000); college degrees (36% versus 29%); and homeownership (64% versus 51%) (Pew Research Center, 2013).

The Growth of the Latino Population in the United States

Another factor affecting the mission of Latino churches in America is the growth of the Latino population in the United States. The 2010 census reported that Latinos were the fastest-growing population in the past decade, with over half of the country's population growth coming from rising numbers of Latinos. Additionally, more than half of all American Latinos were born in the United States and are now English-dominant, making it important for Latino ministries to shift accordingly (Ennis, Rios-Vargas, & Albert, 2011).

Individually, the data gathered in the 2010 census counted 50.5 million Latinos in the United States, making up 16.3 percent of the total population (Passel, Cohn, & Lopez, 2011, p. 1). The nation's Latino population, which was 35.3 million in 2000, grew 43 percent over the decade. Moreover, the Latino population also accounted for most of the nation's growth—56 percent—from 2000 to 2010 (Passel et al., 2011, p. 1).

The available evidence seems to suggest that the Latino population, which was 42 million in 2005, will rise to 128 million in 2050, tripling in size (Passel & Cohn, 2008, p. 1). Recent research confirms this prediction of continued growth among Latinos in America. Flores (2017) reported, "The Latino population in the United States has reached nearly 58 million in 2016 and has been the principal driver of U.S. demographic growth, accounting for half of national population growth since 2000." Passel and Cohn (2008) summarized that "Hispanics will account for 60% of the nation's population growth from 2005 to 2050" (p. 1).

On these grounds, it can be argued that the Latino Church in America must create linguistic models that fit a ministry vision focused on the retention and recruitment of the growing population of Latinos in the United States.

The Rise of the Second Generation

Using a mid-range estimate of immigration flows, Pew Research found that the "Hispanic population will grow by 25 million people between 2000 and 2020" (Suro & Passel, 2003, p. 5). In fact, "during that time the second generation accounts for 47 percent of the increase compared to 25 percent for the first" (Suro & Passel, 2003, p. 5). Equally, they projected that "the second generation more than doubles in size, increasing from 9.8 million in 2000 to 21.7 million in 2020" (Suro & Passel, 2003, p. 5).

Suro and Passel (2003) explained a changing pattern in Latino population growth in the United States:

> As it continues to grow, the composition of the Hispanic population is undergoing a fundamental change: Births in the United States are outpacing immigration as the key source of growth. Over the next twenty years, this will produce an important shift in the makeup of the Hispanic population with second-generation Latinos—the U.S.-born children of immigrants—emerging as the largest component of that population. (p. 2)

The data gathered in recent years demonstrates that the Latino population has reached a new high, but growth has slowed (Figure 7). Flores (2017) wrote, "The Latino population in the United States has reached nearly 58 million in 2016 and has been the principal driver of US demographic growth, accounting for half of national population growth since 2000.

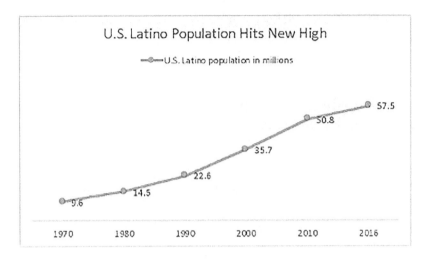

Figure 7. US Hispanic population hits new high. Adapted from *How the U.S. Hispanic Population is Changing* by A. Flores, 2017.

Note: 1990–2016 estimates are for July 1.

For the sake of discussion, it could be argued that the Latino population has changed. Krogstad (2017) explained, "The annual growth rate of the U.S. Hispanic population remained flat between 2016 and 2017" (p. 1). Nevertheless, it appears that Suro and Passel's (2003) prediction has proven right, and Latinos continue to account for more of the nation's overall population growth than any other race or ethnicity.

The Rise of Protestantism Among Latinos

Due to immigration and high birth rates, Hispanics are rapidly growing as a proportion of American society—faster than any other racial-ethnic group—and are widely dispersed throughout the United States. Furthermore, a growing number of US Hispanics are not Catholic but Protestant. Beyond their religious devotion, Protestants, including Pentecostals, capture and channel Latino Protestant religiosity to a greater extent than Roman Catholic churches.

Martî (2015) found that due to immigration and high birth rates, Latinos are rapidly growing as a proportion of American society—faster than any other racial-ethnic group (p. 145). Moreover, these US Latinos are more likely to identify as Protestant, not Catholic. Martî explained, "Recently, Pew Research (2014b) reported a 12 percent drop of Latino adults identifying as Catholic from 67 to 55 percent between 2010 and 2013 and an even greater drop—19 percent—among those foreign-born" (p. 145).

The growth in Protestantism among Latinos matters because of a high rate of religious identity and church attendance among Latinos. Martî's (2015) research found that Latinos tend to emphasize their religious identity over their ethnic identity. He explained, "Latinos have much higher church attendance compared with Whites, and Latino Protestants (whether coming from evangelical, Pentecostal, or mainline orientations) are significantly higher in their church attendance compared with Latino Catholics" (p. 146).

Due to the high capacity to capture and channel Latino Protestant religiosity, Latino churches are strategic arenas for grasping a growing but neglected religious group that will become a more visible and prevalent force in American life.

Latino Intermarriage

First-generation Latinos, like immigrants in general, tend to marry within their ethnic/racial group (Figure 8). That is not true of second- and third-plus-generation Latinos. According to recent estimates (Suro & Passel, 2003), only 8 percent of foreign-born Latinos intermarry, compared to 32 percent of the second-generation and 57 percent of the third-plus generations (Suro & Passel, 2003, p. 9).

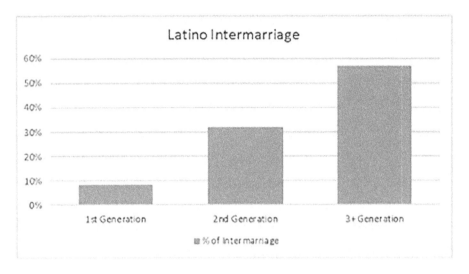

Figure 8. Latino intermarriage. Adapted from *The Rise of the Second Generation: Changing Patterns in Hispanic Population Growth* by R. Suro & J. S. Passel, 2003, p. 8.

There seems to be no compelling reason to claim that this trend has changed in recent years. Pew Research found two trends as early as 2017, "a long-standing high intermarriage rate and a decade of declining Latin American immigration" (Lopez, Gonzalez-Barrera, & López, 2017, p. 4). As a result, some Americans with Hispanic ancestry are distancing "from the life experiences of earlier generations, reducing the likelihood they call themselves Hispanic or Latino" (Lopez et al., 2017, p. 4). The data yielded that in 2015, "25.1% of Latino newlyweds married a non-Latino spouse and 18.3% of all married Latinos were intermarried" (Lopez et al., 2017, p. 4).

This trend can contribute to the silent exodus, as it is likely to become culturally and linguistically difficult for spouses of a different ethnicity to adjust to the language use of a monoethnic Spanish community.

Summary

Important in understanding the silent exodus is recognizing the unique general factors impacting Latino churches in America. A significant change in the composition of the Latino population is underway. It is now an inexorable, undeniable demographic fact. Many Latinos are U.S. citizens by birth and are the products of U.S. schools, and, for that reason alone, they will present a different character and have a different impact on the church than their immigrant parents.

Equally important is the growing number of U.S. Latinos who do not speak Spanish, are highly educated, are intermarried, are not Catholic but Protestant, and seek congregations that meet their needs.

Latino churches in America who are aware of the generational patterns, variances, and increases detailed above can begin to provide avenues for retention by providing church services and ministries that cater to the linguistic, educational, and cultural differences highlighted in this chapter. If Latino churches in America gain awareness of and act to bridge the generational gaps in these areas, they can hope to retain second- and third-plus-generation Latinos.

CHAPTER 3

NAVIGATING TWO WORLDS

*"I attempted to be more Latino, but I was not Latino enough. I tried
to be more American, but I was not American enough. Stuck in a
void, I determined to satisfy both and be twice as good."*

I was born in Bogota, Colombia, to a newly converted couple in
1978. Most of my infant, toddler, and childhood years were spent
alongside my parents in a traditional and strict Pentecostal church
in Colombia.

When I was eight years old, my parents migrated to the United
States and settled in Orange County, California. Religiously, my earliest
memories in the United States felt as if we had just moved into another
neighborhood back home. My parents found a Christian Pentecostal
church almost immediately after arriving, and the religious routine continued. The church we attended was populated by Spanish-speaking
Latinos, so there was no significant cultural or religious shock.

When I enrolled in school, I began to experience a pattern of
peculiarity. Although living in a predominantly Mexican neighborhood,
I felt as if I was always in the minority in one way or another. Be it
language, demographics, ethnicity, religion, I always felt like an outcast.
My Colombian Spanish was dissimilar, my Colombian ethnicity was
not the same, and my strict religious beliefs were eccentric and peculiar.
This atmosphere created a reluctant, shy, and solitary boy afraid to speak
at home, church, or school.

Moving into my adolescence, I opposed my reluctant way of life as an introvert and outsider and looked to be accepted by a group of people who would understand and accept me. I attempted to be more Latino, but I was not Latino enough. I tried to be more American, but I was not American enough. Stuck in a void, I determined to satisfy both and be twice as good. Still, the lack of acceptance and understanding angered me.

I was even motivated by a scene in the movie *Selena*. After receiving an invitation to perform in Monterrey, Mexico, Selena (Jennifer Lopez), her brothers A.B. (Jacob Vargas) and Abraham (Edward James Olmos) disagree on whether or not she should do it.

Like many Mexican Americans, Selena's family lived in the States for decades but sadly would feel that they would never be American enough for Americans and would never be entirely accepted in Mexico. In the scene, Abraham explores and explains the idea of being *"twice as perfect"* in order to please everyone. He says to Selena and A.B., *"We have to be more Mexican than the Mexicans and more American than the Americans, both at the same time! It is exhausting!"* I relate, do you?

Moving into my junior high and high school years, I eventually developed friendships with other young men who had similar childhoods and backgrounds as I did. I finally found a group of people who would accept me and understand me. They, too, came from immigrant families; they also didn't fit the mold and also struggled with their Latino identity in predominantly American culture.

In the mid-1990s in southern California, "party crews" were fashionable and growing. Still working at the newspaper delivery company, going to school, and playing for the school soccer team, my friends and I established our own party crew called "Rebel Familia." Our group intended to promote and organize house parties. The initiation process required its members to be "burned" into the crew by allowing all its members to sting the bicep with a cigarette.

In the interim, my family and I would continue to attend church faithfully. However, everyone at church and my family members had no idea what I was starting to get involved in. Still, I attended church with my parents, respected the services, attended all the youth camps and youth events but never accepted Jesus into my heart. Growing up in church, I reasoned that if I was not going to live for Christ, then I did not have to accept Christ.

Soon after I turned sixteen years old, I was involved in two car accidents as I traveled around with my "crew." At the same time, the local Fox Newscast was doing a special investigation on "party crews," which required its members to be "burned" into the crew by allowing all its members to sting the bicep with a cigarette. On occasion, my parents had seen my burn, and when the newscast was brought to their attention, my mother confronted me about my lifestyle.

Having been through the accidents and realizing the futility of my ways, I began to think deeply about my relationship with God. At the age of seventeen, sitting in a special youth service, I heard a message entitled "It Is a Dreadful Thing to Fall into the Hands of the Living God," based on Hebrews 10:31. I was compelled to answer the altar call. It was on this day when I accepted Jesus Christ. I vowed to follow Jesus, not religiously, as I had seen too frequently in my life, but honestly and genuinely in a personal relationship with God.

Immediately following the church service, God radically began to make changes in my life. I started cultivating a relationship with God through reading the Bible and prayer. I was no longer interested in the party lifestyle or the party crews. This caused the number of my friends to dwindle.

It was at this time that my view of self, the world, and the future began to change. Jesus had changed my heart; I had indeed been reborn. The shy boy yearning for attention was, in fact, a prideful sinner who needed the forgiveness and wholeness that only Jesus could provide. God changed the way I dressed, spoke, thought, and even my future goals.

I have come to realize that my story is not unique. There are thousands of first-, second-, and even third-generation Latinos stuck in a void, trying to navigate two worlds. There will always be a cultural and linguistic tension between who I am and what I am because they run so closely together. Immigrants such as me, are still dealing with the hurts and pains that come either directly or indirectly from a lack of a cultural home. The demands, needs, misunderstandings, and urgency of people can drain their joy and take their toll. Navigating two worlds is not a simple business; it is a calling. It is who you are and what you have been appointed to.

Peace is not the absence of tension, but genuine peace is promised when we trust in God's presence, care, and calling amid tension. I encourage you to learn, as I learn, to navigate the tension rather than remove it. Nothing of significance is ever achieved without it.

The Second Generation Stuck in a Void

For the sake of discussion, it could be argued that the pressure reinforcing the development of a Latino ethnic identity apart from American culture as a whole can also be reinforced by first-generation Latino retraction. This seems to be evident in church experience and exemplified from a theological perspective, which will be discussed ahead in this chapter; however, the data gathered from Crane (2003) seems to suggest that second- and third-plus-generation Latinos are left in a void.

Crane's (2003) research of Mexican-Americans in rural Texas found that many second-generation Latinos are often apprehensive about how they are perceived by both English-speaking Americans and first-generation Mexicans who value the culture and speak the Spanish language. Crane found that second-generation Latinos who lose the Spanish language live with a tension that extends to their family and shoves them toward assimilation with the American culture at large (p. 171), a culture that they cannot entirely appropriate due to ethnic intricacies. In other words, they attempt to reduce the generational clash by restraining their ethnic identity through assimilation, a position that is common with other second-generation, non-white ethnocultural groups (Crane, 2003, p. 171).

As a result, Choi and Berhó (2016) explained, "Second and third generation immigrants, who are mostly youth, often speak little Spanish, and, as these individuals grow up speaking English well, many leave the monolingual Spanish-speaking church for bilingual or English-only churches" (p. 100).

Ortiz (1993) noted that the above-mentioned Latino ethnocentrism described by Crane, Choi, and Berhó inadvertently reinforces "the paradox of living in two hostile worlds" (p. 63). Consequently, second- and third-plus-generation Latinos seem to function at times in a void in American culture and Latino churches in America.

Therefore, choosing a language or languages for worship services and Christian education is an ongoing issue, and the morphological characteristic of a Latino church impacts the members of a congregation. In an attempt to be more Latino, they are perceived as not Latino enough. In an attempt to be more American, they are perceived as not American enough.

A Perspective from Latino Theologians and Educators

Influential theologians recognize population and language intricacies among second- and third-plus-generation Latinos. Arce's (1981) ethnic dependence theory, highlights the importance of a ministry model focused on the recruitment and retention of Latinos who lose the language but keep the ethnic acculturation.

Justo Gonzalez, a prominent Latino Protestant theologian, has noted that even though 60 percent of all Latinos are American citizens by birth, native-born Latinos—second- and third-plus-generation Latinos—are still "made to feel as if they are newcomers" due to cultural and ecclesiastical negligence (as cited in Smith-Christopher, 1996, p. 93). Therefore, Gonzalez encouraged the church to reevaluate its responsibility to include not only a commitment to the gospel itself but also to the citizens and family of God (Smith-Christopher, 1996, p. 109).

Analogously, Presmanes, an assistant professor of practical theology and director of the Institute for Hispanic/Latino Theology and Ministry at Barry University, provided a similar disparagement. He wrote, "Unity is not found in a uniform worship of culturally distinct communities, but in a common baptismal faith that is celebrated and expressed in the context of each community's language and culture" (Presmanes, 2007, p. 139).

This sentiment is not limited to Protestant thought. Father Virgilio Elizondo, one of the most influential Latino Roman Catholic theologians of the past twenty-five years, has summarized the shared legacy of second- and third-plus-generation Latinos. He wrote, "We have always been treated as foreigners in our own countryside—exiles who never left home" (as cited in Bañuelas, 1995, p. 9).

The cultural void of second- and third-plus-generation Latinos is exemplified and evidenced in higher education in the United States. For Galvan Estrada (2018), "One of the major challenges in theological education is the ability to respond to the multifaceted and multilingual identity of the Latino/a community" (p. 146). He summarized, "An assumption often made about Latinos/as seeking theological education is that the curriculum needs to be in Spanish" (Galvan Estrada III, 2018, p. 146).

Correspondingly, Hernández and Davis (2003) insisted that most theological schools and accredited seminaries have neglected the needs and interests of Latinos, based on neglect of cultural awareness. Galvan Estrada (2018) noted that this is one of the primary reasons why these Latinos seek ministerial equipping in Bible institutes instead of formal theological seminaries. He explained, "Formal theological institutes are not perceived to recognize, respond, and address the contextual needs and interests of culturally minoritized students" (Galvan Estrada, 2018, p. 135).

Galvan Estrada described the challenge of higher education institutions seeking to recruit and retain second- and third-plus-generation Latinos: "Bible institutes, including ecclesial based theological seminaries, cannot be disconnected from the network realities of their contextual locations nor fail to observe the student's ethnocultural identities and linguistic preferences" (p. 149).

Along similar lines, Calvillo and Bailey (2015) researched Latino religious affiliation and ethnic identity and found that Latinos are more likely to embrace English monolingualism yet view their religious identity as more important than their ethnic identity (pp. 73–74). This points to the idea that second- and third-plus-generation Latinos seek religious institutions that value and understand their cultural ties while meeting their linguistic preference. At the heart of the discussion on English monolingualism among second- and third-plus-generation Latinos, Galvan Estrada (2015) provided this implication, "We must notice that all education is influenced and interpreted through a subjectivity that is racial, gendered, cultural, as well as ideological and theological" (pp. 341–355).

A Contextualized Hermeneutic

A unique challenge of generational and linguistic blending in Latino churches in America can also be the philosophy and praxis of biblical interpretation as conceptualized by and modeled by religious tradition and interpretation. This is what Galvan Estrada (2015) referred to as a "contextualized hermeneutic" (p. 349–350). He explained that foundationally a person's identity "is both theological and contextual" and "is also actively involved in the construction of meaning with the Spirit and the biblical text" (Galvan Estrada, 2015, p. 349–350).

An excellent example of this is found in the interpretation of Philippians 2:5 where the English Standard Version translation encourages readers to "have the *mind* ... of Christ." On the other hand, a direct translation of the Reina Valera 1995 in Spanish encourages readers to have "este *sentir* ... (in English *"feeling"*) que hubo en Cristo." The word here for "mind" or "sentir" is the Greek word φρονέω (*phroneō*) meaning to judge, discern, or understand. It is also translated, "to feel, (or) to think" (Thayer, 1995).

However, while an English reading leans toward a unique interpretation focused on the mind, the Spanish reading leans toward a unique interpretation focused on the heart. Consequently, two theological perspectives tend to affect church ministry and culture. It is in this context that Martinez (2011) provided this encouragement:

> A meaningful Latino/Hispanic hermeneutic is one that provides serious analysis of the Bible and our society, brings the two analyses together creatively in a hermeneutical blend, gets its nourishment from personal commitment, and communicates the findings so that a large majority of our people can benefit. (p. 139).

This challenge can be an opportunity to be a people of a healthy contextual theology, a people with a healthy balance of both mind and heart, who mend the theological schism by accepting a wholesome and healthy theological approach to both the heart and the mind. Providing practical suggestions to move the field of biblical interpretation in Latino churches in America to a holistic approach can help Latino theology in general, the life and mission of the Church, and society as a whole.

Summary

When asked to reflect on the changing demographics among Latinos in America (i.e., language, intermarriage, culture) an articulate response from a male, second-generation emerging adult in one of our focus groups seemed appropriate to encapsulate the concept of navigating two worlds:

What defined the first-generation was their struggles. Coming from a different country and assimilating to somewhere where they do not know anybody or the culture. And we as a human being are defined by our culture.

But now the struggles of the second-generation are not like the struggles of the first-generation. They have different perspectives. They (second-generation) have heard the stories of their immigrant parents and how they struggled back then and how they struggled to change here. But it is not their story. They have different stories. What will define them is trying to find their place in a country that they are a part of but not completely because of their heritage.

That is what I see; they have a different outlook on life ... Second-generation did not experience having anything to moving to a different place. That affects their theology and what they expect from God and the church.

Probably, the first-generation, they saw God as a provider and refuge, no matter what, God and the church will always be there. But for the second-generation is a different thing ... what does God have to do with my life?

They were not exposed to the (same) struggles; they grew up in a different country. A different experience.

That is what I see among Hispanics (second-generation)... (they are) losing their background in a sense. They are part of them, but they are more defined by (the) here and the values and the morals of here, not their parents. That is the chasm between the first and second-generation.

PART TWO:

PREPARING FOR THE RECRUITMENT AND RETENTION OF EMERGING GENERATIONS OF LATINOS

CHAPTER 4

THE UNIQUE CHALLENGE AND OPPORTUNITY FOR LATINO CHURCHES IN AMERICA

"In churches where the majority of the Latino population is first-generation immigrants, members must realize that their children grow up seeking their own identities and agency."

An underlying challenge for the retention of second- and third-generation Latinos in Latino churches in America is the question of church culture and identity. The nucleus of the challenge in a community like Faro Church and others is the range of ethnic and linguistic characteristics.

Guglani (2016) quoting Zentella explained this dichotomy: "Those who maintain close ties with their land of origin express particular national identities (i.e., Dominican, Mexican, Puerto Rican, etc.) and/or transnational identities, integrating features of their native culture and those of American culture" (p. 345).

A Latino church in America is unique. A congregation can be comprised of multiple generations, and the cultural differences between these groups result in a variety of challenges that must be addressed. For this reason, "These families and churches must face decisions about language, work ethic, and cultural assimilation" (Choi & Berhó, 2016, p. 100).

Also, in churches where the majority of the Latino population is first-generation immigrants, members must realize that their children grow up seeking their own identities and agency. This cultural assimilation is not an easy challenge to address because the impact of multiple generations worshiping together in an immigrant church is complex and results in several opportunities for conflict (Choi & Berhó, 2016, p. 100).

The Latino church leader's perspective on these issues is vital as it has a significant impact on language, culture maintenance, and the retention of subsequent generations in the church. These perspectives strongly influence daily ministry decisions regarding which language or languages to speak at church and, ultimately, help determine if the children of the church community will grow up to be in a Spanish-only speaking church or lose the language, become English monolinguals, and in the process gradually discontinue church attendance or, more seriously, leave the Christian faith.

Among other challenges, Latino church leaders must address the construct of their ethnic and linguistic identities in the church context and how these are affected by the culture, language, and theological orthodoxy at large. The primary issue at hand is the possibility to maintain a native culture without native language. These challenges provide a starting focal point to foster cooperative dialogue and stimulate further scholarship as Latino churches continue to grow in numbers and significance in America.

The Evolution of Immigrant Congregations

Models of change in immigrant, first-generation churches hypothesize that ethnic congregations become more acculturated in response to intergenerational conflicts. As ethnic second- and third-plus-generation church members attempt to meet their personal unique social needs, ethnic churches are forced to amend their mission, vision, and structures in order to ensure the survival of their congregations.

Stevens (2004) found that generational wants and needs can exert pressure for change by showing a strong emphasis on interethnic evangelism through the adoption of monolingual English services (p. 121–138).

Similarly, Goette explained that data gathered from various immigrant ethnic churches demonstrates that they become more assimilated over time, moving from monolingual churches where services are conducted in the immigrants' home language to bilingual or monolingual churches where English predominates (as cited in Kwon et al., 2001, pp. 125–140). Holding services in English is a strategy that these communities use to become more inclusive since English language services allow for participation across ethnic groups and generations within immigrant communities (Ebaugh & Chafetz, 2000).

Yang and Enbaugh (2001) also identified the same transition among other religious communities. They explained that as these immigrant religious communities transfer from "particularism to greater universalism in membership, immigrant Buddhists, Muslims, Christians, and even Hindus have seen increased participation from people outside of their own ethnic groups, including fellow immigrants, as well as native-born black and white Americans" (p. 367).

Mullin's Three-Stage Model of Immigrant Churches

On logical grounds, Mullin's (1987) three-stage model is helpful in understanding the journey of immigrant ethnic churches (Figure 9). The first stage starts when "a strong first-generation leadership establishes an ethnic church in response to their cultural and linguistic differences, as well as discrimination faced in other churches" (Stevens, 2004, p. 122).

As the next generations culturally integrate, churches enter the second stage, "where congregations experience a shift in language and introduce English language services and bilingual ministers" (Stevens, 2004, p. 122).

Finally, the third stage is brought about "as subsequent generations become more structurally assimilated and enter into the cliques, clubs and institutions of the host society. As this happens, the appeal of ethnic churches gradually diminishes for them and the church is transformed into a multiethnic, English speaking congregation" (Stevens, 2004, p. 122).

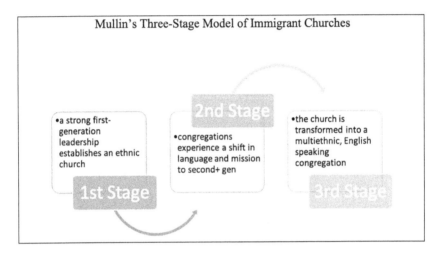

Figure 9. Three-Stage model of immigrant churches. Adapted from *The Life-Cycle of Ethnic Churches in Sociological Perspective* by M. R. Mullins, 1987, pp. 321–324.

Goette's Six-Stage Transformational Model for Immigrant Churches

Goette studied the transformation of first-generation churches into bilingual/second-generation churches in a Korean-American context. Like the Latino churches in America, the Korean church in America is experiencing demographical changes that have moved Korean church leaders to develop monolingual English ministries.

Korean churches in America are shifting from the first-generation focus to an English-ministry focus. However, Goette granted that a smooth transition requires the first-generation leadership of pastors, elders, and deacons to make "cultural concessions" to effectively shepherd the Americanized Korean Americans (as cited in Kwon et al., 2001, p. 139).

Goette explained that this is due to the insistence of most Korean churches in the US to target only "nuclear" Korean Americans who speak Korean fluently and prefer Korean cultural values over American values (Kwon et al., 2001, p. 237).

To solve this problem, Goette provided a six-stage transformational model for immigrant ethnic churches. He explained, "Just as the immigrant family goes through tremendous changes during the first two or three generations after they have immigrated, so does the immigrant church" (as cited in Kwon et al., 2001, p. 237).

According to Goette, six stages and five crises are linked with an adaptation of a church from a first-generation church into a second-generation bilingual church (Figure 10). The critical stages of the transformation derive from the creation of the children's ministry (CM), youth ministry (YM), English department (ED), and English-speaking congregation (EC) while the crises originate from the English-speaking Sunday leadership requirement, part-time trained leadership requirement, language and cultural crisis, decision-making crisis, and power/focus crisis associated between generations (Kwon et al., 2001, p. 128).

Goette's model explained that as children of immigrants grow older, Sunday school and religious services must be conducted in English to meet their linguistic needs. Eventually, this leads to the establishment of two parallel congregations, one in the home language and the other in English, each of which holds equal power and influence. In the final stages, as the older generation dies and becomes less active, the church becomes a predominately English-speaking church with a foreign language department to meet the needs of the remaining first-generation congregants. Goette estimated that it will take the average church between twenty-five to forty years to complete this process (Kwon et al., 2001, p. 128).

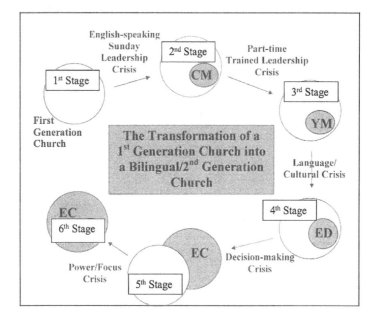

Figure 10. Six-Stage transformational model for immigrant churches (Kwon et al., 2001, p. 128).

Note: Created from the *Six-Stage Transformational Model for Immigrant Churches* by Goette (2001) as cited in Kwon et al.

The models provided by Mullins and Goette contend that "ethnic churches adapt (adopt English language services) in response to larger environmental changes (cultural assimilation of later generations) in order to take advantage of existing resources (second and third generation members) necessary for survival" (Stevens, 2004, p. 123).

Concluding Considerations on the Evolution of Immigrant Congregations

First-generation ethnic churches have a choice between going out of business or developing a new ministry focus. If first-generation churches widen their base of relevance, organizational survival is a possibility. In order to recruit second- and third-plus generations, churches must broaden their original vision and mission to create an environment that would be as equally attractive to them as it was for the first-generation (Mullins, 1987).

It can be concluded that without question, ethnic churches do change in response to the demands of growing second and third generations (Stevens, 2004, p. 123), and in some instances, adopting English services is seen as a way of preventing the silent exodus of these later generations (Chai, 1998).

Subsequently, it can be argued that the Latino church in American must create models that fit a ministry vision focused on the retention and recruitment of bilingual and monolingual Latinos in the United States. Latino churches in American need to recognize shifts in population, sociological factors, and fluency in English and make the necessary changes.

Case Studies of Latino Churches

On the basis of the evidence currently available, it seems fair to suggest that monolingual Spanish ministry models are generally not successful when targeting second- and third-plus-generation Latinos. Alternatively, "the overwhelming majority of Hispanic ministries in the U.S. rely almost exclusively on Spanish and therefore by default primarily target first-generation Latinos (i.e., immigrants)" (Rodríguez, 2009, p. 106).

Sánchez (2010) observed that one of the reasons for refusal of a missiological focus on the second- and third-plus-generation Latinos is the pressure from first-generation Latinos as immigrant parents to pressure their pastors to help them "preserve the Hispanic language and culture" (p. 85). This could stem from a desire to maintain clear ethnic boundaries and distinction from white Americans.

Conversely, given the centrality of this issue, linguistic, cultural, and socioeconomic factors have redesigned ministry models and practices in churches that traditionally targeted first-generation, Spanish-dominant

Latinos. The recognition of these factors has transitioned many churches to target second- and third-plus-generation Latinos successfully.

The pressure to change comes from generational turnover and needs. Stevens (2004) explained, "In current models of ethnic churches' evolution, generational change is the primary catalyst of language and other cultural changes" (p. 123). Along with generational turnover, there needs to be a recognition of transition. Rodríguez (2009) wrote, "Older Hispanic *barrios* in the cities like Los Angeles, San Antonio, Miami, New York, and Chicago, once dominated by first-generation Spanish-speaking *Mexicanos, Cubanos and Puertorriqueños* are now dominated by U.S.-born Mexicans, Cubans and Puerto Ricans" (pp. 104–105).

Additionally, as already highlighted several times in this book, he explained that a growing number of Latinos are English dominant and do not speak Spanish at all. Furthermore, they feel no ties to their ethnic roots and homeland nor their cultural and religious bonds.

Perhaps a dive into Latino church case studies can provide a clear strategic process needed in immigrant, first-generation churches. The extraordinary success of multilingual and multigenerational churches reveals that a commitment to serve, evangelize, and disciple second- and third-plus-generation Latinos obligates church leaders to embrace more contextually appropriate ministry models for English-dominant Latinos. Let me share some examples of this:

Iglesia del Redentor (Church of the Redeemer), Baldwin Park, California

One of the first Spanish-speaking churches in Southern California to transition from a monolingual Spanish ministry model to a multilingual, multigenerational model was Iglesia del Redentor (Rodríguez, 2009, pp. 106–107). Although established in 1961, Pastor Aureliano Flores began to sense a need for assimilation as early as 1962. Pastor Flores began to observe demographical intricacies as personified by his children, and the seed was planted to accommodate changing demographics. He observed that his children preferred to speak English instead of Spanish, and later when they were teenagers, they fancied their friends' English-speaking churches.

Faced by the internal struggle of maintaining present state of ministry and the reality of the acculturation and assimilation of the second-generation congregants in his church, Pastor Aureliano made the difficult decision to provide worship services and Bible classes simultaneously in Spanish and English. Rodríguez (2009) explained, "He could maintain the status quo and inevitably see his children leave for an English-speaking church. Worse still, he could watch them leave the church altogether, a common occurrence among children of other families in the congregation" (p. 107).

The transition was not without challenges. Pastor Flores did not speak English and had to learn the language and overcome his fears and insecurities about cultural reception and recognition. Pastor Flores explained, "I knew that I would have to become proficient in both languages, and since I didn't speak English very well, I would have to be humble, disciplined and work very hard" (Rodríguez, 2009, p. 108).

A significant underlying feature to the transition was Pastor Flores's insistence to not delegate the monolingual English service to an assistant or hired hand but to maintain the same senior leadership. Pastor Flores assumed "jealousy and distrust were certain to plague a multilingual church if it became necessary for him to delegate the English group to an assistant" (Rodríguez, 2009, p. 108).

After a decade-long commitment, Pastor Flores is now fluent in English. In the process, he retained his son's commitment to the church, and his son Paul became an associate pastor for more than ten years. Upon his retirement, Pastor Flores asked his son to assume the role of senior pastor. Along similar lines, Pastor Paul Flores "has dedicated himself to become proficient in Spanish as his father became in English" (Rodríguez, 2009, p. 108). The result over time has been "a dynamic and thriving 500-member multilingual church where three generations of the Flores family now serve the Lord together in a Hispanic church" (Rodríguez, 2009, p. 107).

Iglesia Hispana de Cristo (Hispanic Church of Christ), Western New York

The Latino community of Iglesia Hispana de Cristo in Western New York underwent a similar demographic and linguistic challenge as Faro Church. In Iglesia Hispana de Cristo, the majority of younger parents are first- and second-generation Latinos who were born in the United States or arrived before the age of thirteen. Inversely, older parents are first-generation immigrants, having immigrated to the United States at age thirteen or older.

Guglani (2016) reported, "While most younger parents (71%) are English dominant or monolingual, all older parents (100%) are Spanish dominant, monolingual, or balanced bilingual" (Guglani, 2016, p. 350). These competing lingual ideologies threatened the church's existence and created ministry and missional challenges. If a church does not face these challenges, it may lose its next generation.

When examining the detachment of language from culture, that is, the likelihood of being Latino without speaking Spanish, opinions varied among older parents and younger parents of Iglesia Hispana de Cristo. Guglani (2016) wrote, "For older parents, language and culture are inseparable elements; that is, in order to preserve the native culture, one must also preserve the native language" (p. 353). Alternatively, Guglani reported that younger parents were less concerned with Spanish language transmission than are older parents (Guglani, 2016, p. 353).

Interestingly, although the underlying argument at Iglesia Hispana de Cristo revolved around the language preference, Guglani (2016) described that the "vast majority of participants interviewed reported that they attend the church, at least in part, because it is a Hispanic and Spanish-speaking church that highly values the minority language and culture" (p. 350). Although the church is in New York, being a member of the church community offered these individuals a sense of belonging and cultural identity. To illustrate, all of the participants in the study believed "that passing on Hispanic culture to the next generation is important, and most (75%) believe that passing on the Spanish language is equally important" (Guglani, 2016, p. 350).

Still, Guglani (2016) conceded that opinions did change widely according to age. The study found that younger and older parents expressed quite distinct perspectives. Guglani explained, "Older parents, having spent more time in their native country, generally feel a closer tie to the Spanish language and Hispanic culture than younger parents, who have spent much of their lives in the United States" (p. 350).

One competing ideology stresses the identity of the church as a Spanish-speaking, Latino community above all else. Guglani (2016) wrote about the value and emphasis taught and encouraged in keeping the Spanish language:

This ideology is supported by church policy, church leaders, church elders, and the older members of the congregation. Church policy requires Spanish-only in all formal contexts, including in ceremonies, in services, and in conducting official business; and all church leaders must be Spanish proficient. Church elders cherish the Spanish-language oasis that the Iglesia provides while living in an English-speaking society. They explain that one of the church's main appeals is precisely the fact that it is Spanish-speaking—that many parishioners choose to attend because they want to be part of a Spanish-speaking community or prefer to worship in Spanish. (p. 356)

The competing ideology favors a bilingual or monolingual church environment that creates a place for both languages:

Spanish language proficiency is not a requirement, where English speakers are welcomed and accommodated through English-language programming. This ideology is supported by the younger members of the congregation, who sincerely appreciate the Hispanic,

Spanish-speaking community the church provides but who, at the same time, do not wish to exclude anyone on the basis of language. They emphasize the fact that most of the church's children, as well as members of the surrounding community who the church seeks to evangelize, are English dominant or monolingual and unable to understand religious teachings given in Spanish. They insist that, if the Iglesia hopes to attract and retain these individuals, it must accommodate their linguistic needs. (Guglani, 2016, p. 356)

New Life Covenant Ministries, Chicago, Illinois

Having taken over his father-in-law's Latino monolingual and monocultural church of approximately 125 members, Pastor Wilfredo de Jesus "proposed a fundamental shift in the church's traditional approach to ministry" (Rodríguez, 2009, p. 109). Rodríguez (2009) explained Pastor de Jesus' ministry focus:

> He insisted that if the church was to reach and serve the community, it must immediately begin incorporating English in all its programs and services to meet the linguistic preferences of Latinos who love *"la comida criolla"* (Puerto Rican food) but prefer to speak English. (p. 109).

Similar to the experience of Pastor Aureliano Flores at Iglesia del Redentor, Pastor Wilfredo faced resistance and disbelief from the founding Spanish-dominant members of the church. Pastor Wilfredo explained to Rodríguez (2009), "Their biggest fear was that they would be pushed aside and inevitably be left behind by the younger,

English-dominant majority" (p. 75). This is a common fear among first-generation Latino church leaders.

Although there was much debate about the Spanish-language focus or the English-language focus, the church ultimately adopted a principal English focus that led to renaming the church New Life Covenant Ministries and substantial growth in church attendance. In 2008, New Life Covenant Ministries averaged over 4,000 people. Amazingly and important to note, it was described that "even in the English-language services one can easily perceive the *boricuan* [synonym for Puerto Rican] influence in the music, prayers and preaching" (Rodríguez, 2009, p. 110). These results provide confirmatory evidence and seem to suggest that a large portion of the demographic at New Life Covenant Ministries are Latinos who keep an affinity to the Latino culture but prefer to worship in monolingual English services.

On the other hand, the monolingual Spanish service of New Life Covenant Ministries has also grown. The only Spanish service averages over 500 in attendance. Rodríguez (2009) concluded, "Today, 80 percent of the membership at New Life Covenant is still Latino, the overwhelming majority of whom are native-born and English-dominant" (p. 110).

Mission Ebenezer Family Church, Carson, California

Mission Ebenezer Family Church was founded in June of 1960 by Reverend Miguel and Lupe Canales as a Spanish-speaking church. It has grown from fifteen to 3,000 adherents since their son, Dr. Isaac Canales, implemented monolingual services. It is a Spanish- and English-speaking church with five worship services on Sundays, drawing widely from the Greater Los Angeles Metropolitan area as well as enjoying regular mention in the media, having been featured in both the *Los Angeles Times* and *The Daily Breeze* (Mission Ebenezer Family Church, 2017).

Mission Ebenezer Family Church began as one of the smallest and only Spanish Assemblies of God churches in the South Bay. Over time, a switch was made to include English-speaking worship for English-speaking friends and family in the Spanish congregation. Today, both language experiences are prevailing. It takes five services on Sunday to accommodate the growth of this dynamic church with great ministries to the family.

Similar to the experience of Pastor de Jesus and Pastor Flores, Dr. Canales experienced religious and cultural apprehensions about new linguistic realities. Canales explained that some congregants opposed the implementation of a monolingual English service because it would open the door to the secularism of the American culture at large. Canales recalled hearing members object, "El diablo habla ingles" ("The devil speaks English"), revealing what Rodríguez (2009) called a sense of "cultural superiority" (Rodríguez, 2009, p. 117) or perhaps, a cultural resistance that is endemic among many conservative and traditional first-generation Latinos. Ortiz described this sentiment as Latino ethnocentrism that brings with it an anti-American bias that inadvertently reinforces the previously stated "paradox of living in two hostile worlds" (Ortiz, 1993, p. 63).

Adding further data to the discussion, Canales broadened the scope for the need for monolingual English ministry models among Latinos. According to Canales, "You cannot build a great or financially independent church on the back of immigrants" (as cited in Rodríguez, 2009, p. 115). He insisted that Latino leaders who desire to be unrestricted by denominational jurisdiction or the control of a sponsoring church must reach out strategically to the upwardly mobile, native-born, second- and third-plus-generation Latinos (as cited in Rodríguez, 2009, p. 116).

Templo Calvario,
Santa Ana, California

Dr. Danny De Leon, pastor of Templo Calvario in Santa Ana, California, began ministering at the church in 1976. Within two years, the church grew from sixty to 750 congregants, which was attributed to a transition to monolingual English and Spanish services (Templo Calvario, 2018). In 1985, the church moved to a 1,400-seat facility, with Billy Graham as the keynote speaker (Van Veen, 2017). Then in 2007, the church moved to its current auditorium that seats 2,200 to accommodate its average weekly attendance that exceeds 3,800 (Van Veen, 2017). Templo Calvario is now one of the largest bilingual Latino congregations in the United States (Van Veen, 2017).

Upon the implementation of monolingual services, de Leon experienced similar challenges to the ones already detailed above. However, as it relates to the question at hand and adding to the discussion, de Leon identified an additional challenge to the argument. In his experience, Pastor de Leon observed a fracture between first-generation Latinos and second- and third-generation Latinos. He identified a rejection at the hands of immigrants who criticized US-born Latinos for not speaking Spanish or for speaking it inadequately (Rodríguez, 2009, p. 113). His observation provides further data to substantiate the perceived void among second- and third-plus-generation Latinos who are contributing to the silent exodus. The evidence seems to point to the fact that second- and third-plus-generation Latinos do not usually respond positively to the evangelistic efforts of Spanish-speaking immigrant churches where ethnicity is most often determined by language use alone.

A Word of Caution

Presmanes (2007) provided a word of caution on the use of bilingual liturgy and describes its challenges. He postulated three central concerns to consider before implementing bilingual liturgy.

First, the use of bilingual liturgy is a simple pastoral tool to communicate, but it is not the only way to achieve an ecclesiastical accord. Second, he contended that "the best home for bilingual worship is its celebration among bilingual people" (Presmanes, 2007, p. 139). When bilingual services are celebrated among monolingual people, "the bilingual liturgical text always will impede the full, conscious, and active participation of the liturgical assembly" (Presmanes, 2007, p. 140). Finally, "bilingual liturgy should be the exception and not the rule" (Presmanes, 2007, p. 146).

This word of caution encourages a monolingual approach to ministry that can facilitate liturgical engagement while acknowledging congregational unification challenges among multilingual communities. Further, it points to the success of monolingual English services among Latino churches in America as described in this chapter.

Summary

Meditating deeply on the scholarly work above can help us navigate two worlds. This relevant literature and accepted models of change among immigrant churches and a theological substantiation demonstrated and supported changes in population, fluency in English, and religious attitudes between first-generation Latinos and second- and third-plus-generation Latinos.

This awareness has profound implications for retention and recruitment of second- and third-plus-generation in Latino Churches. This information is significant for the many realms of the mission of Latino churches in America and indeed for anyone seeking to understand the nature of navigating two worlds in a multicultural yet monoethnic context.

The Latino church case studies provided a clear strategic process needed in immigrant, first-generation churches. The implementation of monolingual English services in Latino churches has profound implications for retention and recruitment of second- and third-plus-generation Latinos. However, the linguistic transition is never without cultural challenges and doubts based on religious tradition expressed by the first-generation church leadership.

We must recognize that in the above-mentioned examples, ministry leaders had aspirations to keep their immediate relatives and the families of the church under one roof. They also wanted to provide a ministry environment where discipleship and development of the second- and third-plus-generation Latinos who were English-dominant would occur.

The churches demonstrating the transition to monolingual English services and multicultural ministry models are illustrations of churches who recognized the changing generational and lingual characteristics and made the appropriate adaptations by providing the necessary programs and services in English.

The extraordinary success of these multilingual and multigenerational churches reveals that a commitment to serve, evangelize, and disciple second- and third-plus-generation Latinos obligates church leaders to embrace more contextually appropriate ministry models for English-dominant Latinos. These second- and third-plus-generation Latinos often feel out of place or even unwelcome in churches that are exclusively Spanish speaking, but they are also reluctant to assimilate into English-speaking dominant-group churches. This is both the challenge and unique opportunity for Latino churches in America.

CHAPTER 5

SETTLERS OR DEVELOPERS?

"While not negating their identity as settling immigrants, they must recognize a more real identity (imago Dei) given by God and seek to fulfill God's command (missio Dei) to reach the next generation."

The question of recruitment and retention of second-and third-plus generations in the Latino church in America is a question of motive. Does the church want to be a generation of settlers or developers? Is the Latino church in America willing and ready to set up the next generation of Latinos for spiritual success?

Remember the Sigmoid Curve in the introduction of the book? Developers come to the axis point of the s-shape and recognize the plateau and recognize seasons of restructuring and renewal (Malphurs, 2013, p. 11).

In keeping with the biblical mandate of the church and the redemptive and restorative purpose of God, the church must desire not only personal transformation but also the transformation of emerging generations.

The motive of development in founded on God's redemptive purposes through Jesus Christ as revealed in the Old and New Testament Scriptures. The whole Bible follows a common thread that revolves around God's redemptive purpose and mission for a fallen humanity. This redemptive mission or theology of mission can only be understood when viewed in its historical and scriptural context and origins.

According to Kaiser (2009), "There is a popular misconception that the Old Testament does not have a missionary mandate and that it is a book dedicated only to the Jews and their history" (p. 10). However, God's redemptive purposes for the whole world are evidenced in the Old Testament and throughout the Bible. The Great Commission, as we know it today, is not primarily a New Testament idea.

Among many Old Testament texts that clearly express God's redemptive mission and God's missionary mandate for Israel, Genesis 3:15 and Genesis 12:1–3 exemplify God's redemptive mission and God's missionary purpose through the nation of Israel. Humanity is separated from God, and Israel was meant to communicate to the Gentile world God's redemptive purpose.

Since the fall of man in the garden of Eden, God's redemptive mission has been to reconcile sinners to himself. This is immediately exemplified in God's promise to Adam and Eve after they had sinned. When Adam and Eve rebelled and sinned against God, they severed the perfect fellowship and communion with God, thereby distorting and damaging his image (the *imago Dei*—image of God) in (or on) them. Sin had broken their relationship with God, each other, and even themselves. So, God's redemptive solution to their brokenness is alluded to in Genesis 3:15: "And I will put enmity between you and the woman, and between your seed and her Seed; He shall bruise your head, and you shall bruise His heel" (Gen. 3:15).

As early as Genesis 3:15, God's redemptive blueprint by which salvation would be provided for humanity may be seen. Moreau, Corwin, and McGee (2004) explained that "this initial promise of salvation, known as *protoevangelium,* is the promise that Jesus will come for all people" (p. 31).

Ellison (2009) explained, "The two figures in this conflict are later declared to be Christ, who was the seed born of a woman (Gal. 4:4), and Satan, called 'the serpent of old'" (Rev. 20:2) (p.19). Eve's Seed was to bruise the head of the serpent. This prophecy points forward to the promise of Jesus's redemptive work on the cross, which would destroy the devil. The prophecy that the serpent would bruise the heel of the Seed pictures Satan's "driving force behind the crucifixion of Christ" (Ellison, 2009, p.19). Ellison further explained that Genesis 3:15 gives God's two-fold program for God's kingdom and man's redemption: "He would ultimately reclaim His total kingdom by destroying Satan and Satan's kingdom, and would redeem believing men in the process by the death of Christ" (p.19).

One of the first developments in this redemptive plan included the choosing of men of faith through the offspring of Adam and Eve who would install God's redemptive purposes through the nation of Israel. Moreau et al. (2004) explained, "God's universal intent now is to be manifest through an individual and the people who come from that individual" (p. 31). The first of these men was Abraham, and his calling is found in Genesis 12:1–3:

> Now the Lord had said to Abram: "Get out of your country, from your family and from your father's house, to a land that I will show you. I will make you a great nation; I will bless you and make your name great; and you shall be a blessing. I will bless those who bless you, and I will curse him who curses you; and in you all the families of the earth shall be blessed. (Gen. 12:1–3)

Abraham's call encompasses a covenant and a blessing. God's covenant with Abraham promised to make him into a great nation and bless him to become a blessing to all the families of the earth. Abraham would be blessed for the sake of becoming the nation by which all other nations would be blessed. This blessing is known as the Great Commission of the Old Testament (Moreau et al., 2004, p. 32). God would make Abraham into a great nation and bless him so that through him, "*all peoples of the earth will be blessed*" (Gen. 12:1–3; Rom. 4:13). This was further unveiled when Israel was established in the Promised Land to be light for the Gentiles (Isa. 42:6; 49:6). They were to be God's exclusive treasured possession, to be a kingdom of priests and a holy nation (Exod. 19:5–6).

The whole nation was to function on behalf of the kingdom of God. Israel was to serve as the center to which other nations would come and find God. However, Israel did not obey God, and through the divided kingdom and the exile, a more solidified and clearer picture of the promised Messiah emerges through the writings of the prophets.

Ultimately, Jesus would embody the Old Testament mission of blessing all nations as He gave His life as a ransom for humanity (Mark 10:45; 1 Tim. 2:3–6). Jesus would give Himself as a payment for the sins of humanity on the cross. This is the basic fulfillment of the Genesis 3:15 and Genesis 12:1–3 passages.

However, I do not want us to miss the point. Remember that in the Bible, "the God of Abraham, and of Isaac, and of Jacob" was a title and description of God used in the Old Testament (Exod. 3:6), then referred to by Jesus and the apostles in the New Testament (Matt. 22:32; Acts 3:13) to distinguish the one true God from the gods of the Gentiles and to show him as the God of Israel, the one, only true, and living God.

There was a transgenerational connection between Abraham, Isaac, and Jacob. Through the generations, Abraham's faith transferred into Isaac's foundations and then into Jacob's inheritance.

Similarly, in Joshua's generation, there was a transgenerational link in the time of the Exodus and the conquest. A relationship was formed from the "the God of Moses" (Exod. 6:3) to "the God of Joshua" (Josh. 1:2), but then, this was followed by a loss in connection. A link was lost.

The period of the Judges explains how the link was lost: "After that whole generation had been gathered to their ancestors, another generation grew up who knew neither the Lord nor what he had done for Israel" (Judg. 2:10).

The generation of the Exodus led by Moses took the generation of the conquest to the edge of the Promised Land. However, after having settled in the Promised Land, there was a sort of "silent exodus" that occurred with the generation of the judges. Although Joshua's generation was honored in many ways, they failed to pass the truths to their children that Moses handed down to them.

Joshua's generation were not only the children of the desert, but they were the first recipients of God's inspired law and the first generation to enter the Promised Land. They experienced the miracle of the parting of the Jordan River (Josh. 3).

They experienced the miracle of the tumbling wall of Jericho (Josh. 6). They experienced the miracle of the sun and the moon standing still (Josh. 10:13). They experienced the very first Passover (Exod. 12). They experienced liberation out of captivity.

Nonetheless, after settling down in the Promised Land, they neglected to pass these truths and miracles, along with the knowledge of God, to the next generation. The memory of God's great works gradually faded away and, with this memory, their influence upon the hearts of the people.

The new generation had no personal relationship with God and no personal awareness of his power. God was someone whom their parents related to and who did great things for their parent's generation but had no relation with the next generation. A similar challenge lies ahead for Faro Church and Latino churches in America. They cannot exist alone; they must coexist with rising generations and prepare and develop them for spiritual success.

Abraham's generation had a developer's mentality while Joshua's generation had a settler's mentality.

The Psalmist summarized this challenge like this: "We will tell the next generation the praiseworthy deeds of the Lord, his power, and the wonders he has done" (Ps. 78:4). Correspondingly, he continued, "So the next generation would know them, even the children yet to be born, and they in turn would tell their children" (Ps. 78:6). In another chapter, the Psalmist wrote, "One generation commends your works to another; they tell of your mighty acts" (Ps. 145:4).

Jesus in Matthew 28:18 said, "All authority in heaven and on earth has been given to me." And he continued in Matthew 28:19–20,

"Therefore go and make disciples of all nations, baptizing them in the name of the Father and of the Son and of the Holy Spirit, and teaching them to obey everything I have commanded you. And surely I am with you always, to the very end of the age."

This passage, known as the Great Commission, is given in light of the authority of Jesus in Matthew 28:18. This indicates that this is an authoritative command, not a suggestion.

Therefore, Jesus has bestowed upon us God's redemptive mission. It is his authority that sends, his authority that guides, and his authority that empowers. His work and message continued to the world through his disciples based on that premise. Jesus has all authority to confer upon believers God's redemptive mission to go and spread God's redemptive plan to the entire world.

The relationship between the *imago Dei* (image of God) and the *missio Dei* (the mission of God) is central to the commission of God. In other words, God's intention for humans is to reflect His glory. This only happens when man is in right relationship with God, fellowshipping with Him and enjoying perfect communion with Him.

Therefore, the *missio Dei,* at the core, aims at restoring and renewing the *imago Dei* in man. This restoration mission and project is not solely individualistic; it is corporate and communal. God is on a mission to restore a people unto Himself that they may be a people that bring Him glory, honor, praise, and adoration.

As the church lives in the world on mission, it must not forget that the *missio Dei* is seeking to redeem and restore the *imago Dei* in order that man may once again be in a perfect relationship by which he reflects the glory of God in the created order.

If one generation does not develop the next generation, the gospel's reach and effect must start from scratch. As stated in the introduction of the book, if the Latino church in America cannot produce disciples, they will never reproduce leaders; if they cannot reproduce leaders, they cannot reproduce pastors; if they cannot reproduce pastors, they cannot produce churches, and if they cannot reproduce churches, communities are left without the foundational tool of God's kingdom to reach and disciple the lost.

Latino churches must demonstrate an unwavering commitment to relevance and reaching the next generations. For too many churches, the commitment to certain cultural forms far outweighed the commitment to the function of the message. However, a harsh reminder for the Latino Church in America is that the church does not primarily exist to keep the culture and language of a particular country or ethnicity.

If the first-generation leadership of pastors, elders, and deacons are unwilling to make "cultural concessions" (Kwon et al., 2001, p. 139) to effectively shepherd their emerging adults, another generation will rise who will not know the Lord or what He has done for them.

Latino churches have a choice between going out of business or developing a new ministry focused on the development of the next generations. Latino churches do not have to, as Mullins (1987) described, "de-ethnicize" but instead must widen their base of relevance and envision a multiethnic, multilingual, and multicultural church.

The silent exodus requires a shift in mentality from the first-generation leadership. While not negating their identity as settling immigrants, they must recognize a more real identity (imago Dei) given by God and seek to fulfill God's command (missio Dei) to reach the next generation. Our mindset must change from settlers to developers.

The question is, how do we do it? Perhaps a good starting point is to allow a capacity to welcome change and to seek to mend the schism that are found in Latino churches. I will explain below.

The Capacity to Welcome Change

The central theoretical premise for the following biblical and theological foundations is that there is a silent exodus happening in Faro Church and similarly among Latino churches in America. It is a crisis of infertility and preservation, an inability to retain and reclaim emerging generations due to changing demographics. Unless the Latino church takes emerging adults and their changing demographics and preferences more seriously, the future of the Latino church is in doubt.

Nothing will be more revitalizing to the Latino church in America than change and renewal, focused on the retention and recruitment of second- and third-plus-generation Latinos. However, renewal cannot happen unless the church prepares for it.

This type of ministry focus requires a willingness to welcome change, as renewal is directly connected to the capacity to welcome change. As detailed in Malphurs's Life Cycle of the Church in the introduction, understanding renewal begins with the recognition that change is inevitable and unavoidable (Malphurs, 2013, p. 9–14). However, since change is inevitable and unavoidable, it is also predictable, and since it is predictable, the church can prepare for it.

Malphurs explained that all good things have a shelf life. In a world of constant, turbulent change, many relationships and most organizations do not last. The pattern is that they wax and eventually wane because they do not recognize the need for reformation and revitalization (Malphurs, 2013, p. 10). No matter what person or institution it is, organizational "plateau" sets in. The person or institution becomes brittle, ceases to function, and expires.

This is why it is vital for Latino churches in America to identify plateau or decline and recognize the leading of the Spirit to implement a strategic planning process to avoid organizational death by setting the organization for renewal.

Similarly, Scazzero (2015) explained that every church and leader needs to understand that there is a continuum of endings in leadership (p. 270). To not recognize this natural shift in the life of a church can result in "disintegration, falling apart, a coming undone" of a once-thriving church or ministry (Scazzero, 2015, p. 280).

Correspondingly, Latino churches in America need to prepare for renewal by having vessels ready for a change. Jesus explained this dichotomy: "Neither do people pour new wine into old wineskins. If they do, the skins will burst; the wine will run out and the wineskins will be ruined. No, they pour new wine into new wineskins, and both are preserved" (Matt. 9:17 NIV).

In Jesus's day, people would take an animal skin and sew it to make a container or bag in which people could store and carry wine. Newly made wine would ferment and expand, and thus if it were placed in an old wineskin that no longer contained much elasticity, the seams would tear and cause the wine to spill out. If unfermented wine is put into brittle old wineskins, the gas will burst the skins, and both the skins and the wine will be lost.

The immediate application meant that the Jewish religion of Jesus's time was a worn-out wineskin that would burst if filled with the new wine of the gospel. The new wine of the Spirit could not be forced into the old wineskins of Judaism. Jesus was revealing the Jewish religion was about to be renewed. As a result, today there is no need for sacrifices, priests, the temple, nor ceremonies. Jesus did not come to renovate the Law or even mix law and grace; he came with new life.

Alford (1868) explained the imagery of Jesus's words in Matthew 9:17. He articulated that the words of Jesus "describe the vanity of the attempt to keep the new wine in the old skin, the old ceremonial man, [is] unrenewed in the spirit of his mind," and therefore, "the skins are broken" (Alford, 1868, p. 62). Conversely, he continued:

> The new wine is something too living and strong for so weak a moral frame; it shatters the fair outside of ceremonial seeming; and the wine runneth out, the spirit is lost; the man is neither a blameless Jew nor a faithful Christian; both are spoiled. (Alford, 1868, p. 62)

The principle for today is clear. Jesus reminds us that what is old and stagnant often cannot be renewed or reformed without being ruined and entirely changed. God will often look for or create a new vessel to contain his new work until those vessels eventually wear themselves out.

When Jesus taught that new wine must be poured into new wineskins, he emphasized that the container and the content, both the medium and the message, are new. This is a sober reminder that at times when God wants to initiate a season of renewal, new systems and structures are needed for success and blessing.

The capacity to welcome change is vital for Latino churches in America. To identify plateau or decline and recognize the leading of the Spirit to implement a strategic planning process to avoid organizational death can set up the organization for renewal. Latino churches in America need to prepare for renewal by having vessels ready for a change.

Confronting the Schisms

More contextually appropriate ministry models in Latino churches must mend several ministry schisms. In 1 Corinthians 1:10, Paul wrote, "I appeal to you, brothers and sisters, in the name of our Lord Jesus Christ, that all of you *agree* with one another in what you say and that there be no *divisions* among you, but that you be perfectly united in mind and thought."

The ancient Greek word for divisions is σχίσμα (schisma). Although the English word "schism" is derived from this Greek word, it does not mean a "party" or a "faction"; it properly means, "to tear or rend" (Thayer, 1995).

In the church of Corinth, schisms happened because members of the church or the church leadership demeaned others whom they felt were not worthy to be proportionately treated because they were Gentiles or from a lower socioeconomic level. Paul's plea was to stop "ripping" each other apart and "tearing" up the body of Christ. Gentile Christians in Corinth were being mistreated.

So, Paul encouraged the church not to regard themselves or others as "second-class citizens" in God's kingdom. The Gentiles were not only full citizens of God's kingdom but also full and equal members of God's household. Since all Christians are part of the same body, they have the same access to God.

The mending of the schisms would only happen when the Corinthian church would learn to speak the same thing. The Greek word for *speak* is λέγω (Legō) meaning *to narrate, to describe,* which Paul follows with αὐτός (autos), meaning the *same thing* (Thayer, 1995). The connotation is that the remedy to the tearing apart is to *agree with one another.*

There are schisms, inevitable challenges, and differences that are apparent in Latino churches in America where Spanish is the primary language of communication. When engaging the changing, emerging Latino demographic, how do these churches communicate with a new linguistic reality? How can they speak the same thing when there are distinct linguistic preferences? How does a Latino church in America unite in a multicultural context?

There are clear and present dangers of schism/division as it relates to the specific evangelistic mission of Latino churches in America. The Bible, however, offers some hope and direction. There are at least four biblical examples that can help the Latino church in America navigate through the specific demographical challenges that arise from changing linguistic and cultural realities.

Mending the Language Schism

Perhaps the most evident danger of schism in the Latino church in America is language. A language is a fundamental tool of communication needed for unity. A classic example is found in the story of the Tower of Babel in Genesis 11:1–9. The story explains that the whole earth had one language and used the same words. So, people migrated, settled, and decided in direct disobedience to God's command to spread out over the earth (Gen. 9:1) to build. They said, "Come, let us build ourselves a city, with a tower that reaches to the heavens, so that we may make a name for ourselves; otherwise we will be scattered over the face of the whole earth" (Gen. 11:4).

Surprisingly, the Lord responded with these words, "If as one people speaking the same language they have begun to do this, then nothing they plan to do will be impossible for them. Come, let us go down and confuse their language so they will not understand each other" (Gen. 11:6–7). This confusion, along with their scattering throughout the earth, stopped the building project.

The story concludes, "That is why it was called Babel—because there the Lord confused the language of the whole world. From there the Lord scattered them over the face of the whole earth" (Gen. 11:9).

The Lord makes a prominent statement concerning the unifying power of speaking the same language. He said, "Nothing they plan to do will be impossible for them" (Gen. 11:7). This is a negative situation, teaching a positive principle. The principle is clear; if a group's language or terminology is confused, they will not be able to understand each other and accomplish anything. They will not be able to achieve anything, let alone build God's church. If the church is not proficient at communication, the result is confusion and division.

However, in reality, the problem with the people of Babel was not their language but their hearts. They wanted to get rid of God and make a name for themselves. If people are willing to communicate and work together regardless of their linguistic differences, unity is achievable. This is exemplified in the biblical account of Pentecost.

It can be said that at some level at Pentecost, God did something similar to what he did at the Tower of Babel. He gave people different tongues to spread the gospel. At Pentecost, God poured out his Spirit and filled the disciples, and they began to speak in tongues as the Spirit enabled them (Acts 2:4). As a consequence, Jews who had traveled from "every nation" under heaven were bewildered and asked, "Aren't all these who are speaking Galileans? Then how is it that each of us hears them in our native language?" (Acts 11:7–8).

So, the outpouring of the Holy Spirit resulted in linguistic understanding and ultimately the spread of the gospel message and the expansion of the church across the Roman Empire. Language was no longer a divisive tool, but through the Spirit of God, it was a unifying factor.

If the Latino church in America is to retain the second- and third-plus-generations, they need to communicate and cooperate with one another. To their benefit, they have access to the Holy Spirit who can empower and enable them to examine their ministry models to meet the linguistic needs of emerging Latino adults better.

Often in Latino churches in America where a monolingual Spanish ministry model is utilized, it is said that the language of heaven is Spanish. Whether this is done intentionally or in jest, it is still a prejudicial thing to say. The assumption is that only one sector of the church has access to the language that is spoken in heaven.

However, in reality, what is the language of heaven? Is Spanish the language of heaven? Is English the language of heaven? Fortunately, the Bible provides an answer to these questions.

In John's vision of heaven, he described heaven with these words, "there before me was a great multitude that no one could count, from every nation, tribe, people and language, standing before the throne and before the Lamb" (Rev. 7:9).

A closer look reveals that every language is spoken in heaven. It appears that although on earth, citizenship can change, in heaven, language and ethnicity are never lost. So, the language schism is mended when churches yield to the Spirit of God and follow his leading concerning linguistic realities

Mending the Ethnic Schism

I remind you that although synonymous, it is my preference to use the term *ethnicity* rather than race to stress the fact that human beings are described biblically as one race with different ethnicities (Acts 17:24–28).

In Numbers 12, Moses married a Cushite woman, something that his siblings, Miriam and Aaron, criticized. The account states, "Miriam and Aaron began to talk against Moses because of his Cushite wife, for he had married a Cushite" (Num. 12:1).

The suggestion here could be compounded. Jethro, Zipporah's father, could have been from Ethiopia and could have moved to Midian, making Zipporah, Moses' wife, an Ethiopian by birth who was living in Midian. Also, it may also be possible that the Ethiopian reference was a derogatory one used to criticize Zipporah because of a dark complexion.

It is possible that this was interracial marriage, something with which Miriam and Aaron did not agree. God's response to this apparent discrimination was strong. It states, "The anger of the Lord burned against them, and he left them. When the cloud lifted from above the tent, Miriam's skin was leprous—it became as white as snow" (Num. 12:9–10).

Leprosy was a disease of bodily decay and corruption; it was considered to be a curse. Miriam had an advanced case of leprosy instantly. At this moment, God caused her body to reflect her heart.

The rise of Latino intermarriage has the capacity to stir, not profound ethnic discrimination, but indeed cultural anxieties that can affect the retention of intermarried couples in Latino churches in America. Therefore, the ethnic schism can be mended when the Latino church in America recognizes the changing differences in population and sociological factors, even in the church, and does not allow them to be a source of decay but of life.

Mending the Cultural Schism

A classic example of cultural disparagement is in Acts 6. The account explains that a complaint arose due to a neglect of Hellenist widows in the church. Some of the Christians from a Greek background believed that the widows among the Hebrew Christians received preference in the daily distribution.

Though the titles Hebrews and Hellenists are used in the text, these were Christians and followers of Jesus. Nevertheless, the Hebrews were those Jews more inclined to embrace Jewish culture and were mostly from Judea. The Hellenists were those Jews who embraced the Greek and Roman culture, and most were from all over the Roman Empire.

To oversimplify, Hebrews tended to regard Hellenists as unspiritual compromisers who embraced Greek culture, and Hellenists regarded Hebrews as religious traditionalists.

There is a similar cultural phenomenon in the Latino Church in America. Many times, second- and third-plus-generation Latinos who assimilate with the American culture are perceived as people who are ashamed of their ethnicity, language, and religion. Whereas, first-generation Latinos who refuse to assimilate are perceived as strict traditionalists who are afraid of change.

This cultural schism was mended by seven men who were "known to be full of the Spirit and wisdom" (Acts 6:3) and who gave their attention to the matter while the disciples focused on "prayer and the ministry of the word" (Acts 6:4). It is possible to have an undying devotion to the Word of God while tending to the cultural divides in the church.

Mending the Theological Schism

Linguistic and cultural realities provide different theological perspectives. A unique challenge of generational and linguistic blending in Latino churches in America can be the philosophy and praxis of biblical interpretation as conceptualized by and modeled by religious tradition and interpretation.

As stated in earlier, an excellent example of this is found in the interpretation of Philippians 2:5 where an English reading of the text lends a unique interpretation focused on the mind, and a Spanish reading leans toward a unique interpretation focused on the heart.

Another example can be seen in the meaning of the verb "to know." The English verb "to know" is equal to two verbs in Spanish, *saber* and *conocer. Saber* is to know information and facts. *Conocer* is to be familiar with a person, place, or thing. In Philippians 3:10, Paul said, "I want to know Christ." However, Paul's desire to know Christ was not limited to information and data.

Paul uses the Greek word γινώσκω (ginōskō), meaning "to know," primarily through personal experience or first-hand acquaintance. The word used in the Jewish sense of the day was used to describe sexual relations between a man and a woman, as in Adam knew Eve. γινώσκω is an intimate knowledge of a person or thing.

To know Jesus is not the same as knowing his historical life; it is not the same as knowing correct doctrines regarding Jesus. God is not something to study. God can be known and loved. This idea is perceived in the Spanish rendering where it reads, "Quiero conocerlo" (Phil 3:10 Reina Valera).

The Spanish rendering denotes the idea of knowing someone personally not merely informationally. Jesus is not only a historical figure, provable in history and archeology. He is alive right now. That is what makes a relationship with God so fresh and so real.

Theological schism is mended by accepting a wholesome and healthy theological approach to both the heart and the mind. This challenge can be an opportunity for the Latino church in America to be a people of a holistic theology.

Summary

Remember, renewal cannot happen unless the church prepares for it. Since change is inevitable and unavoidable, it is also predictable, and since it is predictable, the church can prepare for it.

The Latino church has a choice to live at Pentecost or to live in Babel. They either recognize or ignore the changing differences in population and sociological factors. They can choose to keep an undying devotion to the Word of God while tending to the cultural divides in the church.

This is done by accepting a wholesome and healthy theological approach to both the heart and the mind.

Ultimately, I will say it again. The silent exodus requires a shift in mentality from the first-generation leadership. While not negating their identity as settling immigrants, they must recognize a more real identity (imago Dei) given by God and seek to fulfill God's command (Missio Dei) to reach the next generation.

PART THREE:

LEADING A LATINO CHURCH IN THE TWENTY-FIRST CENTURY

CHAPTER 6

LEADING IN A POST-MODERN WORLD

"The challenge of our time is to either be influenced by people with a blue checkmark next to their names or to be saved and transformed by the red letters of Jesus Christ."

The silent exodus is defined as a crisis of infertility and preservation, an inability to retain and reclaim emerging generations in Latino churches. As addressed already in this book, this is due primarily to changing demographics among emerging generations. However, the silent exodus is also reinforced by an increase of influence of post-modernistic thought infiltrating the church, recent challenges with technological and social media advances, and an inability of relevant leadership capable and willing to address these issues. Such is the nature of leading a church in the twenty-first century.

In this section of the book, from a first-hand experience, I will write about how Latino leaders in churches experiencing the silent exodus can respond to postmodernity, globalization, and technology. This will require you to directly engage the culture to understand better the times in which we live.

Additionally, Latino pastors and emerging leaders must understand not only the tools and threats of demographical changes—as we have already studied—but it must also recognize the philosophies and worldviews at war with Christian orthodoxy and the church. Today's

Latino churches not only face the challenge of making space for multi-generational identities, but they must also develop the leadership skills necessary for relevant contextual leadership.

I want to challenge you to critically engage the complexities of postmodernity, globalization, and technology as they relate to Latino multi-generational realities and Latino church leadership.

This chapter focuses on equipping pastors and emerging leaders for positional and non-positional leadership in Latino ministry settings by providing a leadership approach for the Latino leader who directly engages globalization and communicating the gospel in a post-Christian world. This will provide a foundation for further discussion as we move along into the other chapters in this section.

Postmodernism

As it relates to communicating the gospel in the twenty-first century, we do not always think about it, but ministry and preaching concerns the communication of a message that is at least 2,000 years old to a contemporary audience that idolizes artists like Cardi B and Post Malone, all while hiding their vaping devices on their thumb drives and posting a selfie on Instagram or posting a dance on TikTok.

On June 23rd, 2020, when the world was in the throes of a pandemic and mass protests, Twitter was trending with the hashtag #cancelchristianity. Yes! "cancel Christianity" was trending on Twitter. Later, in August, according to the New York Post, protestors were recorded burning Bibles in Portland, Oregon. Furthermore, I witnessed many Latino churches, pastors, and believers being morally questioned and fundamentally challenged by cancel culture and the woke mob.

I understand that perhaps this was people's frustration with Americanized religion, the prosperity gospel, and political evangelicalism. But it has a lot to say about a growing sentiment against Christianity and the Church.

The culture has indeed lost most of its memory of the Christian faith. It has moved on to something new. It is post-Christian. And sadly, there is a void of strong, healthy, and relevant Christian leaders to combat or respond to these challenges from a place of grace and truth.

The challenge of our time is to either be influenced by people with a blue checkmark next to their names or to be saved and transformed by the red letters of Jesus Christ. Today, I have found, believers are more apt to believe Twitter than Scripture. And as a result, we see many who are falling away from sound doctrine and biblical faith.

Cancel culture is rooted in the postmodern assertion that all truth claims are individual and subjective. Each of us interprets our experiences of the world in ways that are unique to us. As a result, we are told there can be no such thing as "objective" truth.

Conventional wisdom claims that there is only "your truth" and "my truth," and that there is no such thing as "the truth." Tolerance is, therefore, the great value of our society. We are told that we must tolerate and affirm any behavior that does not hurt or harm others.

However, our "tolerant" culture is highly intolerant of Orthodox biblical Christianity. If you believe that life begins at conception, many will accuse you of waging a "war on women." If you have stated that marriage should be a lifelong covenant between a man and a woman, you are "homophobic" and a "bigot." If you believe that men and women are fundamentally and biologically different, you are a "sexist." If you have made the biblical statement that Jesus is the only way to heaven, you are "intolerant."

The ideas and practices that overwhelm our culture—in schools, on social media, in homes, on television, in politics, in academia, and even in some of our churches—are no longer orthodox Christian ideas.

Chuck Colson described it like this, "Today a cultural war rages in our nation; the struggle between two conflicting world views." On one side are those who cleave to the Judeo-Christian understanding of truth, with a corresponding view of life and culture based on two central commandments—love for God and love for people. On the other side are those who believe truth can be defined by each individual, with a corresponding view of life and culture based on individual choice—"what's right for me."

"Postmodernism" was a term coined by Arnold Toynbee (1889–1975) early in the century to refer to the last quarter of the nineteenth century (1801–1900), a time where capitalism and imperialism and Western civilization in general began to decline.

The term *postmodern* came into use as a description of certain trends in architecture, art, and literature in the 1970s, although the trends it describes reach back earlier in the twentieth century to Joyce's *Finnegan's Wake* in the case of literature, and to the 1950s at least in the case of architecture. However, in philosophy, postmodernism is a term used to describe the prominent change in how society views and defines truth. In a postmodern culture, truth is relative not objective.

We can categorize how society's view of truth has changed through three major philosophical epochs. First is pre-modernism (beginnings up to 1650s) with a worldview centered around a God-centered universe, God's revelation, and *truth as absolute.* Second is modernism (1650 to 1950s) with a worldview influenced by enlightenment, evolutionary science, where *truth is relative.* And third is postmodernism (the 1950s to current times), where we have perhaps lost all hope for absolute truth. In postmodernity, truth is not discovered, or relative, *truth is created.*

American culture in many ways used to be Pre-modernist. Pre-modernism held to the view of a God-centered universe, revelation, and that truth is absolute. Groothuis explicates, "Premodern cultures typically have little or no cultural or religious diversity, minimal or no social change, have not been affected by secular isolation and are prescientific" (Groothuis, 2000, p. 33).

Then came Modernism, rooted in the enlightenment and science, which believed that truth is relative. Enlightenment and its motto, "dare to know," sparked a spirit of criticism where it encouraged "philosophers to question all received believes in the name of rationality" (Groothuis, 2000, p. 35).

Today, we live in a time of Postmodernism. Postmodernism has lost all of the hope for absolute truth and holds to the value that truth is created. Groothuis explains, "Postmodernists affirm relativism even at the level of language itself. Objective reality cannot be captured by the contingent human invention of language, whether it be language about God, the cosmos or human values" (Groothuis, 2000, p. 40).

The main point of contrast between postmodernism and the Bible is the definition of truth. Ravi Zacharias asserts, "Truth by definition is exclusive. If truth were all-inclusive, nothing would be false" (Small, 2013, pp. 145–146). Groothuis further clarifies that, "Without a thorough and deeply rooted understanding of the biblical view of truth as revealed, objective, absolute, universal, eternally engaging, antithetical and exclusive, unified and systematic, and as an end in itself, the Christian response to postmodernism will be muted by the surrounding culture or will make illicit compromises with the truth-impoverished spirit of the age" (Groothuis, 2000, pp. 81–82).

Post-truth was the Oxford Dictionary's word of the year in 2016, where it means:

> "Relating to or denoting circumstances in which objective facts are less influential in shaping public opinion than appeals to emotion and personal belief."

We are in danger of duplicating what has occurred with the church in Europe. In Europe, churches have become museums because of unrelenting attacks on biblical truth.

In America, for centuries the Christian church has been the *center* of Western civilization. Western culture, government, law, and society were based on explicitly *Christian principles*. Concern for the individual, a commitment to human rights, and respect for the good, the beautiful, and the true all grew out of *Christian convictions* and the influence of revealed religion.

A postmodern culture is a post Christian culture. A post-Christian society is not merely a society in which agnosticism or atheism is the prevailing fundamental belief. It is a society rooted in the history, culture, and practices of Christianity but in which the religious beliefs of Christianity have been either rejected and forgotten, and worse, they are now persecuted.

We now live in a postmodern or post-Christian world. Will Herberg, an American Jewish sociologist, and theologian coined the phrase, "A cut flower generation" to describe today's American culture. He explains that cut flowers retain their original beauty and fragrance, but only so long as they retain the vitality they have drawn from their now-severed roots; after that is exhausted, they wither and die.

Without the life-giving power of the Word of God out of which they have sprung, they possess neither meaning nor vitality. We continue to detach ourselves from the source of our beauty—we are severing our roots. With the bouquet in hand, we say, "See, nothing has changed. They are still beautiful. Everything is just fine." They will be sustained as long as they can live off the vitality of the roots from which they were severed. Then they will wilt and die.

Postmodernism's influence has infected the church today. Christians are toning down their message so that the gospel's clear truth-claims do not sound judgmental to the postmodern ear. Many stay away from unmistakably stating that the Bible is true, and all other religious systems and worldviews are false.

Some who call themselves Christians have gone even further, purposefully denying Christ's exclusivity and openly questioning His claim that He is the only way to God. But the biblical message is clear: Jesus said He was the truth in John 14:6, "Jesus answered, "I am the way and the truth and the life. No one comes to the Father except through me"". Jesus said his Word was truth in John 17:17— "Sanctify them by the truth; your word is truth." The apostle Peter proclaimed to a hostile audience in Acts 4:12: "Nor is there salvation in any other, for there is no other name under heaven given among men by which we must be saved." The apostle John wrote in John 3:36, "He who does not believe the Son shall not see life, but the wrath of God abides on him."

Again, and again, Scripture stresses that Jesus Christ is the only hope of salvation for the world. In 1 Timothy 2:5, Paul wrote, "For there is one God and one Mediator between God and men, the Man Christ Jesus." Only Christ can atone for sin, and therefore, only Christ can provide salvation. And John tells us in 1 John 5:11–12, "And this is the testimony: that God has given us eternal life, and this life is in His Son. He who has the Son has life; he who does not have the Son of God does not have life".

Those truths are antithetical to the central tenet of postmodernism. They make exclusive, universal truth claims, declaring Christ the only true way to heaven and all other belief systems erroneous. That is what Scripture teaches. It is what the orthodox doctrines of the church have proclaimed throughout her history. It is the message of Christianity. And it cannot be adjusted to accommodate postmodern sensitivities.

Instead, many Christians pass over the exclusive claims of Christ in embarrassed silence. Even worse, some in the church, including a few of evangelicalism's best-known leaders, have begun to suggest that perhaps people can be saved apart from knowing Christ. Christians cannot surrender to postmodernism without sacrificing the very essence of our faith.

The Bible's claim that Christ is the only way of salvation is certainly out of harmony with the postmodern notion of "tolerance." We cannot waiver on this, no matter how much this postmodern world complains that our beliefs make us "intolerant." G. K. Chesterton reminds us, "Tolerance is the virtue of men who do not believe in anything." The good news is "that truth is still truth, that it provides a backbone for witness and ministry in postmodern times, and that God's truth will never fail" (Groothuis, 2000, pp. 81–82).

Engage Culture and Understand the Times

In a list of names from 1 Chronicles 12, we find a helpful reference about the men of Issachar. 1 Chronicles 12:32 says that the Men of Issachar understood the times and knew what Israel should do.

It is tempting to read too much into the brief, seemingly unrelated remarks found in the author's genealogies and record-keeping. Still, it is interesting that the author considered it necessary to describe these men as having a profound understanding of the times in which they lived and, as a result, knowing what actions Israel should take.

What were the times they understood? From an administrative standpoint, they knew the future was with David, the shepherd-boy-turned-warrior who had already been anointed king of Israel but had yet to ascend his throne. Because they understood the times, they "cast their lot with David rather than Saul" (Expositor's Bible Commentary). They were, in a sense, in a time between the times. The rightful king had been anointed but not visibly enthroned.

Note the connection between "understanding the times" and "knowing what Israel should do." In other words, a proper understanding of the time in which they lived was essential for the men of Issachar to obtain the wisdom needed to know what Israel should do.

Their leadership was contextual. God not only gave them the Torah to obey, but He also expected them to discern the proper application of the Torah in the context in which they found themselves. They strategized their reality on the timeline of biblical history and, therefore, had the wisdom to make decisions as leaders, to let the people they led know the right course of action.

The men of Issachar were able to interpret God's written Word by recognizing the significance of the present and applying its lessons. The Latino church needs to know the times, utilize all that is at their disposal to advance the Kingdom of God, know what to do to win the lost, disciple the believer, and guide God's people.

Globalization

One of the most substantial challenges and opportunities to the church's survival and, more specifically, the Latino church today is posed by the impact of post-modernism driven by globalization and the commercial revolution of information technology. Globalization has caused human connectedness to be expanded to a truly global level leading to unprecedented "acceleration, compression and intensification of life" (Guinness & Wells, 2012, p. 97).

Myers explains that the Christian church can respond to the threat of globalization in ignorance, resistance, or engage it" (Myers, 2017, p. 187). As it relates to the Latino church and Christians, globalization means that we are called to be in the world but not of the world (John 17). This means that every generation must discern and decide how to engage their culture, and as Paul reminds us, this should be done "by all possible means" (1 Cor. 9:22).

Myers explains that "the mission of the church in the world is not complicated" (Myers, 2017, p. 188); however, it would appear that the "how" of the mission is to be accomplished can be made problematic.

I believe that the church needs to primarily do a *complete hermeneutic* that involves both a good study of the biblical text in its context. It also involves an equally important task of understanding the culture to whom the message is intended. It is a comprehensive scriptural exegesis along with a faithful and complete hermeneutical bridge connecting to contemporary culture.

It is vital to initiate the conversation here to help us think through relevancy in culture. We need to consider the tension of the required internal church changes related to the culture's external demands. This is the art of knowing what changes and what never changes.

The Latino church is not called to be religious in the negative sense, reflecting some religious leaders of Jesus's day, who cared more about being right than doing right (Matt. 23:1–36). The traditionalists and

Pharisees of the New Testament times were spiritual yet ignorant of the complexities of the culture in which they lived.

Nor is the Latino church called to be revisionists, like the progressive theologians who are rewriting what it means to be Christian. Theologians like McGrath and Grenz (Groothuis, 2000, pp. 116–117) provide a spiritual element, but it is wayward as it attempts to change the gospel's message to accommodate culture. They are spiritual but errant.

Instead, the Latino church must seek relevancy, not by trying to change orthodox doctrine, but by innovating the way church is done. The church needs to think about new ministry methods in a new world. We must keep an undying devotion to God's Word and in this sense, we are spiritual yet relevant. Relating to culture while remaining faithful to the scriptures is a balance the church must strive to keep.

In the Synagogue and in the Marketplace

Today the church is waging a war of reason and logic with the rise of secularism and anti-Christian sentiment. As the months and years take their toll, we are becoming more and more post-Christian and postmodern.

In some sense, the best thing that the devil can do in the life of a believer is not to get them to sin but get them to lose their faith. One way that the devil accomplishes this goal is by placing seeds of doubt and disbelief in our reason and logic through deceptive lies about God, God's creation, and God's Word. This is why the ability to preach and defend the gospel inside and out of our church structure is essential for twenty-first-century relevance.

Douglas R. Groothuis, professor of philosophy at Denver Seminary, describes Paul's ability to preach the gospel to the Athenian philosophers in Acts 17 as an excellent example of contemporary evangelistic and discipleship endeavors.

In Acts 17:17, Luke unearths Paul's ministerial ability both inside and outside of the religious circles of his day. He wrote, "So he (Paul) reasoned in the *synagogue* with both Jews and God-fearing Greeks, as well as in the *marketplace* day by day with those who happened to be there" (Emphasis added).

The compounded Greek word for "reasoned" is *dialegomai*, from *diá* denoting transition or separation and *légo*, which means to speak. It could also be translated as dialogue, and it means to engage in an interchange of speech. It means to think about a subject from multi-faceted perspectives and use thoughtful arguments to persuade another.

In the synagogue, Paul would face challenges from Jews who, for the most part, were ignorant of the arrival of Jesus as the Messiah. So, Paul would reason with them, proving that Jesus was, in fact, the promised Messiah. This reasoning was most likely a dialogue with the Jews, using the Old Testament Scriptures. However, in the marketplace, Paul faced a challenging audience of Greek philosophy in Athens. It was a cultured, educated city that was proud of its history. It was an intellectual center. Paul spoke to a city, perhaps different than any other city he had preached in.

Acts Two or Acts Seventeen?

Paul did not ignore or dismiss the use of logic, reason, and intellect. Still, he reasoned from the Scriptures, utilizing philosophical perspectives that agreed with a Christian worldview to demonstrate the Christian position's sense and consistency over Judaism and the pagan Greek and Roman philosophies. This is what some have called an "Acts 17" or "marketplace" approach.

In contrast, many Latino churches, organizations, Bible colleges, seminaries, and so forth in America train believers and students to use only an "*Acts 2*" or "*synagogue*" approach to evangelize and disciple. The Acts 2 method is based on how the apostle Peter preached to the Jews, or how Paul preached in the synagogue to a people who believed in the God of creation and understood the meaning of sin and the Fall. They boldly presented the message of the death and resurrection of Jesus and the need to repent and put faith in Christ for salvation.

In the *Acts 17* approach, Paul was able to reason with both the biblically literate and the biblically ignorant. In this approach, Paul had success in preaching to the Greeks. The Greeks were outright pagans who did not know the true God, the Bible, or the Gospel message. Consequently, they lacked an understanding of the meaning of elementary Christian concepts, like creation, the chaos of sin, the cross, and the promised new creation.

Most Greeks dismissed the Gospel message as foolishness. But when Paul explained who the real God as the Creator God is and explained that every human being is the descendant of one man, Adam, he set the foundation for explaining the Gospel message and the necessity for Christ. By describing the origin of sin and the need for salvation, Paul then dismantled their belief in pagan gods and presented the message of salvation—and some responded.

One of the reasons we are experiencing a silent exodus from Christian churches, including Latino churches, is because we have been committed to an Acts 2 evangelistic and discipleship strategy.

For example, many Christians too quickly dismiss the importance of Genesis and the foundational truth that God is Creator. We, now, for several decades, have been preaching to a generation that has, for the most part, been educated to believe that they have evolved, not that they have been created. Consequently, the well-known verse from Ecclesiastes 12:1—"Remember your Creator in the days of your youth"—has become obsolete. If there is no creator, subsequently, there is no one to remember.

Ecclesiastes 12:1 is an example of a direct contrast to a prevailing view of evolution today. Today, emerging generations are being fed a doctrine of evolution that directly contradicts God's truth as Creator. But if we get the beginning wrong, everything extending from that foundation can be wrong. Accepting the theory of evolution removes the idea of remembering a Creator as a whole and gives it a whole new definition all together—the idea that we have to remember that God is Creator.

We are preaching an Acts 2 message to an Acts 17 audience. We no longer have the foundations that allow us to present the Gospel. To reach Latino emerging adults, we must define and redefine terms. We must be able to answer the attacks on the authority of scripture. We live in an Acts 17 society. Most of the emerging adults we minister to today—including most of those who grew up in our churches—are Greeks who are influenced by the marketplace and consequently are an Acts 17 audience.

Apologetics: Defend, Contend, and Argue

One of the primary ways we engage the Acts 17 audience is with the use of apologetics. Apologetics is the discipline that deals with a rational defense of the Christian faith. Apologetics is the defense of the one true and living God of the Bible against the claims of false gods and competing worldviews. Apologetics is to say why you believe what you believe.

Groothuis explains the necessity for different methodologies of the gospel today: "Scripture makes distinctions between the proclamation of the gospel, the defense of the gospel, and the communal manifestation of the gospel" (Groothuis, 2000, p. 162). The need for apologetics is not only a biblical command but also a ministry essential.

Peter uses the Greek word for apologetics (*apologia*) in 1 Peter 3:15, "But in your hearts set apart Christ as Lord. Always be prepared to give an *answer* to everyone who asks you to give the reason for the hope that you have. But do this with gentleness and respect" (Emphasis added).

In the ancient Greek world, an apologia was a legal defense of oneself, similar to the speech a modern-day defense lawyer makes on behalf of their client. It did not mean "a regretful acknowledgment of an offense or failure" (the Oxford English Dictionary definition of "apology") but a carefully reasoned defense of one's beliefs or actions. It is the biblical mandate not to apologize for the Christian faith and a Christian worldview but to defend it.

The Greek word *apologia* is where we get our English word *apology*. However, apologetics has nothing to do with apologizing for what we believe as propositional truth. Still, it should instead be understood as an intellectual defense against false charges or misunderstood truth (Groothuis, 2000, p. 163).

Thomas Aquinas (1225–1274), a great theologian and apologist of the Middle Ages, was concerned with defending the truth of Christianity. He used reason and logic to reason for the absolute truth and the assumptions of a Christian worldview. In his classic work *Summa Theologica*, Aquinas defines faith with exacting language. He wrote, "Faith is to believe ... with assent" (II, II, 2, 1).

More specifically, he believed that "faith" believes what cannot be proven, or it would not be faith. However, faith is not irrational. It must be made on reasonable grounds and evidence. In Aquinas's thought, faith and reason are two layers of truth that cannot contradict one another. He believed that philosophy is not the enemy but a servant (handmaid) of theology. He thought that man had the capacity for reason as a God-given gift because an infinite God gave finite man the ability to reason and logic as part of God's image. In other words, you do not have to sacrifice your intellect for faith.

Practically speaking, apologetics means to defend, contend, and argue for the Christian faith. First, we *defend* the Christian faith by answering the objections when it is challenged (Col. 4:5–6). Sometimes Christianity is attacked by people who are openly hostile to it, sometimes the attacks are misunderstandings or mischaracterizations, and sometimes someone has an honest question.

An early example of this is Justin Martyr. Justin was a second-century apologist who defended the Christian faith through two written works. In his *First Apology*, he defended Christianity from clear misconceptions. Ironically, Christians were labeled as atheists because they believe in only one God; they were accused of cannibalism because of metaphors of the blood and the flesh in communion. Further, Christians were accused of incest because they called each other brother and sister (in the faith), yet they were married in some cases.

Justin explained that Christians do, in fact, believe in God—the one true God. He admitted that Christians did not worship the emperor or other gods and that most did not participate in the social events associated with pagan religion. But this did not make Christians bad citizens or people who did not believe in God.

The charge of cannibalism, he explained, came directly from the words of the Eucharist, "Take and eat, this is my body broken for you" (1 Cor. 11:24) but was misread in a literal, cannibalistic sense by witnesses ignorant of the metaphor. He also defended Christians by explaining that Christians refer to their fellow believers as brothers and sisters (Jam. 2:15) and should not be misunderstood as incestuous.

Second, we *contend* for Christianity by showing how all other belief systems are false (Jude 1:3). Apologetics is not used just to engage non-Christians. Apologetics strengthens the faith of Christians by answering questions they have about their own belief. These are Christians who are not sure quite what they believe and are often only comfortable only around other Christians because of their insecurity. When they encounter challenges to their faith, rather than being defenders, they become defensive.

Let me give you a personal example. Several years ago, a Latina high school junior struggled to reconcile elements of her faith with what she was being taught in her science class in school. She provided me with the sheet below and asked me for answers from a biblical perspective (Figure 11). She stated that she had never really been taught about these issues in church and struggled to provide a Christian perspective.

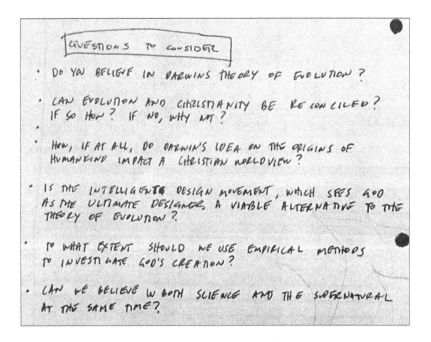

Figure 11. Questions to Consider from High School Student

The church needs to provide reliable biblical propositional responses to these types of questions, but often in Latino churches, we ask our students to "just have faith." This is not enough, President of the Barna Group, David Kinnaman, explains: "Only a small minority of young Christians has been taught to think about matters of faith, calling, and culture" (Kinnaman, 2011), and he elucidates further: "The university setting does not usually cause the disconnect; it exposes the shallow-faith problem of many young disciples" (Kinnaman, 2011).

Third, we *argue* for the truthfulness of the Christian claims. Some use philosophical arguments such as the Cosmological Argument (beginning has a cause), the Anthropic Principle (fine-tuning), and the Argument from Morality(God's nature provides an objective reference point for moral values). Some use historical evidence, such as the case for the bodily resurrection of Jesus Christ or the argument from fulfilled prophecy (1 Cor. 15:12–19).

Furthermore, we cannot forget that in 1 Peter 3:15, Peter addresses the need to prepare and provide a logical defense for the Christian faith with an added emphasis on praxis. We are to defend the hope we have with gentleness and respect. Love is the greatest apologetic. Christian apologist Ravi Zacharias once explained it like this: "If truth is not undergirded by love, it makes the possessor of that truth obnoxious and the truth repulsive."

This is precisely why at our church, three years ago, we started "The Apologetics Forum," an evangelistic and encouraging event that provides discipleship and guidance for college and high school students exposed to secular thought on a day-to-day basis. Each year we focus on a prevalent apologetic topic.

At our initial meeting, we gathered over 250 students and spoke about "The Exclusivity of the Christian Message"; the year after that, we explored "How Did We Get the New Testament?" Later that fall, we gathered about 300 students and answered questions concerning "The Problem of Evil." We have found this event an exceptional tool to provide answers to the skeptics and disciples alike. Often the questions that doubters and believers have are the same. Apologetics provides answers, not only for the seeker but also for the thinker.

The Emerging Generations

Let me share some further information about the journey of emerging generations and the impact of postmodernism to better minister to them. Understanding the emerging generations is critical to the continual survival of the first-generation churches and the retention of second-and third-generation Latinos.

Billy Graham was a legendary American evangelist who preached the Gospel to some 215 million people who attended one of his more than 400 Crusades, simulcasts, and evangelistic rallies in more than 185 countries and territories. Part of his success could be attributed to the fact that throughout his ministry, American culture resembled the Jews in Acts 2, having a biblical foundation and a Christian worldview. But this is no longer the case. We now live in an Acts 17 world that lacks both a biblical foundation and a Christian worldview. The gap between a Christian worldview and a non-Christian view is growing. We are no longer a Christian society but a society of Greeks.

Figure 12. Billy Graham Headline on Yahoo

Graham preached from the authority of the Bible. He was famous for using the phrase, "The Bible says ..." People had respect and recognized its authority. But today, with more and more frequency, people do not respect the authority of the Word; in fact, they do not even know biblical terminology. Today, we live in a different culture and context.

Understanding the times means understanding the generation we are trying to reach from a cultural standpoint. In this sense, it is vital to recognize how postmodern thought is pervasive among the rising generations, such as the millennials and especially Generation Z. You may already have Gen Zs in your church leadership—and if you do not—you will soon.

Before we focus on Gen Z, let me briefly describe the journey that generations have endured. In the book, *Recapture the Wonder*, Ravi Zacharias beautifully and definitively delineates the attacks and challenges that emerging generations have suffered throughout the centuries. He wrote:

> *"In the 1950s, kids lost their innocence. They were liberated from their parents by well-paying jobs, cars, and lyrics in music that gave rise to a new term—the generation gap.*
>
> *In the 1960s, kids lost their authority. It was a decade of protest—church, state, and parents were all called into question and found wanting. Their authority was rejected, yet nothing ever replaced it.*
>
> *In the 1970s, kids lost their love. It was the decade of me-ism dominated by hyphenated words beginning with self. Self-image, Self-esteem, Self-assertion .... It made for a lonely world. Kids learned everything there was to know about sex and forgot everything there was to know about love, and no one had the nerve to tell them there was a difference.*
>
> *In the 1980s, kids lost their hope. Stripped of innocence, authority and love and plagued by the horror of a nuclear nightmare, large and growing numbers of this generation stopped believing in the future.*
>
> *In the 1990s kids lost their power to reason. Less and less were they taught the very basics of language, truth, and logic and they grew up with the irrationality of a postmodern world.*
>
> *In the new millennium, kids woke up and found out that somewhere in the midst of all this change, they*

had lost their imagination. Violence and perversion entertained them till none could talk of killing innocents since none was innocent anymore."

And to appropriately complete the journey, we could add the words of Cohen (2013) here and say that in the digital age, kids have lost their community, "We're collecting friends like stamps, not making a distinction between quantity versus quality, and converting the deep meaning and intimacy of friendship with exchanging photos and chat conversations."

There has been much written about Generation Z and their characteristics and attributes. However, for our purposes, I want to draw your attention to some of the primary keystones that can help us understand this emerging generation as it relates to the Latino Church in America.

First and foremost, we must understand that although Gen Z is between 69 and 70 million strong, interestingly, about half this generation is non-white (The Barna Group, 2018, p. 14). More specifically, 48 percent of Gen Z is non-white (The Barna Group, 2018, p. 34). They are the most ethnically diverse generation in American history. The kindergarten class that started school in 2016 made up the largest minority ever in the United States (The Barna Group, 2018, p. 34).

Additionally, Barna found a notable lack of faith engagement among Gen Z Latino Christians (The Barna Group, 2018, p. 74). They specify that the Latino population "make up more than 13 percent of the U.S. population but represent only 7 percent of engaged Christians among teens (The Barna Group, 2018, p. 74).

Furthermore, Barna offered six forces forming Gen Z that help our endeavor to understand the generation before us (Barna Group and Impact 360 Institute, 2018). Let me briefly highlight them for you.

First, technology: the internet is at the core of Gen Z's development, a uniquely powerful influence on their worldview, mental health, daily schedule, sleep patterns, relationships, and more. Devices are more constantly on their person and their minds. More than half of Gen Zers use screen media four or more hours per day (57%).

Second, worldview: Gen Z's worldview (and, in turn, their moral code) is highly inclusive and individualistic. This diverse, open-minded group of young people is sensitive to others' feelings and experiences and wary of exerting any one view as right or wrong. They are twice as likely as adults to say they are atheist (13% vs. 6%), and only three in five identify as Christians (59% vs. 68%).

Third, identity: their assorted views on gender identity and expression have changed how they accept and affirm other people. They create safe spaces where each person can be herself or himself without feeling threatened or judged. It is important to note that Gen Z, more than older generations, considers their sexuality or gender central to their sense of self. This is due to the pervasive public debate surrounding sexuality and gender.

In fact, about one in eight of all thirteen- to eighteen-year-olds describes their sexual orientation as something other than heterosexual or straight (12 percent). Seven percent identify as bisexual (since Barna has asked survey respondents about their sexual orientation, about 3 percent of all US adults have identified as LGBT). However, faith identity and practice correlate with a higher tendency to identify as straight, with nearly all engaged Christians saying they are heterosexual (99% vs. 86% all Gen Z). Teens with no religious affiliation are less likely than others to describe themselves as straight (79%; 13% consider themselves bisexual) (Barna Group and Impact 360 Institute, 2018).

Fourth, security: Gen Z has come of age in a post-9/11 nation reeling from the 2008 recession, and many teens are anxious about the future. Not to mention the effect that the 2020 pandemic, along with its shutdowns and social distancing, is doing on their psyche and mental health. It is no wonder that their goals revolve around professional success and financial security, and a majority says their ultimate aim is "to be happy"—which a plurality defined as financial success.

Fifth, diversity: Gen Z is used to people with different beliefs and experiences, and they seem to have a greater appreciation for social inclusiveness compared to generations before them. They are the most racially, religiously, and sexually diverse generation in American history.

Finally, parents: access to immediate information through the internet has a complicated dynamic with their family. They admire their parents, but most do not feel family relationships are central to their sense of self—a significant departure from other generations.

Summary

A complete contextually appropriate exegesis involves both a proper study of the text and context but also involves an equally important task of understanding the culture to whom the message is intended. It is a complete hermeneutical bridge reaching the depths of God's Word and stretching toward the current culture and context in which believers live.

Latino pastors and emerging leaders must be equipped for positional and non-positional leadership in Latino ministry settings by providing an approach that directly engages globalization and communicating the gospel in a post-Christian world. Contextual leadership recognizes the relationship between postmodernity, globalization, and the Latino Church. It is aware of the challenges of emerging generations and culture as it strives for relevancy through engagement and understanding.

CHAPTER 7

LEADING IN A
TECHNOLOGICAL CONTEXT

*"Influencers have become the kings, priests, and prophets of our
culture today, taking the place of authority that pastors
and churches once held."*

I t seems to me from personal experience that church leadership,
including leadership within Latino churches, was simpler and more
domesticated in the past. I realize that this is a personal bias. Still, I think
it is fair to say that leadership today is far more complex and challenging
that in prior generations, and emerging Latinos seem to think that a
first-generation leadership cannot measure up to their expectations.

In their day, first-generation immigrant church leaders not only
inspired confidence, but respect and reverence as well. Sure, they had
their flaws, but they were courageous and boldly communicated the
gospel the best way they knew how. This was possible because of the clear
boundaries between the church and "el mundo" (the world). However,
today's social networking, cultural complexities, and political divide
have a multiplicity of voices and influences speaking into the next generation of Latinos. And, it is in this sense that the first-generation Latino
leadership may not inspire the same confidence.

As it has been pointed out in this book, the lack of realization among
first-generation leadership of changing demographics has severely frac-
tured the Latino church. The lack of realization of the clear and present

danger that social pop-culture besets the Latino church today is equally as important.

Allow me to present three clear and present challenges that the Latino leader, both first generation and beyond, must face as it relates to the leadership crisis of relevant church engagement.

The Multiplicity of Influencers

The first clear and present challenge that the Latino leader confronts is the multiplicity of influences on emerging generations. Today, people with the most considerable following on social media are called "influencers." Social media influencers are specialists at tapping into core human interactive needs, which stimulate a response, often in iniquitous action. The terrifying thing is that a lot of this action leans toward immorality and away from biblical moral absolutes and toward progressiveness. As such, influencers are powerful communicators leading, at times, the next generation astray, and they fill the void left by an aging and at times detached, disengaged, and disconnected church leadership.

At a certain level, influencers have become the kings, priests, and prophets of our culture today, taking the place of authority that pastors and churches once held, very similar to the Old Testament's leadership roles. Today's influencers, like the kings of old, lead people into civil battles and disputes. Like the priests of old, influencers provide "spiritual" and emotional support to their followers. Like the prophets of old, influencers speak "truth" from a place of higher authority.

Both church leaders and their adherents must be aware of this. The seduction of social media can suck us in. Before we know it, we are becoming more influenced by the noise around us than by the Word of God working within us. I am all for social media use, but it can be a problem when that is all we are doing. As stated previously, the challenge of our time is to either be influenced by people with a blue checkmark next to their names or to be saved and transformed by the red letters of Jesus Christ.

Allow me a rigid description of emerging generations. Due to the post-modern influence, many have lost their moral compass. Being digital natives, more thought is given to what is trending than to what is true. They live in a world where the belief is: if it is not happening on social media, it is not happening at all. As a result, it appears to be a generation where people want to be liked and followed instead of loved and trusted. They would rather be retweeted and DM'd instead of respected and appreciated. They worry about perception instead of reality and make decisions based on feeling, not on fact. They seek to be the *g.o.a.t.* instead of following the Lamb.

Global Village Missionaries

The challenge of the multiplicity of influences speaking to emerging generations is overwhelming. However, we can begin to understand it and engage it by confronting culture through technology. This is the challenge of becoming global village missionaries.

The idea of a global village is the world considered as a single community linked by telecommunications. We now live in a global village—we are hyperconnected—no one is too far that we cannot reach.

Today, as a church, we do not have a choice on whether we do social media; the question is how well we do it. Social media is a breeding ground for influence and vanity, so a leader must teach what we believe and interpret truth from influence. In a postmodern culture, where truth is relative, we need to know what we believe to help emerging generations navigate through the fog of postmodernism as propagated through social media.

This is particularly true because research shows the best leaders find effective ways to understand and improve the way they handle their own and other people's emotions" (Goleman, Boyatzis, & McKee, 2013, p. 4).

I appreciate Turkle's (2012) approach to technology. I resonate with her honest cautioning about the perils and threats of technology, all while encouraging us to create a "Rule of Life" that can use digital technology "to make this life the life we can love." This is a balance I like to encourage our youth pastors to have personally and teach their students.

An essential understanding for the Latino church to accomplish this goal could be realizing that technology is neither good nor evil. Technology is amoral. Technology is not wrong. It is a question of redemption, not rejection. I often find myself explaining to the older generations in the Latino church that technology is not evil, and the younger generations in the Latino church about technology's malicious dangers.

One of my father's favorite preachers was Yiye Ávila. Yiye Ávila was a Puerto Rican Pentecostal evangelist. He is considered one of the most influential Protestant preachers of the Spanish language of the twentieth century. He was a great man of God whose moral integrity and ardent message resonated with many.

However, my father recalls when he heard him say in a sermon that "the TV was the devil's box." The funny thing is that just a couple of years later, as he was preaching to thousands, if not millions, through a television program. Sometimes we are too quick to condemn a tool that God has provided to expand the kingdom of God. Let me encourage you with these words. Just because it is new, you do not have to be afraid of it. Just because it is different and unfamiliar to you, you don't have to reject it or ignore it. God can use it. Redeem, rather than reject.

Several years ago, as I preached at several youth camps and conventions, some first-generation Latino leaders criticized me for using my iPad tablet when I preached without bringing up a physical Bible to the pulpit.

I have a deep respect for these leaders, so I felt it was vital for me to consider their critique. I took a couple of days to pray about it. I asked the Lord if I was doing anything wrong by taking my tablet to the pulpit instead of the physical book.

In my prayer, I lightheartedly explained to the Lord how, on my iPad, I had the Bible app, which had access to 2,062 Bible versions in 1,372 languages, including audio Bibles. I clarified that I had googled that information. I also explained how I had other tablet applications that would allow me to access the Bible in the original languages. I concluded by saying that I took several Bibles to the stand every time I took my tablet to the pulpit.

As I prayed and wrestled with this critique, the Lord comforted me, and I remember how the Lord impressed in my heart to get my "tablet" and type the following words:

> *Moses used tablets;*
> *David used parchments;*
> *Jesus used scrolls;*
> *Paul wrote letters;*
> *Luther used Gutenberg's press;*
> *The 19th century used books.*
> *Today we're back to tablets,*
> *But it's still the infallible and inspired Word of God.*

I often share these words to encourage our leaders not to take an overly legalistic stance against technology because God can redeem it for His purposes. This is especially true in the global village we live in now. Remember, the Christian's role is to take an ancient message and apply it to a contemporary world. Relating to our culture while remaining faithful to the scriptures is a balance we will always keep.

Roman Roads

God set the stage for the most important event in the history of the world—the sending of His Son. In Galatians 4:4, Paul explained, "But when the set time had fully come, God sent his Son." While God appeared to be silent during the 400 years following the return of the Jews to Israel after the Exile, he was not inactive. Several things were taking place in preparation for the coming of the Messiah.

Although the yoke of Rome was despised by most of the Jews, there were several ways in which Rome's rule was fundamental in setting the stage for the coming of Christ. To keep their empire under control, the Romans built a network of roads throughout the empire. Their roads were so well constructed that parts of them still exist to this day.

By the time Jesus was born, all parts of the vast Roman Empire were readily accessible, with an excellent road system created for control and dominance. Roman soldiers could traverse the entire Roman Empire and reach the very ends of the known world. The ancient Roman roads spanned more than 250,000 miles. The Romans started building these continent-connecting arteries in 500 BC, enabling both their empire to grow and the gospel to advance rapidly.

The disciples were commanded to go to all the world and make disciples (Matt. 28:16–20), and although at first, they were reluctant to leave Jerusalem, God used persecution (Acts 8) to spread them throughout the world. Undoubtedly, they used the Roman roads to significantly extend the gospel message wherever they were scattered (Acts 8:4; 11:19).

There is a similarity between the setting for Jesus's first coming and the present day. Today's Roman roads are found on social media and the internet, ready and waiting for innumerable journeys of faith and witness. While the ancient roads connected hundreds of towns and cities, the new ones join millions of homes and individuals.

We have to get the Latino church out of the church in the traditional sense and the digital sense. As the first disciples were reluctant and accidental missionaries, we, too, may have just become reluctant and accidental missionaries in this new age.

According to Digital Church Hub, after the national quarantine which did not allow churches to meet in person due to the coronavirus pandemic, eight out of nine churches in America were struggling to connect with their people digitally, and only one out of nine were ready with a digital plan as a way to communicate with their people.

During the first couple of weeks of the quarantine, many churches were struggling with the question of how to stream a service online. Many churches had to answer some critical operational questions during the shutting down of church gatherings due to the coronavirus pandemic. How will we worship and praise the Lord? How will we bring our tithes and offerings to the storehouse? How will we have Bible study and Sunday school? How will we hear the weekly sermon? How will we fellowship?

Unfortunately, Christians are so used to calling the buildings where they worship and learn the Bible "church" that they are left feeling orphaned when they cannot assemble at those buildings.

Churches who gained traction were churches who realized they needed to connect digitally Monday through Saturday. An equal effort was placed on reaching people Monday through Saturday with content, engagement, and serving.

The truth is, Christians live and grow outside of the two hours they are in church on Sunday. The other 166 hours of the week are so important to engage people and give them opportunities to be discipled and serve the community.

Again, we have to get the church out of the church, not only in the traditional sense but in the digital sense. The church, when rightly defined, has never been a building. Jesus did not die on the cross to save a building. He died to save a people called to know Him and enjoy Him, who know Him and make Him known. Therefore, we must send missionaries into the world both in the traditional sense and in the digital sense. Today, digitally speaking, no one is too far that God cannot reach. We now live in a global village.

The Emphasis of the Image Over the Word

While there are wonderful opportunities for outreach through social media, I like to remind our emerging Latino leaders that fundamentally, technology and our use of it is not always bringing us closer together. I think it is also essential to consider the dangers of engaging the world in the global village. Turkle explains, "There's plenty of time for us to reconsider how we use it, how we build it." She emboldens us with these accurate words, "I'm not suggesting that we turn away from our devices, just that we develop a more self-aware relationship with them, with each other and with ourselves" (Turkle, 2012).

Like Turkle, I am still excited by technology but believe that we are letting it take us places that we do not want to go. My purpose is not to push our leaders and emerging generations away from using social networking sites but to realize the necessity for face-to-face interaction with God's Word and others.

Consequently, the second clear and present challenge that the Latino leader confronts is the culture's emphasis on the image over the word. As I write this, in California, we are just beginning to emerge from a statewide shutdown. I heard a funny advertisement on our local sports radio that perfectly described our consumption of media. The short commercial congratulated the listening audience for conquering and devouring everything on the internet during the quarantine. It was funny because it was true. But what is it doing to us human beings? And more specifically as believers?

It is crucial to consider the role that social media and technology play in our lives. Its airbrushed photos, edited videos, pleasurable movies, binge-worthy shows, and unbiased newscasts (that last one was a joke) play a significant function in our lives today.

At the very least, we must acknowledge that it affects not only what we think but also how we think. We are inundated with far more entertainment and information than we can cope with. It was back in 2002 that Couchman reminded us, "We see more images in twenty-four hours than people in Jesus' time saw in their whole lives" (Couchman, 2002).

It is vital to recognize that reading a book instead of using our smartphones changes the way we interact with others, and it is changing the way we think. Impressively, Carr believes that "With the exception of alphabets and number systems, the Net may well be the single most powerful mind-altering technology that has ever come into general use. At the very least, it is the most powerful that has come along since the book" (Carr, 2011, p. 116).

If God has revealed the Gospel of Jesus Christ through written words in a book, this confronts us with a real problem. We now move and operate in a world where pictures are more important than words, and feelings are more important than facts. The question for us to consider here is, how do you reach a generation that listens with its eyes and thinks with its feelings? How can we share the Good News in an image-centered society?

Changes in the Brain

There are radical changes that are taking place in our brains and our relationships due to not only the content available through modern technology but also the use of the apparatus itself.

Over the last few years, technology has been tinkering with our brain, remapping the neural circuitry, and reprogramming the memory. The internet seems to be making us its servant, even to the point of rewiring our brains and making us more and more lonely and individualistic. We as humans are becoming content with exchanging reality with virtual reality.

It has been proven that when we engage with our smartphones, our brain releases dopamine, the same chemical that smoking, drinking, and gambling all release in our brains. And what do these activities all have in common? They are highly addictive, and they all have age restrictions. Turkle explains, "Our little devices, those little devices in our pockets, are so psychologically powerful that they do not only change what we do, they change who we are" (Turkle, 2012).

The truth is that many teens and emerging adults confess that they get jealous if another person receives more likes on Social Media. Emotional turmoil and self-esteem are directly connected with the number of likes someone can collect.

There is now a rise in teen suicides blamed on social media. Recently, teens who commit suicide have exhibited high rates of depression caused by unhealthily low levels of serotonin.

I am not a medical doctor, so take this with a grain of salt, but here is what I think is happening. When a person engages with social media for long periods, dopamine is released in their brains. With prolonged use, they are addicted to their phones. Long engagement reduces levels of serotonin. Serotonin affects a person's mood and social behavior. Since the person is always engaging, there is no time allowed for the body to replenish its healthy serotonin levels. So, the body must replace it with adrenaline. However, adrenaline is only meant to be used in emergencies. When adrenaline quickly burns out, the person has an emotional breakdown, leading to depression and suicidal thoughts.

Loneliness

Another price we are paying for assuming the power of technology is alienation. Cohen explains, "As a social fabric in the western world weakens, it is not surprising that more and more people define themselves as lonely. And thus, loneliness has become the most common ailment of the modern world" (Cohen, 2013).

Human beings' tendency is to hide behind an avatar or a screen name and avoid face-to-face relationships. Cohen describes this ailment as a virtual romance, "disguised by the social network, which supplies an impressive platform that allows us to manage our social life most effectively" (Cohen, 2013).

If we fall into the trap of the modern temptations of social media and the internet, we may miss the most important of all things in life: relationships. Social media gives us a false sense of community and relationships and forces upon us a feeling of intimacy and closeness that does not exist.

That is why Cohen warns, "We are collecting friends like stamps, not making a distinction between quantity versus quality, and converting the deep meaning and intimacy of friendship with exchanging photos and chat conversations. By doing so, we are sacrificing conversation for mere connection. And so, a paradoxical situation is created, in which we claim to have many friends while actually being lonely" (Cohen, 2013).

Gallup took a poll in 2001 and found that the average American said they had ten really close friends. The same survey was carried just a few years ago, and the average American said they only had two close friends. So, what happened? Where did everybody go? They are all on their phones. Our new best friend is our smartphone.

I think we have all seen this by now and maybe even been a little guilty of it ourselves. We see families out to dinner, and everyone is on their phones. Think about it; every time we are on our phones when someone is right in front of us, we project that they are not important enough to hold our attention. We are saying that we would rather be with someone else or doing something else.

Mary Meeker did a study that found that we touch our phones or check our phones a hundred and fifty times a day and that about a quarter of people worldwide say they share "everything" or "most things" online. When do we do this with our family and loved ones?

We have become a generation that lacks simple interpersonal skills, living superficially (with filters), and seeking approval from a device. On Instagram, we post pictures that present us as lions, but we are house cats in reality. This is the bottom line: "Texting, email, posting, all of these things let us present the self as we want to be. We get to edit, and that means we get to delete, and that means we get to retouch, the face, the voice, the flesh, the body—not too little, not too much, just right" (Turkle, 2012).

Instead of building genuine friendships, "We're obsessed with endless personal promotion, investing hours on then building our profile, pursuing the optimal order of words in our next message, choosing the pictures in which we look our best. All of which is meant to serve a desirable image of who we are" (Cohen, 2013).

In a world that is becoming more and more socially connected, we must remember that it can never substitute for face-to-face relationships. Baym explains, "Digital media aren't saving us or ruining us. They aren't reinventing us. But they are changing the ways we relate to others and ourselves in countless, pervasive ways" (Baym, 2015, p. 177).

Healthy Relationships

It is true, technology can drive us farther apart, as we know more and more people but know less and less about each of them. In a world that is becoming more socially connected, we must remember that it could never be a substitute for face-to-face relationships.

Relationships are the foundational pillars upon which life is built. That is precisely the reason why paradoxically, technology appeals to us. Turkle explains, "Technology appeals to us most where we are most vulnerable. And we are vulnerable. We're lonely, but we're afraid of intimacy. And so, from social networks to sociable robots, we're designing technologies that will give us the illusion of companionship without the demands of friendship" (Turkle, 2012). So, if our face-to-face relationships are weak, the quality of life is in grave danger.

Today, one of the greatest threats to our relationships' health is social media and its message given to us through modern technology. Turkle agrees, "We're getting used to a new way of being alone together. People want to be with each other, but also elsewhere—connected to all the different places they want to be" (Turkle, 2012).

One of the reasons why social media is so widely popular is that it affords us the ability to maintain contact with others while not seeing each other face-to-face. These social networking sites tend to draw us away from face-to-face interaction.

Social media gives us a false sense of community and relationships; it forces upon us a feeling of intimacy and closeness that does not exist. Human beings' tendency is to hide behind an avatar or a screen name and avoid face-to-face relationships. If we fall into the trap, we miss the most important of all things in life—relationships.

Created for Relationships

Genesis 1:26–27 records the final creative act of the sixth day of creation: Then God said, "Let us make mankind in our image, in our likeness... So God created mankind in his own image, in the image of God he created; male and female he created them."

So, God created man "in his own image, in the image of God he created him; male and female he created them." What does it mean to be created in the image of God? At the very least, it means that God made us out of relationship for relationship. We were created to have a relationship with God, with each other, and with creation.

Notice the "*Let Us ...*" in the verse. God is a trinity; He is three in one, one in three. And out of the complex unity in the community of the trinity, we see a relational being creating humanity in his *likeness* as a relational being.

That is why the next chapter says, "Then the Lord God said, "It is not good that the man should be alone; I will make him a helper fit for him" (Gen. 2:18). For the first time, God saw something that was *not good*—the aloneness of man. God never intended for man to be alone, either in the marital or spiritual and social sense.

We live in a disposable generation. Napkins, cups, forks—and even folks! Sometimes it cheaper to buy something new than to repair something old or broken. We choose to purchase something that carries no baggage, no history, and no stress. We live in a society where we throw away everything that does not work. If a relationship is no good, we amputate; we move to another one and then another one. We erase them from our Facebook or Instagram.

We see this in leadership, in churches, where they do not like one, they move on to the next one. We see this with celebrities all the time. And disposable relationships have become the new normal.

That is why social networking in cyberspace works for us, because we can have relationships without real commitment. That is why cyberporn is so prevalent because men can have a virtual relationship with no obligation and no history.

However, we cannot just throw someone away. "*We cannot butcher the cow when it stops giving us milk.*" We cannot afford to be easily hurt. A hurt heart hurts hearts. A healed heart heals hearts.

We have become a generation of relational wimps who get hurt for any little disturbance in our lives. We cannot be surprised when sinners sin. We must become good at repairing broken relationships. *People are not an interruption to ministry; they are ministry.*

The beloved disciple encourages us to have the courage to have face-to-face interaction. John wrote to the church, "I have much to write to you, but I do not want to use paper and ink. Instead, I hope to visit you and talk with you face to face, so that our joy may be complete" (2 John 1:12).

It is there in that little epistle where John tells us why his letter is so short. There are just some things that cannot be done with paper and pen or cell phone and text. I like to contextualize like this for you. If John would have written this today, he may have written something like this: *"I have much to say to you, but I do not want to use Facebook, Snap Chat, Instagram, or Text you. Instead, I hope to see you and talk with you face-to-face; let's meet at Starbucks so that our joy may be complete."*

One of the reasons John wanted to see his brothers and sisters face-to-face, in a living connection, was because it brought them complete joy, a joy that could not be obtained by the writing of letters. John understood that complete joy in our life is contingent on face-to-face interaction. So, he expresses his desire to see them, not just write to them.

Joy is a barometer for meaning and purpose; that is, the real joy that comes from genuine, raw relationships, with an undertone of love, forgiveness, and grace. If you lack strength, it is because of the lack of joy. If you lack joy, it is because your lacking healthy, committed, accountable relationships.

God's desire for us is to have face-to-face relationships because it meets our human need to be connected. Face-to-face interaction, a living connection, gives us complete joy that does not come through social media. We need each other. That's why we must view people and their problems, not as an interruption to ministry, but as ministry.

The words from Morse resonate: "Our presence and potential for influencing is part of daily life. There isn't a 'now I'm a leader' or 'now I might influence' time. We are always living our lives as an offering of Christ's hospitality—anywhere, anytime" (Morse, 2008, p. 158).

If we want to see God at work, we cannot run from the threat of face-to-face relationships. Turkle reminds us, "Human relationships are rich and they're messy and they're demanding. And we clean them up with technology. And when we do, one of the things that can happen is that we sacrifice conversation for mere connection. We short-change ourselves. And over time, we seem to forget this, or we seem to stop caring" (Turkle, 2012). Will it require vulnerability? Courage? Truth? Yes, but it will allow us to see God in ways we never have seen him before, mending relationships, restoring relationships, and reconciling relationships.

The Size and Speed of Issues

The third clear and present challenge that the Latino leader confronts is the size and speed of the issues. The size and speed that leaders are faced with today have increased considerably. This does not mean that the previous generations of leaders had it easier; instead, they had more time between decisions than leaders have today.

Today, with the dawn of instantaneous communication across the globe, leaders have very little time to think and react emotionally to issues instead of responding biblically to genuine concerns. This was specifically true during the coronavirus pandemic shutdown and the racial tensions that ensued, along with political polarity that followed.

Most of the Latino leaders I have worked with, in both the church and in the educational sectors, are inundated with information and overwhelmed with data and perspectives. They seem unable to move from one issue to the next without frequent interruptions as new influences occur.

The size and the speed at which social media moves today provide people with an unprecedented amount of information. As a consequence, we may be at the cusp of a generation that has lost its ability to think deeply about issues as it struggles to decipher between information and influence.

An interview of the popular Hollywood actor Denzel Washington recently went viral. In the interview, at the premiere of the National Museum of African American History and Culture, Washington said, "If you don't read the newspaper, you're uninformed. If you do read it, you're misinformed." He went on to explain the effects of "too much information," and the sixty-one-year-old Oscar winner concluded by exhorting the news media with these words: "(Today's news is concerned about) the need to be first, not even to be true anymore." He added, "So what a responsibility you all have—to tell the truth ... In our society, now it's just first—who cares, get it out there. We don't care who it hurts. We don't care who we destroy. We don't care if it's true."

The price we pay for leaning toward the more comfortable, more accessible channels of information found on the internet and social media sites are chipping away at our capacity to concentrate and contemplate.

The easy accessibility to fragmented information on social media sites and the internet has numbed us to the time and ability needed to reason through text and truth. Faced with all the contradictory messages, we do not have the time or the ability to sort out factual information. Today's reality is likely to be reversed tomorrow. The result is an all-pervading confusion and a weary cynicism about truth itself. People can twist facts in whatever way they want them to be interpreted.

In Groothuis's book, *Truth Decay*, he delineates how the mass media is promoting postmodernism. In the appendix of his book, he outlines five ways television has contributed to the decay of truth in our culture. Strikingly, although written before the social media boom in the late 2000s, Groothuis delineation applies to social media as we know it today. Judge for yourselves. For our intended purposes, I will only replace the word *television* with the phrase *social media*.

(1) Social media emphasizes the moving image over the written and spoken language. "It is image-driven, image-saturated, and image-controlled. When the image overwhelms and subjugates

the word, the ability to think, write, and communicate in a linear and logical fashion is undermined" (Groothuis, 2000, pp. 283–286).

(2) Social media provides an avenue for the loss of authentic self. "The self is filled with a welter of images and factoids and sound bites lacking moral and intellectual adhesion. The self be-comes ungrounded and disjointed" (Groothuis, 2000, p. 287).

(3) Social media relentlessly displays a pseudo world of discontinuity and fragmentation. "The images appear and disappear and reappear without a proper rational context. This is what Postman aptly calls the 'peek-a-boo world,'—a visual environment lacking coherence, consisting of ever-shifting, artificially linked images. Without any historical or logical context, the very notion of intellectual or moral coherence becomes unsustainable on television" (Groothuis, 2000, pp. 289–290).

(4) The increasingly rapid pace of social media's images makes careful evaluation impossible and undesirable for the viewer, thus rendering determinations of truth and falsity difficult if not impossible. "With sophisticated video technologies, scenes change at hypervelocities and become the visual equivalent of caffeine or amphetamines. The overstuffed and overstimulated soul becomes out-of-sync with God, nature, others, and itself. It cannot discern truth; it does not want to. This apathetic attitude makes the apprehension and application of truth totally irrelevant" (Groothuis, 2000, pp. 290–291).

(5) It promotes truth decay by its never-ending entertainment imperative. "Amusement trumps all other values and takes captive every topic. Every subject—whether war, religion, business, law or education—must be presented in a lively, amusing or stimulating manner" (Groothuis, 2000, pp. 291–292).

Groothuis concludes his appendix by contrasting a modern-day megachurch pastor who advises preachers not to preach longer than twenty minutes in length and to a use "light and informal" approach with liberal sprinklings of "humor and anecdotes" (Groothuis, 2000, p. 292). He continues, "An entertainment mentality will insulate us from many hard but necessary truths. Jesus, the prophets, and the apostles held the interest of their audience not by being amusing but by their zeal for God's truth, however unpopular or uncomfortable it may have been. They refused to entertain but instead edified and convicted. It was nothing like television" (Groothuis, 2000, p. 292).

Deciphering Enigmas

Reading about the clear and present challenges for the Latino leader, might discourage you. However, we can find encouragement and hope from the prophet of old. Daniel 5:12 portrays a leadership trait that is essential today. It reads, "*(Daniel had) an excellent spirit, knowledge, understanding, interpreting dreams, solving riddles, and explaining enigmas*" (Daniel 5:12 NKJV).

There is no doubt that America is at a high-tension point with politics, race, education, freedoms, and more. Each incident that occurs causes the wedge to grow, leading to more arguments where people make points but miss hearts. As this goes on around us, it is clear to me that the leadership spirit of Daniel—the ability to explain enigmas—is needed today more than ever.

Daniel's ability to explain enigma has always captured my imagination and inspired my initiative. Like Daniel during the Babylonian captivity, today's Latino leader must be good at deciphering enigma. An enigma is a puzzle, something hard to understand that requires thinking critically and analytically about the issues at hand.

There is no doubt that the church in America, including the Latino church and especially in Southern California, has "lost their social location at the center of culture" (Roxburgh, 1997, p. 2). The church is perceived as antiquated and obsolete. This is especially true when we think about social discussions at the forefront today. The church is no longer seen as a serious contributor to the significant debate in the general population. The church no longer leads that way.

In past times, the general population would look to the church for a moral compass; they now look to celebrities and other influential media personalities to define morality. In many ways, from my perspective here in Southern California, the church shares some of the blame for what Roxburgh calls "a crisis of identity" (Roxburgh, 1997, p. 4).

The church used to preach a clear and united morality, but it began to present a vague disjointed moral expectation that confused the culture. But think about this. One of the most significant obstacles to the moral formation is their lack of moral compass or ethical awareness. Yet, the observable trend in modern culture concerning the decline of biblical moral values could be described as follows:

1. It is justified and accepted.
2. It is normalized.
3. It is institutionalized.
4. It is encouraged.
5. It is celebrated.
6. It is indoctrinated.
7. It mocks and persecutes the opposing view.
8. Moral objectives are forgotten.

Every sin is forgivable except the ones you do not know you have to repent from. If leaders cannot clearly define what sin is, people will never know what to repent from. If the devil is not successful in tempting people into immoral behavior, he will get leaders to change doctrine to allow for it. We must not allow secular thought to make faith a civil issue.

Injustice and Political Reform

In December of 2019, the Barna Group released a study that revealed that 43 percent of Christians aged eighteen to thirty-five believed that the significant characteristic of a Christ-follower was their care for the poor and vulnerable. This means that for emerging adults, acts of justice are a key and significant subject. But there is a big difference between how first-generation and US-born generations view justice.

I think first-generation leadership operates more naturally toward a *priestly* approach to leadership with a focus on pastoral care. At the same time, second-and third-generation emerging adults yearn for a more *prophetic* style of leadership. Native-born Latinos seem to want their first-generation leaders to speak against the structures they feel or have been taught to believe are systemically oppressing them.

Conn observed that some Latino pastors and churches "confine Christian discipleship to personal piety and the verbal proclamation of the Gospel ... they envision the church at war with secularizing and corrupting influences of *el mundo* which can have an effect on minimizing the role of the church in society as an agent of justice of freedom and peace." Conn seemed to identify that first-generation leadership tends to push the church away from considering issues of justice.

Many first-generation Latino pastors have to respond to the pressure of emerging adults in this realm and find themselves unsure how to react due to the complexities of our contradictory political intersectionality. This is what I call deciphering enigma. What happens when the same structures that most prominently talk and fight about racial injustice are also the ones that speak and most strongly fight for immorality and oppose biblical values and even begin to become anti-Christian?

It would be nice if every issue were black and white—crystal clear. Every single issue. Every subject. Every day. It would undoubtedly simplify decision-making, conscience issues, controversies, and might even prevent some discord. In today's deep thought divide, we must understand that we cannot get rid of the tension; we need to learn how to navigate it. In many ways, Latino church leaders must be ready with answers before the questions come and assault the church. When everything is not black and white, we have to learn how to navigate the depths of complexity with the help of God's Word.

A Short Word on Racism

As a Christian, I fundamentally believe that the government cannot give me something God has already given me. My identity is in Christ. I am against racism, as I already explained several times in this book because a person's race and ethnicity are sacred. You cannot violate it. The biblical perspective is not that we have different races (Acts 17:25–26). We are *one* race—the human race—with different ethnicities. All human beings are created in the image of God and have innate value (Gen. 1:27).

This stands in contrast to some evolutionist ideas that, in the past, have used evolution as a way to teach the supremacy of individual races. Even scientists today admit that, biologically, there is only one race of humans; *all* human beings in the world today are classified as *Homo sapiens*.

In the 1800s, before Darwinian evolution was popularized, most people, when talking about "races," would be referring to such groups as the "English race," "Irish race," and so on. However, this all changed in 1859 when Charles Darwin published his book *On the Origin of Species*. Darwinian evolution was (and still is) inherently a racist philosophy, teaching that different groups or "races" of people evolved at different times and rates, so some groups are more like their apelike ancestors than others.

The Wholistic Prophet

The prophet Jeremiah stands out as a great role model for deciphering enigmas and speaking out about injustices while standing for truth. In Jeremiah 22:3 he spoke about injustice, "This is what the Lord says: Do what is just and right. Rescue from the hand of the oppressor the one who has been robbed. Do no wrong or violence to the foreigner, the fatherless or the widow, and do not shed innocent blood in this place."

But he equally spoke about the evil of child sacrifice. In Jeremiah 19:4–5 he said, "For they have forsaken me and made this a place of foreign gods; they have burned incense in it to gods that neither they nor their ancestors nor the kings of Judah ever knew, and they have filled this place with the blood of the innocent. They have built the high places of Baal to burn their children in the fire as offerings to Baal— something I did not command or mention, nor did it enter my mind."

He additionally spoke about sexual immorality. Jeremiah referenced the goddess Asherah in Jeremiah 17:2, "Even their children remember their altars and Asherah poles beside the spreading trees and on the high hills." Asherah was considered a goddess of fertility. She is portrayed as a nude female, sometimes pregnant, with exaggerated breasts that she holds out, apparently as symbols of the fertility she promises her followers. The Bible indicates that she was worshiped near trees and poles, called Asherah poles. Hence, Jeremiah spoke against ritual sexual immorality and prostitution with every imaginable lewd practice that accompanied it.

Jeremiah's example teaches us that we can categorically denounce racism and stand in solidarity with peaceful protests (not rioting) fighting for justice. Still, at the same time, we can equally stand for life and marriage and sexual integrity. We cannot value one without devaluing the other.

Summary

Contextual leadership recognizes the relationship between globalization and the church. We have to get the Latino church out of the church in the traditional sense and the digital sense. An essential understanding for the Latino church to accomplish this goal could be realizing that technology is neither good nor evil. It is a question of redemption nor rejection.

The Latino church must understand the balance between the command to be a global village missionary, all while striving toward healthy relationships. We recognize that one of the greatest threats to our relationships' health is social media and its message given to us through modern technology. Therefore, we must remember, we are created for relationships. People are not an interruption to the ministry; they are ministry.

CHAPTER 8

LEADING THE LATINO CHURCH

"As an eleven-year-old boy, I had to make a choice. Would I succumb to my circumstances or get up and keep going?"

I n this chapter, I want to personally provide you with the most critical leadership lessons that I have learned in the past eighteen years of full-time ministry and fifteen years of teaching in a Latino context. These lessons have rescued me from burnout while reaming true to my ministerial assignment. From one Latino leader to another, I want to share with you five practical lessons that have contributed to the health of my leadership and the success of our ministry.

Refuse Victimhood

My family emigrated to the United States when I was nine years old. For many years our family of eight lived in a small garage a generous family opened for us in Anaheim, California. This garage was home to us, and we endured a cold winter and a hot summer there.

As you can imagine, my parents did many jobs to feed the family. The children helped too. I remember I began working when I was about ten years old. I helped my mom deliver newspapers in a retirement community. Every morning from 1 a.m. to 6 a.m., we collated, organized, packed, and delivered over 800 newspapers. We worked there for about seven years, and many "character building" stories can be told, but one sticks out the most.

I remember on a scrupulous Saturday when the paper was heaviest, we packed my mother's truck to the brim. Usually, I would sit on the truck's tailgate and deliver the newspapers as my mom drove and yelled out the numbers. On this particular day, I was sitting on the gate's edge and held on for dear life.

Early in the paper route, when the truck was still full, my mother stopped and then accelerated quickly, and, in the process, I fell hard at about 30 mph, and many of the newspapers crammed into the truck fell on top of me. I was cut, scraped, and perhaps concussed. I looked up to see if my mom had noticed, but she didn't and continued along the way for a long time. Finally, at the end of the block, I saw the brake lights shine red through the darkness of the early morning hours and then white as the truck was immediately put into reverse. She quickly came to what I thought was my rescue.

When she finally made it to me, she got out of the truck, and as I was barely licking my wounds and making my way out of a mountain of newspapers ready to feel sorry for myself, she said to me in a loud voice, "What are you doing on the ground?" and "Why are you crying? Get up, pick up the newspapers, and let's go—we have a long route ahead of us." No sympathy, no checking for wounds, it was as if it was expected and a part of life.

In his book *The Road to Character, David Brooks* explains how President Eisenhower's mother, Ida Stover Eisenhower, developed character in her eleven children. Ida believed that character was shaped by self-conquest. Her own life was filled with a series of catastrophes that included being orphaned early in life and the death of two of her teenage brothers during the Civil War. Still, Ida raised five boys who would go on to live remarkable lives.

Character was developed according to Ida, through small, constant self-repression. For instance, Anger was dealt with by quoting a verse from the Bible, "He that conquereth his own soul is greater that he who taketh a city." This was a significant moral ecology in which the Eisenhowers grew up (Brooks, 2015, p. 48–53). Ida's maxims explain this concept: "God deals the cards, and we play them," Sink or swim," "Survive or perish." Ida emphasized the importance of practicing small acts of self-control like going to church, keeping the Sabbath, using formal diction, and avoiding luxury. Like the culture of the time, the Eisenhowers believed that manual labor was a school for character building.

Although Ida was strict in her faith, she was fun-loving and humane in practice. Her character-building method had a tender side. She understood that love is a tool for building character too.

As an eleven-year-old boy, I had to make a choice. Would I succumb to my circumstances or get up and keep going? On that day, my mother taught me the greatest lesson I have ever learned: do not settle for victimhood. You have to find the courage to face your environment and challenges. You have to choose between staying down and blaming the unfair circumstances of life or get up with the help of God and rise above it and move forward.

Refuse victimhood. Remember, "in all these things we are more than conquerors through him who loved us (Rom. 8:37). There is no need to give in to the temptation of victimized mentality. A "poor is me" attitude focuses on the victim instead of the one who loved us.

Victims seek out sympathy under challenging circumstances. They want everyone around them to feel sorry for themselves. This victim mindset will keep you immobile and unable to lead.

There is no doubt, ministry and leadership are difficult and painful, but we are not alone. Christ can set us free from vicious cycles of victimized living. Christ is your confidence and the object of your faith. He gives you the security and strength to carry on even when you feel misunderstood, marginalized, or rejected.

Often, we do not serve because we have victimized ourselves to the point that we are only thinking about ourselves. Victimhood is self-preserving, but love is self-sacrificing. We must get rid of our fears and allow the love of God to fill our hearts with love so that we may lead the body of Christ. Therefore, do not let your circumstances define you. Christ has already defined you as more than a conqueror through Him. You are victorious in Him.

1 John 4:18 reminds us, "There is no fear in love. But perfect love drives out fear." Love takes the focus off you and puts it on the other person. Their circumstances do not define people who embrace victimless living. They do not feel sorry for themselves and serve others freely. When victimhood enters a room, it fearfully thinks, "What will people think about me?" But when love enters a room, it freely thinks, "I wonder who needs me. How can I serve?"

Help those seduced by and stuck in a victim mindset. Be patient while they process what possesses their thinking. Help them break what may be a family trait of defeatist living. Their parents may have been victims. Their grandparents may have been victims. For generations back, their legacy may have been marred by a victim mindset.

Through Christ, lead them to break the chain of this destructive thinking. Help them discover that they need people to pray for them, not to feel sorry for them. They need the power of God to triumph in their lives; they do not need manipulation from man. They can rise out of the mire of a victim mindset by placing their family, faith, and friends in the care of Christ.

The Elephant in the Room

Similarly, from a practical standpoint, another leadership lesson that I have learned is acknowledging the elephant in the room. It takes faith and courage to enter a space you do not know. That is why leadership is not about power, pride, or popularity. It is about developing a posture of genuine love for your people while maintaining a dedication to the truth of scripture and morality.

A church split, or a church problem, does not start when it is manifested, but it begins when it tolerated unhealthy relationships for the sake of ministry. A church that tolerates broken relationships will die. That is why healthy relationships are a priority over programs.

Latino churches must strive to maintain genuine and healthy relationships because healthy relationships are more critical than doing ministry or doing church. According to Jesus, striving toward unity is more important than doing ministry for ministry's sake (Matt. 5:23–24). Greer explains that mission-true organizations "recognize that it is not just what they do, and not just how they do it, but how they talk about it that matters" (Greer, Horst, & Haggard, 2014, p. 166).

That is why, as a community, we must learn to prioritize reconciliation rather than ministry. Remember, God cares more about the servant than the service, and people are not an interruption to ministry; they are ministry.

Many times, we want to institute ministries and programs. But first, we need to make every appropriate step to fixing relationships. You cannot do the work of Christ if you tolerate broken and unhealthy relationships.

Church leaders must be like an elephant—thick-skinned and big-hearted. The combination of thick skin and a thin layer of fat beneath the skin enables the elephant to tolerate cold temperatures and harsh environments. Also, because of the elephant's body's size, the heart has to be healthy, sizeable, and efficient to ensure that blood reaches every extremity at suitable blood pressure. Leaders cannot afford to be easily hurt; therefore, they must have thick skin. Likewise, they must be patient, forgiving, and loving; consequently, they must have a big heart.

Let me explain with an example from the apostle Paul in 1 Corinthians 4. The Corinthian church experienced internal conflict rooted in selfish liturgical preferences and external pressures from the influential pagan culture surrounding them. The epistle deals with Christian behavior within the church walls and conduct in a secular world.

In the first part of the letter (Chapters 1–4), Paul deals with division in the church of Corinth. After Paul left, other teachers had come to town, a scholar named Apollos and then the apostle Peter. And people had picked their favorite teacher and became groupies around those leaders and started to disrespect and talk about people who favored another leader or teacher. So, Paul's response is a long-winded explanation of who he was, who they were, and what the Gospel of Jesus Christ truly is.

In 1 Corinthians 4:1–5, Paul provides three ways to assess church leaders correctly. (1) Church leaders must prove faithful as servants and (2) authentic stewards, and (3) church leaders must have thick skin and a big heart. About this last point, Paul wrote, "I care very little if I am judged by you or by any human court; indeed, I do not even judge myself. My conscience is clear, but that does not make me innocent. It is the Lord who judges me" (1 Cor. 4:3–4).

From this passage, we learn from Paul how to deal with trivial matters. Many times, we do not go to God until something is completely destroyed or rancid. It is not until it is broken that we say that we need God's help. However, sometimes we lose our battles in the trivial things of life, not the major war zones of life. When we respond well to the trivial things of life, we can have a healthy heart that can lead others. If you do not deal with the trivial, it will poison and toxify your heart.

So how does Paul deal with the trivial? How does he deal with internal issues and external pressures? How does he exemplify the leadership characteristics of thick skin and a big heart? He provided three statements for us to think about.

First, "I care a little about what people think about me. You should care what people think about you—but very little. The idea of judging here is one of *examination*. Paul insists that their low estimation of him mattered little; it is what God judges that is important. In this manner, church leaders must have thick skin, meaning that they should not be so easily influenced by others. They should not be people-pleasers but vision pleasers.

People's thoughts about them do not easily persuade good leaders, but they are persuaded by what God thinks about them, and they are relentless for His vision. Some will praise; some will criticize. They will love you one minute and judge you the very next. One can provide a big head; the other a possible depression, or at the least, make you second-guess yourself. Sometimes the more you try to defend yourself; the more entrenched people get in their positions.

In Bible times, cities had walls to protect their inhabitants from their enemies. Often, enemies would surround cities, set camp and siege, and wait them out. When their supplies ran out, they were in a precarious state.

Sometimes enemies would clog the city's water source with "slingers." In Israel, there are rocks everywhere. So, these slingers would sling these rocks over the walls and into the wells inside their camp. Eight-hundred stones at a time, all day long. They would aim and pelt the city square because that is where the most significant well was. Once they clogged the water source, eventually, people would have to exit the city for water, where they would meet their demise.

Similarly, a leader's heart is like a well from which the church draws sustenance. But the enemy wants to clog their well—their heart. He intends to clog their well for the church, for their family, for their marriage, and their future. So, when the enemy launches rocks, and they enter your heart, do not let them clog it. Paul wrote that you should renew your heart every day, and if stones do get into your heart, do not delay getting rid of them. Second Corinthians 4:16 says, "Therefore we do not lose heart. Though outwardly we are wasting away, yet inwardly we are being renewed day by day."

Many times, we do not go to God until something is completely destroyed or rancid. It is not until it is broken that we say that we need God's help. No, be renewed day by day. Answering the call of God is not just something you do one time; it is something you do regularly.

A person's words can poison your life if you allow them to. A paraphrase of Psalm 140:3 says, "A gossiping, fault-finding tongue is like a venomous snake." The more you dwell on unjust criticism; the more venom comes into your heart. The more you dwell on it, the harder it is to shake off.

There is a "people-pleasing" temptation. Leaders ask, "What is it that I am doing that people do not like about me," and they will write it down and dwell on it. Then they do the same thing with another person who does not like the changes they make. In the process, leaders become everyone's frustration receptacle. Ultimately, they lose themselves and never commit to the recruitment and retention of the next generations.

Some people are going to find fault regardless. There is the story a man on his death bed, who was in a coma. He had one last lucid moment, saw his wife faithfully there by his bed, and turned to her and said, "Honey, you have been with me through all the tough times, through the thick and thin. You were there when I broke my leg, when we lost the house, when I was fired from work, when our dog died, and now you are here with me again at my death bed. Today I realize that the problem wasn't me; you are just bad luck." He took his last breath and died.

There is great freedom when we realized that not everyone is going to like us. So, there something worth giving greater priority to over getting everyone to like you and pleasing everyone. Paul said, "I care a little about what people think about me."

Second, "I care very little what I think about myself." You should care what you think about yourself—but very little. This deals with the idea of *self-esteem*. Even our estimation of ourselves is usually wrong. We are almost always too hard or too easy on ourselves. Paul recognized this and so suspended judgment even upon himself. In the end, He who judges us is the Lord.

Growing up as an immigrant in the United States can be frightening if you care too much about what people think about you or what you think about yourself. If you speak Spanish, Spanish speakers will say, "He does not speak it well." If you speak English, English speakers will say, "He does not speak it well." You become too American for the

Hispanic and too Hispanic for the American, and you can grow up to have insecurities and insufficiencies about yourself.

We are terrible at judging ourselves. It is easy to fixate on warts and wrinkles that are inconsequential. We find it difficult to move on from past failures or humiliating defeats. Conversely, there are times when we refuse to acknowledge hard hearts and stubborn selfishness. There is much to which we are blind, and even a clear conscience may be misleading.

Years ago, I realized that I was very sensitive to how people responded during my sermons. So, if I caught someone dosing off during my sermon, I would get angry, and my sermon became very sharp and loud. I would dwell on it and think, why would anybody waste their time and come to church and sleep? I just do not get it. Why not just stay at home? Am I not a good preacher? I must be a really bad preacher. However, the Lord spoke to my heart and said, "You are a people pleaser. And you think too much of yourself. Shake it off, and do not damage my sheep because of your fault-finding tongue."

Whatever problem you focus on, you will become like it. That is why Paul said, "I care very little what I think about myself."

Third, "I care very much what God thinks about me." You should care very much about what God thinks about you. So, here it is: let God guide your life and care what He thinks about you. Focus on the God-given assignment of reaching the second and third generations. So, when people pull and tug, even when your insecurities try to pollute your heart, you must remember who God has called you to be. Get back to pleasing an audience of one. Answering the call of God is not just something you do one time; it is something you do regularly.

Paul goes on to say that his conscience is clear but that does not make him innocent (1 Cor. 4:4). That is why we need the Lord to judge us. Paul recognizes that he does not stand in a perfect state of justification or innocence just because his conscience was clear. Paul knew his righteousness came from Jesus, not from his own life—even though he had a godly walk. In 1 Corinthians 4:5, he wrote, "Therefore judge nothing before the appointed time; wait until the Lord comes. He will bring to light what is hidden in darkness and will expose the motives of the heart. At that time each will receive their praise from God."

For the most part, people's true motives are hidden deep in the heart. However, they will not be hidden forever. God will judge the heart's motives at the appointed time and give praise to those whose reasons were pure and right. This is another reason why human judgment is often wrong and why Paul feels free to disregard the harsh critique of the Corinthian Christians toward himself.

Sometimes we think that success means less criticism, but I realize that success is not determined by how many complaints are sent your way, but what you do with them. I have found that we seem to scale the highest heights but die in the smallest hills. Sometimes we can navigate tremendous financial obstacles and physical setbacks, but we let simple, insignificant things hold us back. It is not the big things; it is the small things.

In 1912, when the Titanic hit an iceberg and sank, many precious lives were lost. However, James Crutch was one of the few survivors of this horrific tragedy who escaped on one of the lifeboats. While in the Navy three years later, he was aboard the USS Lusitania when a German submarine fired a torpedo. He escaped death for the second time in the middle of the ocean. He was a man who survived huge obstacles. One day, he slipped in the creek next to his house, hit his head, and drowned in one foot of water.

James Berkley, a hunter of man-eating tigers and lions, did not die from a dangerous animal's claws during a safari. No, he died after being scratched by his barnyard cat in the backyard. He developed blood poisoning from the incident and died one year later.

The great Charles Blondin, the famous tight ropewalker, had crossed Niagara Falls numerous times by walking on only a rope. He even traveled across with a wheelbarrow full of sand. He died from a fall on his porch, fracturing his leg, and subsequently developed complications. The fall on his porch led to his death.

So many people can overcome enormous obstacles in life and trip over minor issues and misunderstandings with others. Leaders need to pay more attention to elephants in the room, minor relational problems, and work toward reconciliation. It is best to deal with them while they are little, as, in the long run, they can cost us more than we realize at the moment, and they will have a profound impact upon our futures. So, trivial things are not small things; they are far more critical than you realize. Be like the elephant and have thick skin and a big heart.

Good Orthodoxy and Good Orthopraxy

One of the most crucial ministerial lessons I learned was to strive toward a salubrious stability of sound doctrine along with healthy service. As a church, we need to have and teach sound doctrine. Titus 2:1 says, "Teach what is appropriate to sound *doctrine*." When a church is committed to teaching sound doctrine, they have good orthodoxy.

Orthodoxy is a compounded word meaning "good doctrine." *Ortho* is a Greek word meaning "straight, and/or correct," and, *Doxy* is a Greek word meaning "doctrine" or "teaching."

Every church needs to have good orthodoxy, but each member has to have an equal orthopraxy. Romans 12:4–5 says, "For just as each of us has one body with many members, and these members do not all have the same *function*, so in Christ, we, though many, form one body, and each member belongs to all the others."

The Greek word for function is the word *praxis*. When a church is committed to correct function, they have good orthopraxis. Every church, for the sake of their souls and their communities must strive toward good orthodoxy and good orthopraxy. Let me explain what I mean.

We often talk about when churches stray in doctrine (orthodoxy) and pinpoint some teaching as heresy. In some cases, when orthodox scriptural doctrines are altered and contradict scriptural truth, we call them cults. But when it comes to churches or believers straying in terms of practice (orthopraxy), we do not show the same courage, and we lack a theology.

Gatherings Do More Harm Than Good

Paul wrote to the Corinthian Christians the way he might write to many congregations today. In 1 Corinthians 11:17, Paul wrote, "I have no praise for you, for your meetings do more harm than good." The reference here to "meetings" can refer to "agape feasts" that would include the practice of the Lord's Supper and fellowship in Corinth.

A good thing can become a bad thing when it loses its central meaning. In the modern church, the Lord's Supper is commonly celebrated in an atmosphere of dignity. But the Corinthian Christians came from a culture where the pagans typically had wild, riotous banquets given in honor of a pagan god. It is, in this sense, that their meetings did more harm than good. Their meetings became opportunities for gluttony, drunkenness, and favoritism.

I repeat, the truth is that some churches lose their way in doctrine, but others in practice. When they lose their way in doctrine, we call them a cult. When they lose their way in practice, we call them *crazy*! If we falter, either way, our gatherings can do more harm than good.

Remember, a pastor or a leader who is really interested in your holiness wants you to look more like Jesus. This is good orthodoxy. A legalist wants you to look more like them because they are the standard of righteousness. If you do not look like them, dress like them, and act like them, you are obviously not holy. When the pastor and the elders become untouchable, a movement is in danger of crossing the line into becoming a cult.

When blind allegiance to the leaders' wishes is required, and questioning is not allowed, an ordinary church can become cultic from a leadership perspective. The difference may be subtle, but the implication is profound. I will follow my pastor as God leads him, but there is a problem if loyalty is demanded.

Similarly, we often see well-intentioned pastors who are sincere but sincerely wrong. They are the one-pastor-does-it-all pastor. Only he and his wife do everything in the church. It is one person doing 100 things. When one person does 100 things, they will not do them well and quickly burn out and lose the joy of serving.

I believe in pastoral authority, but I do not believe in religious autocracy. Good orthopraxy strives toward a 1:1 ratio—one person doing one thing or a few things. It is not one person doing one-hundred things badly; it's 100 people each doing one thing and doing it well. When more are serving, the burden and the weight of ministry are evenly distributed, and the manifold grace of God is more easily perceived (1 Pet. 4:10). When the pastor and the elders hog ministry, the church is in danger of crossing the line into burnout and disillusionment among the church members.

Today the church needs both good orthodoxy and orthopraxy, and the theology of the laity has a lot to contribute toward a good orthopraxy. In the church, it's not one person doing one hundred things, but one hundred people each doing one service with the gift and talent God has given to them.

Doing Church as a Team

Understanding the theology of the laity is crucial because it determines in significant part how God has called all believers to live out their faith. The concept of church has been watered down to a place one goes to for inspiration every week.

However, in simple terms, if you are a Christian, you are the church.

In technical terms, the word translated "church" in the Bible is *ekklēsia* (ἐκκλησία). It is a compound word in Greek from the Greek words *kaleo* (to call), with the prefix *ek* (out). Thus, the word means "the called-out ones." The connotation is that every believer is called to live out their faith in service to one another and to the world.

Laity is a description of all believers, including the non-leading figures of the community. Theologically speaking, laity refers to "the group described as 'the people of God' (Greek, *laos*)" and "refers to the whole body of Jews or Christians" (Banks, 1993, p. 26). This Greek term preserves the Old Testament idea of the Hebrew word, *am*, meaning "the people."

The connotation of this theology, according to Banks, correlates several truths: (1) All Christians have a "calling"; (2) all Christians are "priests"; and (3) all Christians are "saints" (Banks, 1993, p. 27). Nevertheless, the primary collection of terms used to describe the ministry in the New Testament believer is "serve," "servant," "service," (in Greek *diakoneo*) (Banks, 1993, p. 28), meaning that ultimately, (4) all Christians are "Ministers." The ramifications include the following: All Christians are to engage in caring for one another, all Christians are to engage in teaching one another, and all Christians are to engage in prophesying to one another (Banks, 1993, p. 29).

Beyond liberating the laity to fulfill their ministry in the church and the world lies the challenge of empowering them for their tasks. We must assist ordinary members of a congregation in equipping themselves in critical areas of the Christian life, including the appropriation of their spiritual gifts, how they can contribute toward building community in the church, and understanding ministry in the workplace. In the process, we can have a Christian spirituality that effectively empowers the people of God for ministry.

The theology of the laity rests on clear biblical principles and the Reformation principle of *the priesthood of the believers*. Peter wrote, "you also, like living stones, are being built into a spiritual house to be a holy priesthood, offering spiritual sacrifices acceptable to God through Jesus Christ" (1 Pet. 2:5). Here, Peter's picture is that God builds a spiritual house using living stones (Christians), those who have come to the ultimate living stone (Jesus). Jesus is first called the living stone; then, we are called living stones. As we are connected to Jesus, He wants to join us to others. As much as Israel was chosen by God, so is the church. As much as they had a priesthood, so Christians are a holy priesthood. And as much as they had sacrifices, so Christians offer up spiritual sacrifices acceptable to God.

Peter expounds on his initial thought, "But you are a chosen people, a royal priesthood, a holy nation, a people belonging to God, that you may declare the praises of him who called you out of darkness into his wonderful light" (1 Pet. 2:9). Peter says that we are chosen by God, but we are chosen to be a royal priesthood. We are a royal priesthood. Christians are called priests because they have access to God, and they are to offer spiritual sacrifices. As priests, we offer our lives as sacrifices to God in the form of worship, but we also offer our lives as sacrifices by serving God in serving others.

Peter reminds us that God has gifted us for such a task, "Each of you should use whatever gift you have received to serve others, as faithful stewards of God's grace in its various forms" (1 Pet. 4:10). This means that every believer has a God-given gift to steward, but that gift is just a piece of the picture of God's multifaceted grace. Each believer plays a role in the image of grace that God wants to display to the world. Every part is essential; each has its job to do. Even the smallest, seemingly least important part of the body of Christ is important.

Every Christian is a full-time minister. The great C. H. Spurgeon once said, "Grace makes us the servants of God while still we are the servants of men: it enables us to do the business of heaven while we are attending to the business of earth" (Spurgeon C. H., 1879). In other words, the moment someone becomes a Christian, they become a servant of God by grace. God did not start paying a salary, but He brings us to the realization that it is God who provides so that we can participate in the kingdom of God as His servants. That is why Paul wrote, "Whatever you do, work at it with all your heart, as working for the Lord, not for men" (Col. 3:23).

In other words, the Lord is our employer, so do everything as unto God, not unto man because He is our real employer. God has a place of ministry for all of us. It is a place where we belong, a place where we must serve Christ in the church or the world. It might not be the pulpit, and it might not be preaching, teaching, or singing, but it is the work of ministry in the church or the world.

Skillful Hands and Heart of Integrity

Foundationally, and perhaps a good reminder to anyone in multi-generational leadership, is that God cares more about the servant than the service. God is more interested in developing messengers than messages. It is true, on the one hand, God cares about our hearts, but on the other hand, the quality of our service demonstrates the quality of a servant. That is why the fourth lesson for leadership in a Latino church is to endeavor toward skillful hands and a heart of integrity.

In Psalm 78, we have a song about the history and journey of Israel's people in the desert. The Psalm reveals how time and time again, how even when the children of Israel rebelled against the Lord in the desert, God responded with kindness, giving opportunity after opportunity for them to line up with His best plans. The Psalm progresses to explain how David entered through the servant's entrance and how he stayed in the servant's path. Psalm 78:70–72 details, "He chose David his servant and took him from the sheep pens; from tending the sheep he brought him to be the shepherd of his people Jacob, of Israel his inheritance. And David shepherded them with integrity of heart; with skillful hands he led them."

These verses point out some essential insights into the Lord's assignment and requirements for ministry leaders. There is both a spiritual and technical preparation for ministry. How we prepare ourselves for service and how we present ourselves in service are equally important in the eyes of God.

David's story teaches us that we have to work on our anointing to serve the Lord with all of our hearts. David did not sit back and rely upon his "anointing," but he worked hard at his craft. David developed as a musician, as a fighter, and as a leader.

God cares not only about our hearts being right but also what we do needs to be done right. The goal is not to have heart but no skill. The goal is not to have skill and no heart. It is not "either/or" but "both/and."

Heart of Integrity

What was the difference between David and his brothers, or Saul? First Samuel 13:14 tells us that the king that God would choose would have a heart after his own. He told Saul, "The LORD has sought out a man after his own heart and appointed him leader of his people because you have not kept the LORD's command."

David is described as a man after God's own heart. God chose him because of his divine sovereignty, but He used him because of his heart of integrity. What does integrity mean? It means wholeness. A heart of integrity is a whole heart, a healthy heart, a true heart.

An important distinction is that because of Christ and His redemptive work on the cross, God does not choose based on our hearts' integrity, but instead, he chooses us to have hearts of integrity. Ezekiel's prophecy reminds us, "I will give you a new heart and put a new spirit in you; I will remove from you your heart of stone and give you a heart of flesh" (Ezekiel 36:26). So, God does not choose perfect, healthy hearts, but He chooses those who have broken, sick hearts so that He can make them whole.

But how do we cultivate a heart of integrity? Follow Jesus, not your heart. Do not follow your heart! Matthew 15:19 says, "For out of the heart come evil thoughts, murder, adultery, sexual immorality, theft, false testimony, slander." C. H. Spurgeon reminded us, "We must not trust our heart at any time; even when it speaks most fair, we must call it liar; and when it pretends to the most good, still we must remember its nature, for it is evil, and that continually."

Someone once said, "Everybody is corrupt; some people just do not make the news." Apart from Christ, our hearts are corrupt. Apart from the Holy Spirit, our desires are deceitful. The heart promises something that it cannot deliver. To follow your heart is to follow your deceitful desires. If your heart is not right, you are following your deceitful desires.

Willpower is not going to work because our will is broken. We must be committed to building our character, doing what is right in the eyes of God and not man. We should be doing what is right in secret and in public. Remember the word of Paul to the young minister Timothy, "Flee the evil desires of youth, and pursue righteousness, faith, love and peace, along with those who call on the Lord out of a pure heart" (2 Tim. 2:22).

Gifts and talents open doors, but integrity keeps you there. Remember, God has given us the ability to live a life of integrity, so let us do it so that we might shepherd God's people as David did. Do not follow your heart; instead, guard your heart. Do not follow your heart; follow Jesus.

Skillful Hands

But remember, Psalm 78:70–72 describes both the inward and outward qualities of King David's life. It says, "David shepherded his people with a heart integrity and led them with skillful hands" Notice two crucial observations. First, David was a man of character (integrity) and competence (skill), and second, notice how character was needed for shepherding and competence was required for leadership. Meaning, you can be a person of character and consequently be a good shepherd who pastors and nurtures their church. Still, you can also lack the necessary skill to lead and subsequently be very poor at organizing and administrating. But the opposite can be true as well. You can have the skill required to lead and subsequently provide fantastic systems and structures but lack the necessary character to minister and empathize with people.

Let me briefly explain the contrasts and comparisons between integrity of heart and skillful hands:

- Integrity of heart: an excellent pursuit (of the God who gave us those talents and abilities)
- Skillful hands: the pursuit of excellence (in our God-given talents and abilities)
- Integrity of heart: taking root below (invisible resources)
- Skillful hands: bearing fruit above (visible results)

- Integrity of heart: the shaping of our hearts (something God does)
- Skillful hands: the shaping of our hands (something we do)
- Integrity of heart: needed for shepherding (pastoring, nurturing)
- Skillful hands: needed for leading (organizing, administrating)

Often, God needs skilled men and women who meet some set of standards. To be skillful means to have the intelligence, understanding, and wisdom necessary for that task. It is to have a sense of professionalism and expertise. At Faro Church, we often say that we not only have to grow deep in character, but we must increase our gift competency, our service capacity, and our relational chemistry. This will often place us in a place where God can use us.

Let me give you an example, when an evil spirit was tormenting Saul, Saul's servants said in 1 Samuel 16:16–17, "'Let our lord command his servants here to search for someone who can play the harp. He will play when the evil spirit from God comes upon you, and you will feel better.' So Saul said to his attendants, 'Find someone who plays well and bring him to me.'"

Essentially, Saul's servants were advising that he find what we would call a "worship leader." They would seek out a man who could, using music, bring the love, healing, and freedom of God to Saul. David was chosen for the service of the king because he was able to play the harp and because he loved God.

To lead Saul in worship and to minister to him in music, David had to be skillful in playing the harp. David knew how to play the harp, and this ability made him not only a candidate to the service of the king, but the chosen instrument of God.

Long before he had this opportunity to serve the king, David had to work hard and be ready for the opportunity. He learned, he practiced, he grasped, he become skilled at the art. David had spent long hours perfecting his gifts and talents because he wanted to be good at what he did for God. David became a great musician.

153

The technical aspects of our gifts and talents make a difference in being effective, and it also reveals our true motivation to give God the best. In other words, our desire to work on our technical ability shows that we want to give God our best.

David wrote, "Sing to him a new song; play skillfully, and shout for joy" (Ps. 33:3). David teaches us that if we want to be used in the service of the King, then we must be good at what we do and do it with the right attitude.

Notice that David is encouraging us to continually come up with new songs. God is just too big, too majestic, too holy, and too awesome to be worshiped with just *one* song or a *few* songs or the *same* songs over and over again. God must be worshiped continually with *new* songs. As you can imagine, this requires an imaginable amount of time and effort to develop new songs.

However, David says that it must be done skillfully. The Hebrew word for skillful is *yatab*, and it is defined as good, well, or pleasing. The idea is that you are to play with intelligence, understanding, and wisdom. The word reflects ability as much as it reflects attitude. That is why David follows the playing skillfully with the shouting for joy. David is not talking about perfection but effort. Does your heart reflect ability as much as it reflects attitude?

Some might think, "I do not need to work on my talents or gifts; I'm a natural." You might even justify your actions by saying, "I've done it without practicing, and it came out good, so why practice or learn more?" It is because we should sing to the Lord a *new* song, not a *few* songs. You do not have to be a virtuoso before you can be used of God, but it does mean that you cannot tolerate a too casual, unconcerned, lazy, «we do not need to practice» attitude.

Playing skillfully is not only a matter of skill but a matter of attitude. Whatever you do or want to do, you have to become the best you can be at it. Dr. Martin Luther King Jr. said, "If a man is called to be a street sweeper, he should sweep streets even as Michelangelo painted, or Beethoven composed music or Shakespeare wrote poetry. He should sweep streets so well that all the hosts of heaven and earth will pause to say, here lived a great street sweeper who did his job well." (MLK: What Is Your Life's Blueprint? 10:49)

So, what I am saying is that whatever ministry it is that you do, you have to find ways not only to improve your inner self but also to improve the technical aspect. We need to be developed and equipped for ministry both spiritually and technically.

Most things, especially in ministry, thrive or die based on their preparation. Passion never makes up for a lack of preparation. Gifting never makes up for lack of preparation. As believers, we need to develop spiritually and technically. Our service reflects ability as much as it reflects attitude.

Some people say, "All that matters is if I do it with the heart." Yet, they have failed to equip and prepare for their service. However, the technical aspects of our gifts and talents make a difference in being effective, and it also reveals our true motivation to give God the best. In other words, our desire to work on our technical ability shows that we want to give God the best.

When we practice and rehearse to play skillfully unto the Lord, we serve him with all our hearts. Colossians 3:23 says, "Whatever you do, work at it with all your heart, as working for the Lord, not for men." We might not be the best, but we will do it with all of our hearts. We do not have to expect perfection, but we have to strive toward excellence.

In 2 Samuel 24:24, David said, "No, I insist on paying you for it. I will not sacrifice to the Lord my God burnt offerings that cost me nothing." David knew that it would not be a gift or a sacrifice unto the Lord if it did not cost him something. He did not look for the cheapest way possible to please God. Clarke challenges us, "He who has a religion that costs him nothing, has a religion that is worth nothing." And, John Henry Jowett reminds us, "Ministry that costs nothing, accomplishes nothing."

Does God have you tending the sheep right now? Are you in a humble, lowly, servant's place but feel that God has called you to greater things? If He has, it will only be fulfilled as you are faithful in keeping the sheep right where you are. This is not waiting time; this is training time. David was a great man and a great king over Israel because he never lost his shepherd's heart.

The story ends in this manner in 1 Samuel 16:21–22, "David came to Saul and entered his service. Saul liked him very much, and David became one of his armor-bearers. Then Saul sent word to Jesse, saying, "Allow David to remain in my service, for I am pleased with him."

Remember, there is both a spiritual and technical preparation for ministry. How we prepare ourselves for service and how we present ourselves in service are equally important in the eyes of God. Foundationally, God cares more about the servant than the service. God is more interested in developing messengers than messages. God cares not only about our gifts and talent, but also our hearts. The quality of our service demonstrates the quality of a servant.

Emotional and Self-Awareness

The emotional intelligence of a leader must be their primal task, "It is both the original and the most important act of leadership" (Goleman, Boyatzis, & McKee, 2013, p. 5). The leader of any organization or church is the group's emotional and spiritual example. People look to the leaders, not only for what they say but more often for emotional cues and responses. Research shows, "The best leaders have found effective ways to understand and improve the way they handle their own and other people's emotions" (Goleman, Boyatzis, & McKee, 2013, p. 4). That is why the fifth leadership lesson is emotional and self-awareness.

In a world that lacks godly exemplars, God calls Latino church leaders to be examples of emotional health and intelligence. Emotional intelligence is vital to the spiritual formation development process because leaders wield the power of the physiological *open-loop* design of an organization's emotional stability.

According to Goleman, Boyatzis, and McKee, this physiological phenomenon is called mirroring. They explain, "People in groups at work inevitably 'catch' feelings for one another, sharing everything from jealousy and envy to angst or euphoria" (Goleman, Boyatzis, & McKee, 2013, p. 7). When a leader brings out the best in others, it is called *resonance*, but when the leader undermines people's emotional foundations, they instigate *dissonance*

Perhaps that is why in 1 Timothy 4:12, Paul motivated Timothy with these words: "Set an example for the believers in speech, in conduct, in love, in faith, and purity." Since a leader's life sets the standard for others to follow, Paul encourages Timothy to develop an excellent spiritual resonance. Since an unqualified leader inevitably lowers the standard of godliness in the church, Paul urges Timothy to avoid a life of dissonance. Anyone who cannot set a resonance of godly virtue in these areas does not belong in church leadership.

"Great leadership works through the emotions" (Goleman, Boyatzis, & McKee, 2013, p. 3); therefore, the success of leadership depends on how well they strategize and mobilize a team, as a leader is a group emotional guide. It is not just what they do but how they do it. People tend to follow how a leader lives, not only what they teach. A life of emotional intelligence and spiritual health brings power and authority to a leader's message. Remember this, you can teach someone what you know, but you will replicate who you are.

In 1 Corinthians 4:15–16, Paul said to the Corinthians, "Even though you have ten thousand guardians in Christ, you do not have many fathers, for in Christ Jesus I became your father through the gospel. Therefore, I urge you to imitate me." Here Paul tells us that the Corinthians had thousands of examples in Christ, but not many fathers. So, he took it upon himself to be their father and gave them a model to follow. Even though many in the Corinthian church had been dealt a lousy hand, Paul encourages them to look for better examples to resonate with.

Paul's emotional intelligence drove him to lead people from dissonance to resonance. Paul understood, "if people's emotions are pushed toward the range of enthusiasm, performance can soar; if people are driven toward rancor and anxiety, they'll be thrown off stride" (Goleman, Boyatzis, & McKee, 2013, p. 5).

The spiritual formation development process of any church has to include exemplars. In 1 Corinthians 11:1, Paul alludes to this idea, "Follow my example, as I follow the example of Christ." The emotional dysfunction that is present in many believers and churches provides a fantastic leadership opportunity. Providing an example of spiritual health and intelligence that can be seen and heard can make all the difference in the world.

Practicing Sabbath Principles

Since keeping the Sabbath day is one of the Ten Commandments, many have the tendency of thinking about it as a prohibition. The command to keep the Sabbath holy reminds us that God's commands are not merely restrictive but protective.

In the Fourth Commandment, we are directed to enter delight and rest and flee our infatuation with busyness (Allender, 2009, p. 6). It is in this context that I discovered an important fact that I had overlooked in the Bible. The precise idea, that the Sabbath Day must be *made* holy— that is, to be sanctified as holy is key to understanding this principle.

Allender explains, "The holy is not located in a one designated and agreed-upon space, such as a church, a monastery, or a stunning vista that captures a breathtaking view of a mountain range" (Allender, 2009, p. 3). Instead, the Sabbath is an invitation to enter delight and experience it, and in doing so, we enter it and sanctify it.

I was brought up with the incorrect teaching that Sundays were our Sabbath, that somehow, somewhere, Sunday took the place of the Old Testament command of the Sabbath. Therefore, we had to dedicate Sundays to attending church services. If, by chance, we had time in between, we rested.

Years later, I understood that Christians decided to meet on the first day of the week because Jesus rose from the dead on the first day of the week—not to replace Sabbath. The early church gathered on the first day of the week in celebration and remembrance of the resurrection (Acts 20:17).

Christians under the new covenant can have a healthier understanding of the Sabbath, not just as a "day" but a "way." This "way" is one that Allender understands as an invitation to delight, rather than only "the endless cycle of religious tedium and chronic exhaustion" (Allender, 2009, p. 9). He wrote, "Sabbath is not about time off or a break in routine. It is not a mini-vacation to give us a respite, so we are better prepared to go back to work. The Sabbath is far more than a diversion; it is meant to be an encounter with God's delight" (Allender, 2009, p. 12).

The Sabbath as an invitation to delight is an essential concept to Allender that he paints a clear picture of both a legalistic and lenient perspective. He writes, "Many who take the Sabbath seriously intentionally ruin it with legislation and worrisome fences that protect the Sabbath but destroy its delight" (Allender, 2009, pp. 7–9).

I was brought up to think that an annual vacation was vital because it was a time to rest and refuel, and while I still believe that it is essential to vacation, we must be careful not to fall prey to two extremes. One, being busy and in a hurry even on vacation, to the point that we are exhausted from our vacations and need a vacation from our vacation. Two, to think that the only time for delight is during vacation. Sabbath reminds us and provides for us a healthy view of delight, both for an annual vacation as well as a week-to-week practice.

Allender explains that we—in the Western world—make an incorrect correlation between Sabbath and vacation. In our modern understanding of vacationing, we have fallen prey to "the principalities of consumerism and self-serving capitalism" (Allender, 2009, p. 12). In the Western world, we use our vacation not to seek God's delight but to fill "sugary diversions" that do not satisfy.

Allender advocates something that is along the lines of play and delight. Sabbath in the right framework means not a day off, time off, or vacation time, but rather a day of celebration and delight. He explains, "The holy comes in a moment when we are captured by beauty, and a dance of delight swirls us beyond the moment to taste the expanse of eternity in, around, and before us" (Allender, 2009, p. 3).

Additionally, legalistic views of the Sabbath have a tendency, as Jesus taught, of making "the man for the Sabbath" rather than "the Sabbath for the man" (Mk. 2:27). Any attempt to make the Sabbath a list of dos and do nots adds to what Allender calls the "indulging in idolatrous overwork" (Allender, 2009, p. 12). This is perhaps why Allender invites us to view the Sabbath from a historical and eschatological perspective. When we enter Sabbath, we must remember "our leisure in Eden" and "anticipate our play in the new heavens and earth" (Allender, 2009, p. 5).

Conclusion

This chapter provided you with the five most critical leadership lessons that I have learned in a Latino context and for a Latino church. These lessons have rescued me from burnout while reaming true to my ministerial assignment. I view these lessons as an attempt to have a holistic approach to ministry as defined in the theology of the whole person.

The theology of the whole person can be defined as an all-inclusive approach to life. It is having an integrated Christian life (doctrines and ethics) in a modern-day lifestyle. Bank explains that theologians tend to reside in theological compounds that keep them away from the reality of ordinary everyday life and its predicaments. A theology of the whole person is necessary because modern-day theology seems to trivialize "the emotions, imagination, and will as much as of the intellect" (Banks, 1993, p. 135).

I teach students, in my Introduction to Youth Ministry class, that Jesus is our model of a holistic approach to life. I think this approach has something to contribute to Banks's take on a theology of the whole person.

Luke 2:52 provides for us a unique look at Jesus's all-inclusive development, "Jesus grew in wisdom and stature, and in favor with God and men." I like to analyze this verse as follows: "Jesus grew psychologically, physically, spiritually, and sociologically."

This description of Jesus's childhood into adulthood resonates with Banks description of a fully integrated Christian life (Banks, 1993, pp. 134-135). The growth in wisdom, or psychological growth, speaks of the challenge of accepting and adapting to the changes that take place in a person's intellect and mind. Although "we are constantly in danger of overstressing the role of the intellect in our lives" (Banks, 1993, p. 135), what is stressed here is the application of head knowledge into daily practice. Biblical wisdom is the practical application of knowledge.

The growth in stature, or physical maturity, deals with the challenge of accepting and adapting to the changes that take place in the person's body. This is not only true when a teen is going through puberty but also the idea of aging well.

For example, I played in soccer leagues as a small boy, played in club teams, played for my high school soccer team, and played through my young adult years and into full adulthood.

Just recently my knees and my ankles have not responded as I am used to, and I have come to understand that everything has a lifecycle even your body. When you are younger and more fit, you run through "the wall," but later you hit the wall. As life goes on and you grow older, the wall becomes more and more pronounced. Things that worked for you in the past may work against you in the future, so you have to rethink your strategy. You are still in the game, but now you do not put on the cleats. You may not be able to play but you can still coach. The idea is that there are times where we have to quit being enamored with being the star athlete and rethink our leadership strategy.

The growth in favor with God, or spiritual development, is the challenge of accepting and living life according to the Word of God. This includes the daily spiritual practice of reading scripture and prayer, but it also includes the important discipline of fellowship.

Banks explains that we will never get very far in developing an integrated Christian life "unless I am in a real relationship with a small group of fellow Christians, opening myself up to them and learning how to love them, sharing my dreams with them and growing in sensitivity to them, reflecting on what God is saying and open to their correcting" (Banks, 1993, p. 137).

Conclusively, to growth in favor with man, or growing sociologically, is the challenge of accepting and living life according to the laws of man. This is perhaps where the idea of *covenant* is significant. The covenantal life is pertinent "to the work situation, especially with respect to promises, obligations, and contracts" (Banks, 1993, p. 142).

Ultimately, the theology of the whole person is where "we are reminded of the possibility of change in social, economic, and political structures as well as personal life (Banks, 1993, p. 141). From one Latino leader to another, I pray these lessons contribute to the health of your leadership and the success of your ministry.

EPILOGUE

FARO CHURCH: RESEARCH FINDINGS

B ased on the research and substantiated by the applicable literature, the research methodology assessed whether the implementation of a monolingual English service served as a foundational ministry tool for the reduction of the silent exodus of second- and third-plus-generation Latinos at Faro Church. Consequently, this chapter will aim to describe the data collection findings, along with other related issues encountered during the data collection process.

Research Findings

The following two hypotheses provided a framework for the subsequent research design. First, this study hypothesized that the implementation of a monolingual English service might provoke a response from the second- and third-plus-generation Latinos with a desire to maintain a connection with Faro Church and to continue to worship at the monolingual service. Consequently, this trend would steadily and solidly reduce the silent exodus of second-and third-plus-generation Latinos by allowing for emerging adults of Faro Church to worship at their native congregation without having to seek monolingual English alternatives or stop church attendance altogether. Subsequently, in keeping with the church's mission, the retention will aid the incremental quantitative growth of church attendance by drawing disengaged, disillusioned, and disconnected emerging adults into the community.

Second, this study hypothesized that implementing a monolingual English worship service at Faro Church would provide worship space for intermarried Latinos to worship alongside spouses who may find the bilingual service linguistically challenging to adjust to but who still appreciate the multicultural atmosphere that draws their Latino spouse. Thus, the implementation would allow for more second-, and third-plus-generation intermarried Latinos to worship at Faro Church without seeking monolingual English alternatives or stopping church attendance altogether. As a result, in keeping with the church's mission, the retention will aid the incremental quantitative growth of church attendance by drawing disengaged, disillusioned, and disconnected intermarried Latinos into the community.

The intervention and the foundational portion for this research took place at Faro Church. Faro Church implemented a monolingual English Sunday service and surveyed and observed the changing demographics in the reduction of the silent exodus and in the retention of second- and third-plus-generation Latinos, including intermarried Latinos.

Faro Church continued to provide its current bilingual Sunday service at 9 a.m. but implemented the monolingual English service in place of its existing 11 a.m. bilingual service. Since the implementation of the monolingual English service superseded a current bilingual service, not many logistical factors were affected except the removing of the Spanish element from the bilingual service. The bilingual service already had an established, trained bilingual staff and, therefore, English speakers. Additionally, the 9 a.m. and 11 a.m. bilingual services already provided the English elements needed for worship songs, lyrics, video, and print. Only appropriate edits and alterations were made to accommodate an English-speaking audience with a monolingual English service. Also, on average, an existing bilingual service at Faro Church lasted about an hour and forty-five minutes; however, as explained in Chapter 3, no significant time decrease was expected in the new monolingual English service, as the bilingual service allowed time for translation and inter-pretational needs and challenges.

Implementation and Attendance

The implementation of the monolingual English service taking the place of the 11 a.m. bilingual service at Faro Church began on Sunday, January 6, 2019. This launch date registered the highest attendance during the fifteen-week research period with a total of 135 people (Table 1).

Week	Date	Attendance
1	01/06/19	135
2	01/13/19	85
3	01/20/19	97
4	01/27/19	100
5	02/03/19	97
6	02/10/19	88
7	02/17/19	100
8	02/24/19	71
9	03/03/19	81
10	03/10/19	97
11	03/17/19	91
12	03/24/19	100
13	03/31/19	98
14	04/07/19	67
15	04/14/19	109
MEAN		94
MEDIAN		97
MAX		135
MIN		67
RANGE		68

Figure 13. Table 1—*Faro Church Fifteen-Week Attendance to the Monolingual English Service*

Although many efforts were made as early as August 26, 2018, to announce the implementation of the monolingual English service as of the first Sunday of 2019 (January 6, 2019), it appears that some adherents inadvertently attended the monolingual English service. The average attendance of 157 people at the 11 a.m. bilingual service in 2018 provides evidence of this inadvertence. The first service demonstrated a similar attendance to the 2018 average with 135 people (Table 1). Therefore, it took this initial service to completely confirm to some adherents that the 11 a.m. service was indeed a monolingual English service moving forward. Ultimately, the research period ended on Sunday, April 14, 2019, with an attendance of 109 people. The fifteen-week average attendance was ninety-four people with a range variance of sixty-eight people (Table 1).

Comparatively, the average attendance range variance between the 9 a.m. bilingual service for the 2018 year to the same fifteen-week research period of the 9 a.m. bilingual service was +91 people (Table 2). Whereas, the average attendance range variance between the 11 a.m. bilingual service for the 2018 year to the fifteen-week research period of the implemented 11 a.m. monolingual English service was −63 people (Table 2). However, the average attendance range variance between the 9 a.m. bilingual service plus the 11 a.m. bilingual services for the 2018 year to the fifteen-week research period of the 9 a.m. bilingual service plus the 11 a.m. monolingual English service was +29 people (Table 2). This number is central to the research at hand as it determined that church attendance grew by twenty-nine people with the implementation of the monolingual English service as compared to the prior year's church attendance average (Table 2). This only considers a comparison to the previous year as it is the closest comparable and does not take into account any other factors that could influence a change in attendance from one year to the next.

Faro Church Services	2018 15Wk Average Attendance	Faro Church Services	2019 15Wk Average Attendance	Range
9am Bilingual (Spanish and English)	279	9am Bilingual (Spanish and English)	359	80
11am Bilingual (Spanish and English)	167	11am Monolingual English	94	-73
Total Average	446	Total Average	453	7

Figure 14. Table 2—*Faro Church Attendance: 2018 Total Year Average Attendance vs. 2019 Fifteen-Week Average Attendance with Range*

More definitely, the average attendance range variance between the 9 a.m. bilingual plus 11 a.m. bilingual services for the same calendar period of the first fifteen weeks of the 2018 year to the fifteen-week research period of the 9 a.m. bilingual service plus the 11 a.m. monolingual English service was +80 for the 9 a.m. service and −73 for the 11 a.m. service, demonstrating a total range variance of +7 people (Table 3). This number is central to the research at hand as it determined that church attendance grew by seven people with the implementation of the monolingual English service as compared to the prior year's church attendance for the same fifteen-week period (Table 3).

Faro Church Services	2018 15Wk Average Attendance	Faro Church Services	2019 15Wk Average Attendance	Range
9am Bilingual (Spanish and English)	279	9am Bilingual (Spanish and English)	359	80
11am Bilingual (Spanish and English)	167	11am Monolingual English	94	-73
Total Average	446	Total Average	453	7

Figure 15. Table 3—*Faro Church Attendance: First 15 Weeks of 2018 vs. First 15 Weeks of 2019*

The least-attended monolingual English service was Sunday, April 7, 2019, with sixty-seven adherents (Table 4). This could have been, but is not confirmed, due to the conclusion of the church's annual Doing Church as a Team (DCAT) conference, which recorded the largest 9 a.m. bilingual (English and Spanish) service attendance during the fifteen-week research period with 448 adherents (Table 4). In comparison, the average attendance to the monolingual English service did not seem to be affected by the possible scheduling disturbances such as Super Bowl Sunday (February 2, 2019), with an attendance of ninety-seven people or Daylight Savings Time (March 10, 2019), with an attendance of ninety-seven people (Table 4). Additionally, the speaker on any given Sunday did not seem to affect the attendance to the monolingual English service as the research period did not display any major disturbances to the attendance average, based on the speaker (Table 4).

The implementation of the monolingual English service created an unexpected consequence in the increase of attendance to the 9 a.m. bilingual service as it increased from an average of 268 people in 2018 to an average of 359 in the first fifteen weeks of 2019.

	Date	9am Bilingual	11am English	Total	Speaker	Event
1	1/6/19	311	135	446	Josh	Launch Date
2	1/13/19	351	85	436	Saul	
3	1/20/19	368	97	465	Saul	
4	1/27/19	370	100	470	Saul	
5	2/3/19	400	97	497	Josh	Super Bowl
6	2/10/19	329	88	417	Josh	
7	2/17/19	375	100	475	Josh	
8	2/24/19	385	71	456	Saul	
9	3/3/19	381	81	462	Josh	
10	3/10/19	298	97	395	Josh	Time Change
11	3/17/19	356	91	447	Josh	
12	3/24/19	371	100	471	Josh	
13	3/31/19	314	98	412	Josh	
14	4/7/19	448	67	515	Josh	DCAT
15	4/14/19	330	109	439	Josh	End Research
	Mean	359	94	454		
	Max	448	135	515		
	Min	298	67	395		
	Range	150	68	120		

Figure 16. Table 4—*Faro Church Attendance Combined for the fifteen-week Research Period.*

The increase on average of ninety-one people created an augmented sense of comradery and synergy in the 9 a.m. bilingual service as many adherents reported feelings of enjoyment because the services were filled to the brim, creating an enthusiastic worship experience. Consequently, this could have affected the attendance to the monolingual English service as some were drawn to the new and unexpected allurement of the 9 a.m. bilingual service as evidenced by some of the focus group findings later in this chapter.

Logistically, however, the elders and pastors of Faro Church had to create a sense of reprieve as the meeting space was straining at capacity during the 9 a.m. bilingual service. Therefore, the first option of relief was the resolution to implement a monolingual Spanish service on April 21, 2019, after the fifteen-week research period of the monolingual English service. This was decided, early in February, based on the opportunity to serve the monolingual Spanish-speaking adherents of the church community while keeping the desired focus on retaining and recruiting second- and third-plus-generation Latinos, including intermarried Latinos, through the monolingual English service. Consequently, since Easter Sunday, April 21, 2019, Faro Church has provided three services: 8 a.m. monolingual Spanish service, 9:30 bilingual (English and Spanish), and 11 a.m. monolingual English service.

Research Findings I:
Survey of Emerging Latino Adults at Faro Church

The survey participants were first-, second-, and third-generation Latinos, aged eighteen to twenty-five, who attend Faro Church. This demographic is the primary focus of the research purpose and provided pertinent data for the research at hand. The two prerequisites for this survey were age and observed continuous Faro Church attendance. The age parameter was eighteen to twenty-five years of age in order to meet the emerging adult demographic central to the research.

Faro Church is a congregation comprised of multiple generations, and the cultural differences and ministry needs of these groups result in a variety of challenges that must be addressed. Thus, participants were selected for this survey as randomly as possible within the parameters of this survey to eliminate bias and prohibit the research findings from being inadvertently associated with a particular group of humans.

Therefore, this survey gauged the views of emerging first-, second-, and third-plus-generation Latino adults aged eighteen to twenty-five on the challenges of retention and recruitment at Faro Church and the role of language preference. Further, this survey provided vital qualitative data concerning the changing demographics and ministry preferences of the emerging Latino adults of the church at large. Also, this pre- and post-survey measured changing perspectives, opinions, and ideas about the implementation of a monolingual English service at Faro Church. This survey yielded quantitative support for the need for a monolingual English service to meet the emerging needs of Latino emerging adults.

A pre-survey was conducted before the implementation of the monolingual English service at Faro Church on January 6, 2019. A post-survey was conducted after a fifteen-week period ending on April 21, 2019. Both the pre- and post-surveys were available in English and Spanish and took place at Faro Church. The surveys acquired necessary demographic data including gender, age group, ethnic origin, generation/country of origin, language use, education, marital status, employment status, and church attendance. In addition, the surveys included two research questions, using a four-item Likert scale to gauge the most significant challenges facing Latino emerging adults and the most considerable ministry model challenge that Latino churches have in retaining second- and third-plus-generation Latinos.

Accumulatively, the pre-survey asked seven questions gathering data on opinions and perspectives on the implementation of a monolingual English service at Faro Church. The questions primarily attempted to collect an understanding on issues and concerns, the efficacy or lack thereof in retention, attendance to the English service, and the likelihood of attractiveness to other second- and third-plus-generation Latinos.

Subsequently, the post-survey asked seven questions gathering data on opinions and perspective on the implementation of the monolingual English service at Faro Church. The questions primarily attempted to collect changes in perspectives, opinions, or behaviors after the implementation of the monolingual English service and to assess whether it was successful in the retention and recruitment of emerging adults and intermarried couples.

Comparison of the Pre- and Post-Survey Research Findings I

The range in this survey looked for independent and identically distributed continuous random variables between the pre-survey cumulative distribution totals and the post-survey cumulative distribution totals. The difference denotes the range of the sample size in any given question distribution. The range in this survey comparison is the size of the smallest or largest interval, which contains all the data and provides an indication of statistical dispersion. It is measured in the same units as the data collection. The range is useful in representing the dispersion specifically in small data sets as represented in the twenty-two pre- and post-surveys collected for this research.

Pre/Post question 1. Research question one asked respondents to indicate the importance of challenges for emerging adults in Latino churches using a four-item, three-point Likert scale (Extremely Important—3, Moderately Important—2, Mildly Important—1, and Not Important at All—0). Respondents were asked to rate the following possible items: lack of personal commitment, moral issues (i.e., drug, alcohol abuse, sex, etc.), the lack of spiritual development (discipleship), shortage of positive role models, problems related to immigration, English worship services, contemporary church services (worship music), sermon format and content, small groups or ministries, and connectivity (friends at church, hospitality).

Concerning the question of ranking the importance of the challenges of emerging adults in Latino churches, although there were no variations beyond a point, the data comparison revealed that the need for monolingual English services had the most extensive negative range reporting a –.41 variance from the pre-survey to the post-survey but still demonstrating a moderate vitality rating (Figure 17). The most significant positive range was +.18 for the lack of spiritual development (discipleship), but the factor still kept an extremely vital rating (Figure 17).

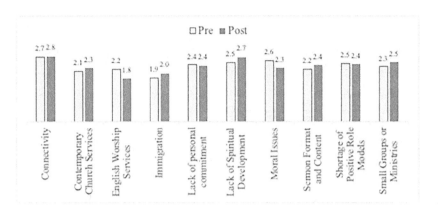

Figure 17. Average response to pre- and post-survey question 1

Pre/Post question 2. Research question two asked respondents to indicate the most significant ministry model challenge that Latino churches have in retaining and discipling second- and third-plus-generation Latinos using a four-item, three-point Likert scale (Extremely Important—3, Moderately Important—2, Mildly Important—1, and Not Important at All—0). Respondents were asked to rate the following possible items: refusal to accommodate linguistic needs of emerging adults, the lack of spiritual development (discipleship), contemporary church services (worship and music), relativity (friends at church, hospitality), a belief that the church exists to maintain the Latino culture, a belief that Latino churches exist to provide ministry to the Spanish speakers, fear in the first-generation to share or expand leadership roles, cultural anxieties and capabilities to reach English speakers (relevance), not recognizing the growth of Latino intermarriage, and inability to answer difficult theological questions.

On the question ranking the most significant ministry model challenge that Latino churches have in retaining and discipling second- and third-plus-generation Latinos, the data comparison revealed that the fear in the first-generation to share or expand leadership roles had the most extensive negative range, reporting a –.23 variance from the pre-survey to the post-survey, but the factor still demonstrated a moderate vitality rating (Figure 18). The most significant positive range was +.28

variable for the inability to answer difficult theological questions, rising from moderately vital to extremely vital (Figure 18). Central to the study at hand, there was no variance on the refusal to accommodate linguistic needs of emerging adults with the factor keeping a moderate vitality by averaging 2.4 points (Figure 18).

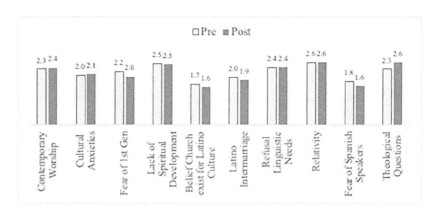

Figure 18. Average response to pre- and post-survey question 2

Pre/Post Survey Question 3. The third pre- and post-survey research question asked respondents to indicate, in their opinion, why many Latino emerging adults are uninterested in church, including youth or young adult activities, by checking all the issues that applied. Respondents were asked to rate the following possible items: lack of personal commitment, moral issues (i.e. drug, alcohol abuse, sex, etc.), the lack of spiritual development (discipleship), shortage of positive role models, no Spanish worship services, no English worship services, contemporary church services (worship and music), sermon format and content, small groups or ministries, and connectivity (friends at church, hospitality).

Concerning the third research question dealing with the reasons why many Latino emerging adults are uninterested in church, including youth or young adult activities, the data comparison revealed that sermon format and content had the most extensive negative range, reporting a −6 point variance from the pre- to the post-survey (Figure 38). The most significant positive range was +4 points for moral issues (i.e., drug, alcohol abuse, sex, etc.) (Figure 19). Central to the study at hand, there was a –5 point variance on the lack of monolingual English worship services, demonstrating a decrease in importance (Figure 19).

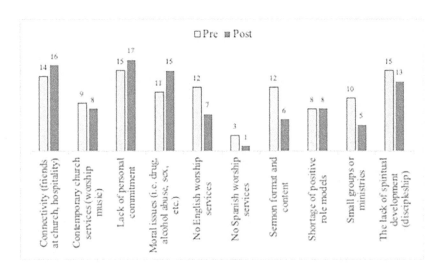

(*Figure 19*. Total response to pre- and post-survey question 3)

Pre/Post survey question 4. The fourth survey question asked respondents to indicate, in their opinion, why some emerging adults are leaving the Latino church (many after attending church for most of their lives) by checking all the issues that applied. Respondents were asked to rate the following possible items: lack of personal commitment, moral issues (i.e. drug, alcohol abuse, sex, etc.), the lack of spiritual development (discipleship), shortage of positive role models, no Spanish worship services, no English worship services, contemporary church services (worship music), sermon format and content, small groups or ministries, and connectivity (friends at church, hospitality).

Concerning the second research question at hand, measuring why some emerging adults are leaving the Latino church (many after attending church for most of their lives), the data comparison revealed that small groups or ministries and the lack of spiritual development (discipleship) had the most extensive negative range, reporting a –5 point variance from the pre-survey to the post-survey (Figure 20). The most significant positive range was +3 points for contemporary church services (worship music) (Figure 20). Central to the study at hand, there was a −2 point variance on the lack of monolingual English worship services (Figure 20), demonstrating a decrease in importance.

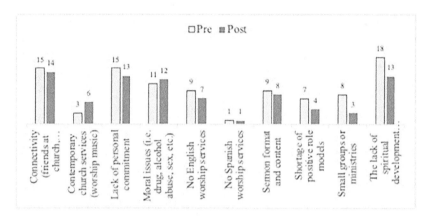

(Figure 20. Total response to pre- and post-survey question 4)

Pre/Post survey feelings and concerns. The pre- and post-survey asked respondents to gauge their initial and conclusive feelings about the implementation of a monolingual English service at Faro Church by checking all the emotions that applied. Respondents were asked to rate the following possible items: excited, reserved, optimistic, pessimistic, anticipation, doubtful, pleasantly surprised, and disapproving.

Gauging the pre-announcement of the installment versus the implementation of the monolingual English service at Faro Church, the emerging adults generally demonstrated positive feelings with little to no disapproval. As expected, after the monolingual English service had been implemented, the data comparison revealed that anticipation had the most extensive negative range, reporting a −3 point variance from the pre-survey to the post-survey (Figure 21). The most significant positive range was +7 points for the feeling of optimism, reflecting a positive outlook on the monolingual English service moving forward (Figure 21).

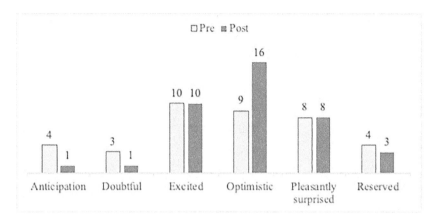

Figure 21. Total response to pre- and post-survey questions about initial and definitive feelings

The pre-survey asked respondents to gauge their initial questions or concerns about the implementation of the monolingual English service at Faro Church, and the post-survey asked if they were actualized. Both surveys asked participants to respond by checking all the issues that applied. Respondents were asked to rate the following possible items: the senior pastor's ability to preach in English, an effect on the primary Spanish-speaking ministries of the church, first-generation feeling "left behind," the inability to attract English-speaking emerging adults, insufficient English-speaking volunteers or staff, a separation of the congregation, what about a monolingual Spanish service, and an unnecessary change.

Gauging the initial concerns versus the actualized concerns, the data revealed the fear of the first-generation feeling "left behind" diminished in importance, demonstrating the highest range variance of –5 points (Figure 22). The highest range was reported in the pastor's ability to preach in English, demonstrating a +2 variance (Figure 22).

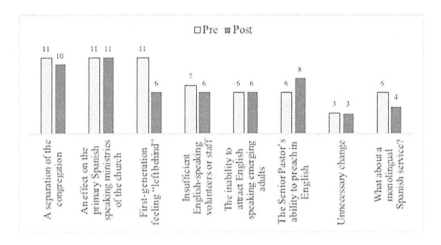

Figure 22. Total response to pre- and post-survey questions about questions and actualized concerns)

Pre/Post-survey attendance and invite questions. Subsequently, the pre- and post-surveys asked by providing a yes or no option whether the respondents would consider attending the implemented monolingual English service at Faro Church. While the pre-survey data yielded by this study provided convincing evidence that the emerging adults of Faro Church would attend the new monolingual English service, evidenced by a 73 percent affirmative response to the prospect of attending, the post-survey revealed a 14 percent range variance (Figure 23).

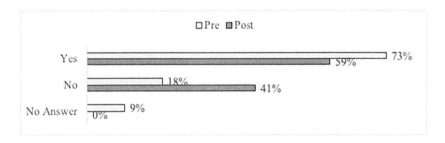

Figure 23. Pre- and post-survey percentage of emerging adults who would and did attend the monolingual English service

Incongruently, although there seemed to be a decline in interest in the monolingual English service, 73 percent of respondents did agree that the implementation of the monolingual English service would facilitate the inviting of friends and family (Figure 24).

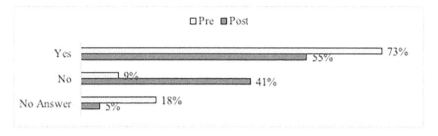

Figure 24. Pre- and post-survey percentage of facilitation of invitation to the monolingual English service

Ultimately, the question measuring the vitality of the implementation of a monolingual English service to the retention and evangelizing of emerging adults demonstrated a slight increase in importance from a 2.50 average in the pre-survey to a 2.57 average in the post-survey representing a +.07 point range with the factor maintaining a moderate vitality rating.

Research Findings II:
Survey of Intermarried Couples at Faro Church

Eleven pre- and post-surveys of intermarried, first-, second-, and third-generation Latinos of Faro Church couples were conducted to gain and gauge evidence supporting the need for bilingual (English and Spanish) or monolingual English services (see Appendix C). "Intermarried" refers to a marriage between a Latino and a person of different race or ethnicity. This demographic is another primary focus of the research purpose and provided pertinent data for the research at hand.

First-generation Latinos tend to marry within their ethnic group; however, second- and third-generation Latinos demonstrate higher intermarriage percentages. Thirty-two percent of second-generation and 57 percent of third-plus-generation Latinos intermarry with other ethnicities (Suro & Passel, 2003, p. 9). Twenty-five percent of Latino newlyweds married a non-Latino spouse, and 18 percent of all married Latinos intermarried (Lopez et al., 2017, p. 4).

Consequently, pre- and post-surveys of intermarried couples at Faro Church were conducted to gain and gauge evidence supporting the need for bilingual (English and Spanish) services for this demographic. The assumption was that these intermarried couples chose to attend Faro Church because it provides bilingual services that they can enjoy together. Nevertheless, this research measured whether they have a preference for a monolingual English service over the bilingual (English and Spanish) service. A post-survey followed to determine whether a bilingual (English and Spanish) or the monolingual English service better met their marital and family needs. This survey provided quantitative evidence to indicate whether Latino intermarried couples prefer to attend bilingual (English and Spanish) services or monolingual English services.

The pre-survey was conducted before the implementation of the monolingual English service at Faro Church on January 6, 2019, and the post-survey after a fifteen-week period ending on April 21, 2019. The surveys took place at Faro Church.

Comparison of the Pre- and Post-Survey Research Findings II

The range in this survey comparison is the size of the smallest or largest interval, which contains all the data and provides an indication of statistical dispersion. It is measured in the same units as the data collection. The range is useful in representing the dispersion specifically in small data sets as represented in the eleven pre- and 11 post-surveys collected for this research.

Pre/Post-survey intermarried couples question 1. Question one asked respondents to indicate the importance of the primary reasons for choosing to attend Faro Church using a four-item, three-point Likert scale (Extremely Important—3, Moderately Important—2, Mildly Important—1, and Not Important at All—0). Respondents were asked to rate the following possible items: bilingual worship services, children's ministry (in English), sermon format and content, friendliness and hospitality, location, contemporary church services (worship and music), small groups or ministries, connectivity (friends at church, hospitality), your spouse's choice, and Latino culture.

Concerning the question indicating how important were/are the primary reasons for choosing to attend Faro Church, the data showed that the spouse's choice demonstrated the most significant decrease in importance, showing a range of –.5 points lowering in importance of rank from third with 2.6 points in the pre-survey to tie for seventh in the post-survey, and representing a change from extremely vital to moderately vital in the Likert scale (Figure 25). Central to the research at hand, the provision of bilingual services (along with location) demonstrated a range variance of +.5 points, increasing in rank from fifth with 2.2 points in the pre-survey to third with 2.6 points in the post-survey and representing a change from moderately vital to extremely vital in the Likert scale (Figure 25). Apart from a +.3 range for friendliness and hospitality, all other items from the pre-surveys to the post-surveys demonstrated minor range variances (Figure 25).

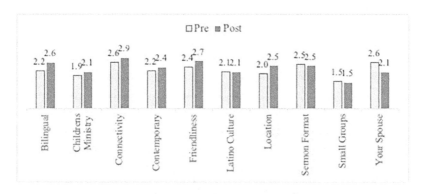

Figure 25. Average response to intermarried pre- and post-survey question 1

This evidence seems to point to the perceived preference of the bilingual service among intermarried couples, even after having experienced the monolingual English service. The data appear to suggest that although intermarried couples seemed to value their spouse's choice as one of the primary reasons for choosing to attend Faro Church, after having experienced a monolingual English service, the provision of bilingual service is a higher value. Therefore, the data provide evidence toward a bilingual service preference over a monolingual English service among intermarried couples of Faro Church.

Pre/Post-survey intermarried couples question 2. Question two asked the intermarried respondents to indicate their worship service and classroom language preference by selecting from a (1) monolingual Spanish service, (2) bilingual (English and Spanish) service, and (3) monolingual English service.

When measuring the range of language preference, the survey demonstrated a drop of –27 percent for the monolingual English service and an increase of +33 percent variance for the bilingual service (Figure 26). This data provides further support for the preference of a bilingual service over a monolingual English service among the intermarried couples of Faro Church.

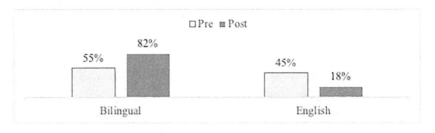

Figure 26. Percentage of intermarried pre- vs. post-survey question 2a

Incongruently, however, in the opinion of the intermarried couples of Faro Church, their children's preference for a monolingual English service increased +18 percent while dropping –18 percent for a monolingual Spanish language preference (Figure 27). Given the centrality of the issue and with the assumption that the children of intermarried couples would be considered second- or third-generation Latinos, this survey seems to support the idea that these children would prefer a bilingual or monolingual English service over a monolingual Spanish service.

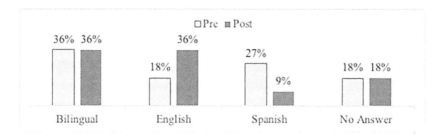

Figure 27. Percentage of intermarried pre vs. post-survey question 2b

Pre/Post-survey intermarried couples question 1. The first pre-survey question asked intermarried respondents to indicate, in their opinion, why many Latino emerging adults are uninterested in church, including youth or young adult activities, by checking all the issues that applied. Respondents were asked to rate the following possible items: lack of personal commitment, moral issues (i.e., drug, alcohol abuse, sex, etc.), the lack of spiritual development (discipleship), shortage of positive role models, no Spanish worship services, no English worship services, contemporary church services (worship music), sermon format and content, small groups or ministries, and connectivity (friends at church, hospitality).

Concerning the question dealing with the reasons why many Latino emerging adults are uninterested in church, including youth or young adult activities, the moral issues (i.e., drug, alcohol abuse, sex, etc.) option demonstrated a –6 point variance, the highest in this survey question, demonstrating a change in rank from first with 9 points to tie for fourth with 3 points (Figure 28). Shortage of positive role models demonstrated the second largest range variance but kept the same rank as tied for fourth with 6 points in the pre-survey and 3 points in the post-survey (Figure 28).

As it relates to the research at hand, the lack of monolingual Spanish services remained as the lowest rank for both surveys, garnering only a single point in both surveys (Figure 28). Similarly, the need for mono-lingual English services demonstrated only –2 variances, falling from the sixth rank with 3 points in the pre-survey to seventh with a single point in the post-survey (Figure 28). The data seem to indicate that wor-ship service language preference is not a primary reason why emerging adults are uninterested in church, indicating that factors like personal commitment and a better discipleship program would be more indica-tive of interest in church.

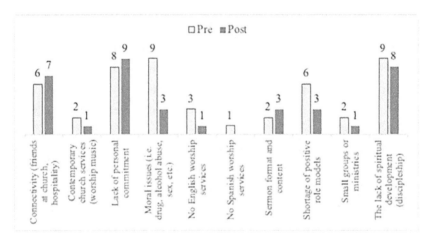

Figure 28. Total intermarried responses to pre- vs. post-survey research question 1

Pre/Post-survey intermarried couples question 2. The second pre-survey question asked respondents to indicate, in their opinion, why some emerging adults are leaving the Latino church (many after attending church for most of their lives) by checking all the issues that applied. Respondents were asked to rate the following possible items: lack of personal commitment, moral issues (i.e. drug, alcohol abuse, sex, etc.), the lack of spiritual development (discipleship), shortage of positive role models, no Spanish worship services, no English worship services, contemporary church services (worship and music), sermon format and content, small groups or ministries, and connectivity (friends at church, hospitality).

Concerning the question measuring why some emerging adults are leaving the Latino church (many after attending church for most of their lives), moral issues (i.e. drug, alcohol abuse, sex, etc.) demonstrated the most significant range variance, losing six points (–6) from the pre-survey to the post-survey (Figure 29). As it relates to the research, the need for a monolingual service increased in rank while dropping a point, demonstrating fifth in rank with 5 points in the pre-survey and tied for fourth in rank with 4 points in the post-survey (Figure 29). Reporting the lowest rank with no variance and no points in each of the surveys was the need for monolingual Spanish services (Figure 29).

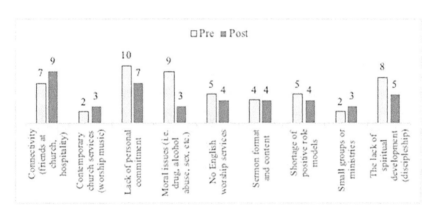

Figure 29. Total intermarried responses to pre- vs post-survey question 2

Pre/Post-survey feelings and concerns. This question asked respondents to check all emotions that applied to the fifteen-week implementation of a monolingual English service at Faro Church. Respondents were asked to rate the following possible items: excited, reserved, optimistic, pessimistic, anticipation, doubtful, pleasantly surprised, and disapproving.

Gauging their emotions regarding the announcement of the installment versus the implementation of the monolingual English service at

Faro Church, the intermarried couples of Faro Church generally demonstrated positive feelings with little to no disapproval. The most significant point range variance between emotions was an increase in excitement from a pre-survey ranking of third with a total of 3 points to a ranking of second with 8 points in the post-survey (Figure 30). Optimism continued to rank high from the pre- to post-surveys, demonstrating the second largest range (+4) from 5 points to 9 points (Figure 30)

Furthermore, although the pre-survey demonstrated a point each for pessimism and doubt concerning the implementation of the monolingual English service, there were no such feelings reported (0) in the post-survey (Figure 30) This data yielded strong emotional support for the implementation of the English service among the intermarried couples of Faro Church.

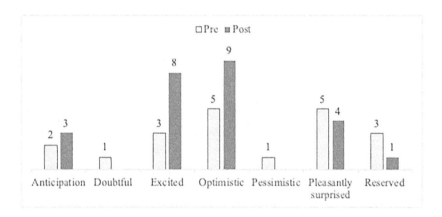

Figure 30. Total intermarried responses to pre- vs. post-survey question about initial feelings

The question of the first-generation feeling "left behind" was the primary initial concern among intermarried couples of Faro Church before the implementation of the monolingual English service, with responses totaling 8 points (Figure 31). However, it demonstrated the most significant range variance of –5 points, weakening to the fifth rank with three points in concern actualization. Similarly, the worry about the effect on the primarily Spanish-speaking ministries of the church decreased from second in concern rank with 7 points to fifth in concern actualization with 3 points (Figure 31). Conversely, the concerns dealing with the senior pastor's ability to preach in English, the inability to attract English speaking emerging adults, and the implementation as an unnecessary change, all increased in concern actualization with each demonstrating a +3 variance (Figure 31). The data seem to suggest a shift from peripheral concerns to targeted concerns relating to the monolingual English service. Volunteerism and concerns for first-generation Spanish speakers were replaced by concern regarding the church's ability to provide a quality English service.

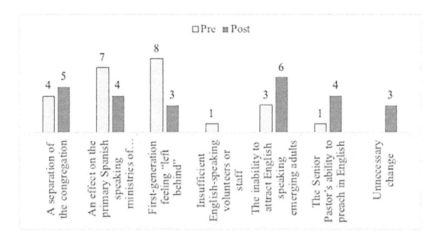

Figure 31. Total intermarried responses to pre- vs. post-survey question about primary concerns

Pre/Post-survey attendance and invite questions. The surveys asked whether the respondents would attend and if they attended the implemented monolingual English service at Faro Church. Although initially eight intermarried couples (73 percent) of the pre-survey participants responded that they would attend, ten did (91 percent) attend the implemented monolingual English service, representing a +18 percent variance (Figure 32).

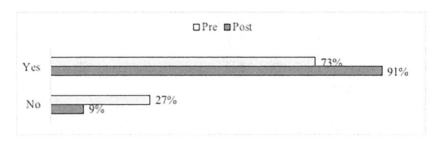

Figure 32. Pre- vs. post-survey percentage of intermarried adults to attend the monolingual English service

Contrariwise, while 100 percent of the pre-survey participants agreed that the implementation of a monolingual English service would facilitate the inviting of friends and family to church, only 73 percent agreed in the post-survey, representing a –27 percent variance (Figure 33).

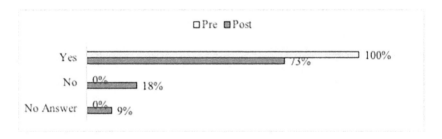

Figure 33. Pre- vs. post-survey percentage of facilitation of invitation to the monolingual English service

Ultimately, the question measuring the vitality of the implementation of a monolingual English service to the retention and evangelizing of emerging adults increased in importance among the intermarried adults of Faro Church from 2.36 points in the pre-survey to 2.45 points in the post-survey, representing a +.09 point variance. This data demonstrates a slight increase in moderate vitality; however, the implementation of a monolingual English service marginally misses an extremely vital rating by .05 points, according to the Likert scale.

Research Findings III:
Focus Groups of Intermarried Couples
and Emerging Adults

Two pre- and post-focus groups were conducted among first-, second-, and third- generation Latinos, including intermarried couples, who attend Faro Church (see Appendix E). These demographics are the primary focus of the research purpose and provided pertinent data for the research at hand. The focus groups were used to measure and develop qualitative evidence for changing demographics and the need for bilingual and monolingual services in Latino churches while documenting differences in outlook about the implementation of a monolingual English service at Faro Church.

The three prerequisites for this focus group were age, Latino intermarriage, and observed continuous Faro Church attendance. Intermarried refers to a marriage between a Latino/Hispanic and a person of different race or ethnicity. The age parameter for emerging adults was eighteen to twenty-four years, and the intermarriage demographic was central to the research. Still, participants were selected for research as randomly as possible within the parameters of the focus group to eliminate bias and prohibit the research findings from being inadvertently associated with a particular group of humans. The focus groups were all actualized in English as none of the participants required translation or interpretation.

A third-party surveyor conducted the focus groups before the implementation of the monolingual English service at Faro Church on January 4, 2019, and at the conclusion of the implementation of a monolingual English service at Faro Church after April 21, 2019, to determine the effectiveness of the monolingual service. The focus groups were audio- and video-recorded for analysis. The focus groups took place at Faro Church.

The focus groups had eight pre-survey prompt questions and seven post-implementation prompt questions, quantifying attitudes, opinions, behaviors, and variables of the monolingual English service. The questions served to gauge the benefits of a bilingual service versus a monolingual English service and documented opinions, reasons, motivations, and the perceived success of the service or lack thereof.

Findings from Pre-Focus Groups

The pre-survey focus group demonstrated affirming attitudes toward the benefits of a monolingual English service. It provided optimistic feelings while demonstrating realistic concerns concerning the implemented monolingual English service. This focus group provided vital qualitative data concerning the changing demographics and ministry preferences of the emerging Latino adults in the church at large.

Question 1: The question of benefit. When asked to express opinions on the most significant benefits of attending a bilingual church, most respondents expressed linguistic enrichment, missiological fulfillment, familial unification, intermarital interest, and generational linkage as the primary driving factors.

A female, second-generation emerging adult explained that the translation (from Spanish into English or vice versa) as generally done at Faro Church in the bilingual service provided linguistic enrichment because it helped her understand the sermon better. She said, "When they say it in Spanish and then I will hear it in English, I feel like it clicks. There are words in Spanish that I do not understand and vice versa. So, I get a double message." Similarly, a female, second-generation Latina agreed, "You know a certain language, but sometimes you understand certain words only, but when you hear them in both languages, you can combine both of them and understand the whole subject that is at hand."

A second-generation, emerging adult, intermarried male expressed that Faro Church's bilingual (English and Spanish) services provided missiological fulfillment because they helped reach a broader Hispanic population who demonstrate different linguistic preferences.

Similarly, a married, emerging female Latina expressed that the bilingual commitment of Faro Church encourages the Latino at large to connect with other cultures, ethnicities, and languages. She explained that the bilingual service "makes you think about how to connect the bridge between both people because we speak Spanish with one culture, and we speak English with a different culture ... it makes you think outside the box on how you can be an example."

Others expressed how the bilingual service is in keeping with the missiological command to preach to all nations as the preaching can meet the linguistic needs of the Latino community uniquely. A non-Hispanic intermarried male explained:

> It opens up doors to reach to a certain demagogic [sic] that maybe are not believers. For example, if you have a bunch of American guys walking the streets of Santa Ana (a city in in Orange County that is predominantly Hispanic), trying to reach non-believers ... they'll get treated differently because they do not look like them, they do not sound like them. There's no connection.

He added, "When you have a bilingual church when you have a lot of migrant families and workers, what are they looking for? They are looking for people that look like them, that speak the same language, the common bonds that you need to feel comfortable."

Similarly, an intermarried couple expressed how the service gave them intermarital benefit by allowing them to worship together in the same church. The wife explained, "Well in our case, [my husband] does not speak Spanish ... It would have been very difficult to remain at Faro if it was not bilingual." A female, intermarried adult explained how the bilingual service was beneficial because the message was being presented in the languages that both could understand. She said, "I think that for mixed couples, it is really important because at the end of the service we are able to talk about it, to communicate, and we hear it in both languages." Similarly, a first-generation, intermarried Latina expressed, "My husband and I can come together and be able to understand the same message."

Additionally, the bilingual services provided familial unification. This familial appeal was experienced by a Latino, second-generation emerging adult who explained, "We were brought here by our parents, and this was a church we could all attend because they are Spanish speaking, and we prefer English, so it was accommodating to us." An intermarried Latina with four Latino emerging adult children said she decided a bilingual church was beneficial for her family because her "kids were able to understand in English what I was learning in Spanish."

This familial bonding seemed to be enriched by the live translation. A non-Latino, intermarried male explained, "You know there are churches where you can go and get headsets where they translate. That, I would say, does not promote unity because you can tell ... I think by going to a bilingual church, you feel more included. It is not more segregated. English speakers and Spanish speakers worship together."

Others expressed that the bilingual aspect of the church helps expose second- and third-generation Latinos who may be losing the Spanish language to Spanish. One female participant explained, "...youth overall, and small children... they'll start learning the language as they hear it more." Comparably, a white, intermarried adult explained that he chose to attend a bilingual church due to the "exposure for the kids to dual languages." This sentiment was echoed by a female, white intermarried adult who clarified:

> Now having kids, to be able to have them around their culture, I feel that if we just went to an English church, which we could manage, because both of us speak English, but the likelihood of the church having the same culture that Faro does, does not exist there.

Moreover, a second-generation emerging adult explained that the bilingual service favored generational linkage by keeping his multigenerational family together. He described, "I think for my family, we stayed because my mom and family liked Spanish. My brothers and I liked English." Multiple participants expressed that the bilingual service allowed the younger generations to worship alongside the older generations. Another emerging adult female added, "I also think that it creates unity since you are listening to the same message."

Another second-generation emerging Latina expressed the inclusivity favorability of a bilingual church. She revealed, "I think that (the bilingual aspect) allowed for my siblings and I to both be able to serve within the church ... if it were Spanish, I would not be comfortable with my level of Spanish being able to serve someone." Counterwise, she explained, "the same thing with my mom or my dad; they would not be able to reach certain people in English because they are not as comfortable in that language ... it allows them to serve better."

Question 2: Initial feelings. When asked to express their initial feelings about the implementation of the monolingual English service, responses varied among eager expectation, evangelistic hopefulness, and reserved fear about the effects on the Latino first-generation, Spanish-only speakers.

Initially, most, if not all, received the news of the implementation of a monolingual English service with pleasant anticipation. One emerging adult simply remarked, "Good timing." A white female, intermarried emerging adult expressed enthusiastic expectation. She indicated, "I was so happy, I never thought that it would happen. I only speak English." A married, Latina emerging adult expressed her eagerness: "I think that it is going to give more people the opportunity to dream about the church ... intermarried couples, teenagers, and emerging adults may feel even more included, to be able to give an opinion. So, I am excited to see what may come, what may unfold in people."

Others expressed excitement for the evangelistic opportunities. A female emerging adult expressed eagerness about the possibility of inviting English speakers to Faro Church. She explained, "I was excited to invite people that I know who only speak English because I love my church, but sometimes the bilingual aspect of Faro can get lost in the translation. So, I was very excited to invite my coworkers or friends to all-English services." A female, intermarried adult echoed the sentiment, "I was excited to invite people to church, thinking they would be more comfortable in an English-only service."

Understandably, some expressed concerns over the impact on the Latino first-generation. A white, intermarried adult expressed his concerns upon hearing about the implementation of the monolingual English service: "I felt that the people that had been coming to the church and solely Spanish speakers were probably going to be a little doubtful, I do not know, almost a little upset, that they are breaking into an English service ... that there would be some level of anger potentially."

Question 3: Initial questions or concerns. When asked to categorize their initial questions or concerns about the newly announced monolingual service, logistic curiosity and church culture uncertainties dominated the discussion.

Enthusiastic feelings seemed to be linked to curiosity. Many of the focus group participants wondered how the new service logistics would materialize. A Latina, female, second-generation, emerging adult posted a concern that would be actualized in the process of the implementation of the research. She wondered if the implementation would overwhelm the church's facilities: "What is going to happen when we grow? Or if all the people from the second service comes into first, how are we going to fit everyone in there?" Correspondingly, an intermarried male questioned the elasticity of the church's facilities to accommodate the potential stress on the first service. He enhanced the conversation saying, "You guys have all been around the first service, right? Where it is full? Now imagine if the second migrates to the first service ... if maybe 70 percent of the second service goes to the first service, it is going to be at maximum capacity."

Additionally, an emerging adult wondered how the change of the second service from bilingual to monolingual English would affect those who attend church based on time of service. She quipped, "I am worried because there is a lot of Hispanics that like to come into the second service ... They like to sleep in."

Furthermore, and also central to a post-focus group concern, a white, female, intermarried adult speculated, "I was worried that Josh was not going to be preaching the English service and that Steve was going to do it. That made me concerned the feeling of two separate congregations." A Latina, female, intermarried adult echoed this concern with a focus on the senior pastor's ability to preach in English. She said, "I have never heard Pastor Josh speak in English, always in Spanish, so I was concerned if the younger kids would get the message ... if the delivery would be the same."

An intermarried male was curious about how the monolingual service would affect ministry volunteers. He imagined:

> Would they even want to serve (first-generation Spanish speakers) because they know, "Oh the second service it is all English speaking," and let's say they were greeters or at the front desk, connect center, help desk, at the front where you do not have the availability to use your native language. People may want to serve less. Do we need a different and/or separate first service crew and a second service crew?

A female, first-generation, bilingual, emerging adult provided a summary of her conundrum. She exclaimed, "I was just wondering what service I was going to go to. The bilingual one or the English one. For me, it was kind of easy because I could understand both languages." While some faced unexpected but welcomed decisions, others wondered how the English service might be or feel different from the bilingual service. A female emerging adult speculated if the English service would be "a full-on young adult kind of church service. Will the same messages be preached for first and second service?" She detailed, "Are they going to fill it up with different things? Is worship going to be shorter? Will the second service (the monolingual English service) appeal more to the young adult crowd, and with the youth?"

Concerning the effects of the monolingual English service on the children's ministry, the focus group wondered if the classes were going to be provided only in English. One asked, "The children's ministry, are they going to do all English or all Spanish, or are they going to be still bilingual because I help out sometimes."

Logically, there were initial concerns about the culture of Faro Church being altered and distorted. The concern was abridged by a male, second-generation, emerging adult, Latino who summarized, "You (may) feel like they are going against the roots of Faro traditions, which is bilingual." A male, second-generation, emerging Latino adult wondered, "What if the culture will change or what could happen? A first-generation Latina expressed a similar concern: "I wonder how that is going to play out, like if the church is either going to build up or stay the same." She posed a question that would become a point of importance in the post-focus groups. She suspected, "I guess it depends on the speaker." Also, an intermarried male expressed his concern about unintended consequences. He explained, "Something that we intend to be inclusive might be exclusive ... the Spanish speakers may feel excluded." He expressed that some who at the point of implementation may accidentally attend the monolingual English service could come to reason, "This is an only English-speaking thing."

A first-generation, Latino, bilingual, emerging adult questioned:

> I was kind of worried because there is a lot of Spanish-speaking people in second service (bilingual service which would become the monolingual English service).

I wonder if they are actually going to make it to first service (bilingual service), or if they actually leave the church because it is their only time slot to come to church. Will people from the second service move churches? Will they move to an all-Spanish church, or will they quit going to church in general?

Although some expressed that a monolingual service would provide opportunities for generational familial unity, others wondered if it would foil family ties. A female, second-generation, emerging adult pondered, "For my family and me ... are we all going to stay together? Sunday is the day we all hang out. So, I was like am I still going to see my siblings, or are we going to go to different times, or what is going to happen?" A female, second-generation, emerging adult also wondered, "For youth, what if the parents want to go to first (service), but they want to go to the second (service). Are they just supposed to stand around the first service?

Question 4: Church's demographics. When asked how the implementation of the monolingual English service was going to change the church's demographics, the focus group felt that it would bring greater diversity, higher economic prospects, and an increased attendance among intermarried couples and Latino emerging adults. However, some expressed a decline in the first-generation, Spanish-only-speaker demographic might be possible.

There seemed to be a consensus among the focus group that the monolingual English service would create greater diversity as it would have the potential to draw people from different cultures. A Latina, intermarried female explained that Faro Church could become "more diverse, not just more from Latino countries but others." She continued, "Maybe more interracial couples that do not speak Spanish. Like those second- and third-generation couples ... who do not know any Spanish, and they marry someone who is second- and third-generation

... they would want to come." Simply stated, "We are going to get more English monolingual people attending," said a male, second-generation emerging adult.

Interestingly, a male, second-generation emerging adult assumed that the implantation of the English service would draw people from a higher economic demographic. He explained that the church would draw a different "social class ... richer people who speak English."

Ultimately, the focus group commented on the ability to draw inter-married couples and a potential increase in Latino emerging adult atten-dance. A second-generation, male Latino rationalized, "I think that having an English service is going to draw more of a younger crowd, I think over time it will." Others agreed, "I think, with the youth, it will help them invite their friends." Furthermore, a female, first-generation, married emerging adult said, "Having the younger generation, we are going to see a lot of young leaders, having them step up as well. I mean a lot of young people are coming in."

A specific concern was expressed about a potential decline in first-generation Spanish-only speakers. A second-generation married emerging adult said, "I think that it will slowly fade out the older gen-erations because they ... fear change." Another concern was voiced by a female, intermarried, first-generation Latina: "I feel like it is very important, but selfishly I like this church because it's bilingual and it gets my kids exposed to Spanish a lot, and when I see that the second service in only English, I feel we cannot come together as a family ... That is just my perspective as a mother."

Question 5: Vitality on retention and evangelization of emerging adults. When asked to speak on the vitality of the implementation of a monolingual English service to the retention and evangelizing of emerging adults, the focus group expressed an established agreement on its significance.

While some thought the monolingual service would provide familial generational links, others questioned its effectiveness in drawing new emerging adults at large. A female, intermarried adult expressed this concern, "We have large churches around us that are English only, so is that going to be possible, or are we going to have the same impact?"

A Latino, second-generation emerging adult honestly indicated, "I feel that more emerging adults will stay if it was not Spanish and English (bilingual). I am an emerging adult, and I get tired of sitting through the Spanish and English." A male, intermarried emerging adult concisely consented, "Having an English service would attract the emerging adults."

Others agreed that taking away the bilingual element would remove distraction and facilitate understanding the sermon and drawing their attention in worship. One intermarried male adult remarked, "No matter how well you do the translation, it is a distraction. It is just human nature." A male, first-generation, bilingual emerging adult agreed:

> A lot of people that listen to Spanish and English (Bilingual service) ... it is hard for them to understand some parts in Spanish and some parts in English. It is a distraction for them, trying to translate it yourself and understand it, instead of listening to the message.

A Latina intermarried adult imagined, "Even just worship, you know worship gets them ready for the message, but if you do not know the Spanish, you get tired and zone out ... hopefully, we will get them to a point where they want to be closer to God."

Others conveyed that the monolingual English service provided a more auspicious opportunity not only in retention but also in discipleship and leadership opportunities. A female, second-generation emerging adult revealed, "I think we would be pouring more into them ... they possibly would want to serve and lead."

Reiterating the need for a monolingual English service, a male, intermarried adult rhetorically asked, "Like ninety percent of emerging adults are highly educated, (they) are going to college, going to school in English. So, how do we evangelize them?"

Question 6: Will you be attending? When asked whether they would attend the monolingual English service, most responded affirmatively while others expressed some unrelated hindrances. A female, second-generation emerging adult stated, "Yes, to see what it would look like and to see the growth of it. It would be cool." A female, intermarried emerging adult responded, "I decided to attend both. I am excited to see the difference." A male, intermarried emerging adult said, "I will for sure frequent the (English) service." Another married emerging adult agreed, "I think yes, just because for me it will flow better. Everything. Work is English. Friends are English. Life is English." A white, female, intermarried emerging adult said, "Yes because I can sing the songs all the way through."

A female, second-generation emerging adult explained, "I am stuck in between yes and no. I say no just because my parents are very into unity, and they probably would want me to attend the Spanish (bilingual) service rather than the English service." Similarly, a male, first-generation emerging adult said, "I will personally say no because I actually fellowship with the people that come to the first service ... Plus, it is when my family decided to go."

A male, intermarried adult expressed some indifference due to familiarity with Faro Church. He indicated, "For us that have grown up in the same church, we really do not favor one over the other. It is the same message."

Perhaps the vacillation of some can be encapsulated by two remarks. First, a female, second-generation emerging adult expounded, "I think no. I just need to see how it plays out and kind of get a feeling for it just because I have grown up with bilingual." She continued with some uncertainty, "Maybe I am open to an all-English service because I would understand the service, but I do not know." Second, when asked if she would attend the monolingual English service, a second-generation emerging adult pondered:

> No, the reason I came to Faro was to keep up with my Spanish, but I do understand both languages ... But maybe also, just in case my boyfriend and kids want to attend the second service (English) because they only speak English, then I would transition to sometimes attending the English service.

Question 7: The question of recruitment. When asked to evaluate whether the implementation of a monolingual English service would facilitate or impede the inviting of friends and family to church, the focus group agreed that the monolingual English service would provide an added benefit to the evangelistic efforts of Faro Church.

Simply stated, a male emerging adult implied, "We got options." A male, intermarried emerging adult added, "I think it is going to benefit ... More of my friends are geared towards English. It is easier to invite them." A female emerging adult indicated, "It is easier for people to come into the English service because I feel like the bilingual language is a disservice; it is intimidating to hear both. So, I think it would be easier to invite friends and family." A female, second-generation emerging adult said:

> I think it would be good for me to invite my younger cousins. They speak both English and Spanish but would enjoy the service better since (in English). They understand English as their first language; Spanish is their second language. They use it (Spanish) just to communicate with their parents.

The monolingual English service seemed to facilitate the inviting of friends and family among intermarried couples. A white, intermarried adult explained, "I know that I will be inviting more English-speaking attendees. My father, hoping my brother and sister will come. They did not care for the bilingual aspect of it ... but I think my family members did not."

Similarly, a white, female, intermarried adult agreed, "I am an English speaker, and a lot of my friends and family are English speakers. It just another opportunity to invite people."

A female, first-generation emerging adult clarified, "I can invite my coworker, and I know her family is all English speakers ... it definitely opens up that window with other coworkers." However, she continued, "I know her mom speaks Spanish, but she can come to the first (bilingual service), and I think that it opens up a window."

In contrast, some expressed some apprehension. A male, second-generation emerging adult thought, "If we are strictly talking about the monolingual English one, I think it facilitates for friends and impedes for my family." A female, second-generation emerging adult added, "I say that it impedes most for first-generation, for first-generation families with second-generation kids." A male, first-generation emerging adult said, "I feel like for me it facilitates for my friends because they do speak English often, but it impedes on my family bringing them here because I am first-generation and most of them only speak Spanish." Similarly, a female, first-generation intermarried adult added that the removal of the 11 a.m. bilingual service would impede the ability to invite her Spanish-speaking family. She described, "It impedes when I invite people from my country that do not speak English or my family who live in Miami that only speak Spanish. So, we would have to wake up early and come to the 9 a.m. service."

Question 8: Changing demographics. When asked to evaluate feelings about the changing demographics among Latinos in America (i.e., language, intermarriage, culture), most appreciated the newfound awareness and the urgency to build bridges.

A second-generation Latina explained that the implementation of the monolingual English service made sense due to the special sermon series and meetings leading up to the implementation, which explained the need to reduce the silent exodus of emerging adults in Latino churches. She understood, "Those services and some meetings before that announced it … It just made sense when he showed all the stats, and it made you think." A male emerging adult approved: "I think that it is inevitable because of where we live, and there is a bunch of (changing) demographics (among Latinos). A female, intermarried mother explained that the data agreed with her experience as she thought "about not seeing a lot of the (young) people that used to be here (Faro Church) since they were little. And I was asking, where did they go?"

Encapsulating the linguistic generational pattern, a female, second-generation emerging adult expounded, "In regard to language, my brother is only four years younger than me, but he does not speak Spanish; it is kind of, not sad!"

A female, second-generation emerging adult explained the effect of the changing demographics among generations. She emotionally explained, "I think that it is hard sometimes for parents and young adults and youth to connect on certain grounds because of the differences in culture." She continued, "Even in understanding parts of the language or the way things are done. I grew up with my grandma being strict and seeing things that were not bad to some other people was bad to her growing up. So, it is hard sometimes." In agreement, a white, female intermarried adult explained the differences in worldview among generations. She said:

> I think that the younger generation in the Latin communities are starting to develop a different theology than what their prior generations had. I know that older Hispanic communities are more conservative and have a very black and white way of looking at things whereas Millennials and post-millennials are wanting to adopt things that they really believe in, so I think that is a change.

A female, second-generation, intermarried adult provided a personal experience concerning the challenge of intermarriage, and it sheds light not only on the changing demographics among Latinos but also the sentiment and outlook of such relationships. She shared:

> When [my husband] and I got together, that was hard. It was hard ... it was not just family, it was the church, who thought they could give their two cents. It was hard, that whole intermarriage ... It was like racism and dealing with it when I had not had to deal with much racism, even growing up within a white neighborhood. It was hard, and when people said certain things joking around, like it was not funny. (My daughters) are half Chinese and half Latino. (When) I started having my own kids, the kids in class (church class) would sometimes laugh when you say (the kids were) Chinese. I am like what is so funny about that? ... I hope that it is getting better, but it takes people educating that we should not put that race barrier among people in it ... Latinos in America, those are the ones that are mostly open to different languages, to intermarriage, to keeping the roots of our culture and the theology, but I do not know because they are saying stuff, like I do not know if you guys get into those conversations but maybe it is just me.

Findings from Post-Focus Groups

The post-focus groups confirmed affirming attitudes toward the benefits of a monolingual English service while providing ongoing questions and concerns. The post-focus group provided positive stories and testimonies of new and returning emerging adults and intermarried couples who attended Faro Church as a result of the implemented monolingual English service. The focus group provided vital qualitative data concerning the changing demographics and ministry preferences of emerging Latino adults in the church at large.

Question 1: Have initial feelings changed? When asked to gauge their change of feelings, if any, about the implementation of the monolingual English service, most participants communicated enthusiastic responses along with expressions of unexpected benefits while voicing certain concerns and remaining questions.

A female, second-generation emerging adult summarized her feelings over the fifteen-week research period. She said, "I think there has been a slight change. I have seen new people and faces—also, a bit of a younger crowd. But slightly, not like a ginormous change. Obviously, it is not going to happen right away." A male, second-generation emerging adult summarized his experience: "I was skeptical about the established service, I thought maybe it would backfire and not work as well. But I think they have been good thus far." Others similarly expressed enthusiastic reactions. A male, second-generation emerging adult explained, "This is something that did not cross my mind initially; I was more focused on the demographics and how it would affect the culture of the church. I did see new people that I have never seen before."

Some participants noted welcomed unexpected benefits from the monolingual English service. A male, second-generation emerging adult contrasted his experience between the bilingual service and the English service. He said that previously at the bilingual service, "I understand both (languages), but I found myself zoning out from English to Spanish. Now that it is English only, I find myself paying attention and not zoning out." Another male, second-generation emerging adult expressed a newfound enhanced ability to comprehend the message and better-uninterrupted worship experience. He said, "I like the English service, and it gives those who do not speak Spanish a better understanding of what the sermon is all about. I think that worship flows better."

Question 2: Initial questions or concerns. When asked to describe if any of their initial questions or concerns were actualized, most agreed that the senior pastor's ability to preach in English was a primary concern. A male, intermarried adult expressed his concern: "It is ... an apprehension moving forward. I think that Josh (senior pastor) is giving everything he can from the English standpoint but if I am thinking about growing the English service and attracting pure English speakers." He clarified, "So, when they are church shopping and they walk through the doors, they are comparing our service with other English services, and from that standpoint, there is a difference. This is his second language; it is not his native language."

A male, second-generation emerging adult voiced one exception to this concern. He said, "I have not been affected by Josh's English. Yes, it is a little broken, but I have not been affected." However, he was consenting. He said, "Moving forward, for people that I know that only speak English it would be a better idea to have someone that does not have a broken English. If you go to a different (English-speaking) church and then come here, it is way different."

A male, second-generation emerging adult voiced a similar hopeful sentiment: "I did notice that Pastor Josh is a bit more nervous. That is understandable. But over this period, I have noticed that he has gotten so much better in his messages." Others agreed that the pastor's ability to preach in English grew over time. A female, third-generation emerging adult said, "The pastor was nervous starting, but he has gotten better. It slowly grew." A male, second-generation emerging adult shared a similar reaction. He said:

I have been to the service. It is really apparent that Josh is not speaking his primary language. He is able to elucidate in a way we can understand him, but, in a way, it feels a little bit forced. But I am hopeful that over time, it will get a little bit better.

An initial concern voiced in the pre-focus group revolved around the danger of church division. For a white, female, intermarried adult, this was not actualized. She said:

At the beginning, one of my concerns was that the church would feel split and feel like two separate churches. But I have not really witnessed that. I think it has been a good divide of people ... I have not seen a divide in cultures.

A Latina, female, intermarried adult agreed:

I think that people were commenting that people are actually hanging out more to see everybody. Hanging out talking to each other, although it was an initial concern, I think it had an opposite effect to what we thought it would. Instead of division, it seems to bring people together.

The implementation of the monolingual English service caused many church attendees to migrate to the 9 a.m. bilingual service. This created an amazing, full, and united worship experience. The result was not division but adhesion. A female, second-generation emerging adult explained, "There was a lot of people in the bilingual (service), but I remember people thought that the culture would change, but it has not."

Ultimately, to the focus group, the implementation of the monolingual English service did not have any significant disruptions of church culture. A Latino, male intermarried adult said he did not think the culture of the church changed. He said, "I think it is going to (continue to) have the feel and values. I think all of that is going to stay the same. I do not think the English service is going to (change) that. That was an initial concern."

One of the initial concerns revolved around the impact the monolingual service was going to have on the children's ministry. However, it seemed that due to excellent preparation on the part of the children's ministry staff, this concern was not actualized. An intermarried Latina explained, "In the kid's ministry, the question was whether teachers were going to feel comfortable, but we did not lose any teachers. We have gained a couple of helpers." She continued, "The feeling of losing people or not feeling comfortable has been taken more as a challenge ... they took it upon themselves to go for it."

Another initial concern was the possible effect of the monolingual English service on the first-generation Spanish-only speakers of the church. All focus group participants seemed to agree that this was not an actualized concern. A male, second-generation emerging adult said:

One of my initial concerns was what would happen to the original pioneers, like the people who have been used to this being in a Hispanic space. People who have a commonality in race, ethnicity, culture, and language ... But I have seen that that is not the deal.

He went on to explain the most if not all of the Spanish speakers moved over and assimilated to the bilingual service with no major disruption to the church culture. Similarly, a white, female, intermarried adult elucidated:

I thought about the older generation and those who serve. We are used to having that Spanish core, so I felt they could feel discouraged to serve the English service. But a lot have received it really well. I see them serve the same way. They have accepted that the church needs to grow and span.

The pre-focus group delivered questions concerning the division of familial unison. This in some ways was an actualized concern with some unexpected positive opportunities. A female, second-generation emerging adult explained, "My concern was my family ... we liked coming to the same service and hanging out together after the service. Now that there is another service, we are just everywhere." However, she went on to explain, "My siblings (now) serve in all services. It affected us, but it is great that my siblings are serving. It was a concern, and it was actualized but were ok with it."

Question 3: Church's demographics. When asked to describe how the implementation of the monolingual English service changed the church demographics, most participants responded by pointing to some of the research focuses and findings.

One of the primary research focuses was the retention and recruitment of emerging adults through the implementation of a monolingual English service. A female, second-generation emerging adult seemed to agree that the implemented English service is, in part, accomplishing this goal. She said, "There is a lot of people showing up, new faces which is great. I thought it was going to bring different ethnicities, but it was mostly Hispanic with a little Caucasian and Asian." Additionally, it has also been observed that some first-generation Latinos prefer the monolingual English service. A female, second-generation emerging adult observed:

It is just another language. I have seen people in the English service whose primary language is Spanish, yet they sit there just fine. I do see people in the English service more engaged. People whose primary language is English are also engaged, and it gives people the opportunity to invite English only. We have come full circle.

A Latina, female, intermarried adult offered a timely comment concerning the implementation of the monolingual English service as it relates to changing demographics. She explained that the fact that she has observed so many emerging adults attend the monolingual English service proves there is a need for such services. She said, "I think that this proves that there is such a thing as a Latino that does not speak Spanish who need these kinds of services." A white, female, intermarried adult agreed that there is such a thing as a Latino who appreciates an English service. She explained, "They (Latino emerging adults) want the English service and be surrounded by Latinos who can relate and understand them."

Others specifically observed that the monolingual English service did attract emerging adults and intermarried couples. A Latina, female, intermarried adult witnessed:

I see that it is the younger ones (emerging adults) who are coming, so attendance to the kid's ministry is kind of low. Young people who just got married and have not started their families. It is the generation that is in there right now. So, it makes sense.

A female second-generation emerging adult similarly detected, "The service is younger people and intermarried couples ... it would make sense for them to go."

Another way the church has changed due to the implementation of the monolingual service is the length of services. A female, second-generation emerging adult explained, "I think it helps that it is flowing. And you are getting the same amount of Word; it just not being translated." A white, male, intermarried adult equaled the sentiment: "It is nice to have an hour and fifteen-minute service instead of two hours."

Question 4: Vitality on retention and evangelization of emerging adults. When asked about their thoughts about the implementation of the monolingual English service as to the retention and evangelizing of emerging adults, most participants responded with positive feedback. A Latino, male, second-generation emerging adult spoke about the vitality of the monolingual English service at Faro Church as to the retention of emerging adults. He witnessed some of his church friends leave the church because there was not a monolingual English service at Faro Church. To them, the bilingual service was not enough. He clarified:

There have been people my age group that has left because they do not speak Spanish as their parents did. To them it is pointless, so why would they stay. It is easier for them to go to a service at Mariners (church nearby) or other churches in English and not worry about it.

Correspondingly, a female, second-generation emerging adult commented, "The importance is bigger than we know because there is a lot of young adults who are getting lost. Now that there is an English service there is no excuse to not come to church and receive the Word."

A second-generation, intermarried Latino reported that before the implementation of the monolingual English service, she witnessed some people who stopped attending the church because of the bilingual services. However, she detailed, "The English service, it has brought them coming back ... So, it helps in those situations where the bilingual part was too hard."

A first-generation, intermarried Latina suggested that the family can still be united even though they attend different services. She explained, "I think it keeps the families together. If you have a monolingual English service, you could attend the same church. They may be in different services, but they are still here." Similarly, a female, second-generation emerging adult explained that the English service has allowed families to stay together. She stated, "It has a lot with keeping the families together. My boyfriend can come with his kids that do not speak Spanish, and they are in the same service."

A female, second-generation emerging adult explained that while the language aspect is essential, the relevancy of the service is equally vital. She illuminated:

I think it is important to keep those who speak English. Since it is a younger generation, the topics should be a little bit different. Talking with my brothers, certain topics are not being spoken about, and that is affecting why (more) people do not come (to the English service).

Similarly, a white, female, intermarried adult commented, "In terms of retention, I think it is helping ... But in terms of inviting people, I do not think just having an English service is going to have a big impact." She explained that since the audience is in part emerging adult and leaning more toward an Americanized culture, the message relevancy must be adjusted. She noted:

They need to preach on different things that millennials are passionate about, and our church does not talk about those subjects. So, having an English service is great, but it still not going to be as interesting to that generation, so it is limited unless the subject matter/speaker is not changed.

According to the focus group participants, the ideas of relatability and relevance seemed to be on par with language as they relate to the church's ability to retain and evangelize. Relating to culture seemed to be a reoccurring theme and need for the monolingual English service. A white, male, intermarried adult added:

It seems like pastor Steve (associate pastor) is really good at relating to that population, and if you are looking for growth it would be beneficial for him to speak more at those. That way, the youngest population is more enthusiastic to come and invite others.... I like Josh's (senior pastor) format in terms of theology and style, but I am not sure the younger people have that approach.

One male, second-generation emerging adult made a poignant observation concerning relevancy. He said, "I wanted to see if the people were engaged and if they wanted to come back. Was the speaker engaging? And it was a concern for me. Is Josh able to engage with the younger generation?"

Nevertheless, after having experienced the monolingual English service, most agreed that it would make evangelistic endeavors easier. A Latina, intermarried adult commented, "I think that it is easier for young adults to invite their friends, classmates, and coworkers and talk to them about Jesus and spread the gospel. They would be more comfortable in an English service."

A male, second-generation emerging adult encapsulated the discussion by providing a futuristic outlook to the implementation of the English service. He said:

I think that moving forward, we may not see it now, we are sowing seeds. People are still attending with their families but we're thinking about the future. If you interact with these young adults, they are more English and American oriented; they have adapted to this culture. The children are more in tune with this culture and not the Latin American culture of their parents. I think we may not see the fruits of the English service right now, but it is for the future. Eventually, those parents will not be there for long, and the children have to make the choice of going to church. When that decision comes, they can think about the commonalities they have with the people that attend their church. They speak English and (have) the American culture, but they have same (Latino) background.

Question 5: Did you attend? When asked if they attended the implemented monolingual English service, everyone responded in the affirmative with varied responses. A white, female, intermarried adult commented that she attended but did not like the 11 a.m. start of the service. She preferred the early start of the 9 a.m. bilingual service, and the language preference was not enough to make the change.

Most emerging adults in the post-focus group enjoyed the service and are attending the service now. A male, second-generation emerging adult said, "I like the English service. I only go to the English service. Usually, my brothers come with me. I go because I can focus and concentrate and not drift. And its shorter, and I like that too." Similarly, a female, second-generation emerging adult noted, "I like the (English) service ... I am glad that it is there for people who really need it."

Others attended for the sake of younger family members who prefer the English language. A female, second-generation emerging adult explained, "I come to the English service mainly because of the time and my brother. He retains it more, and he is less on his phone. He is more attentive and engaged."

One male, second-generation emerging adult confessed he attended but was dissuaded by the lack of relevancy. He said, "I attended, but a problem with the monolingual service was the speaker."

Only three of the post-focus group participants did not attend the monolingual service. All three explained that it was due to family reasons. One female, second-generation emerging adult explained, "I have not attended. I want to, but my family goes to the bilingual. I am just used to going to the church at that time." Another female, second-generation emerging adult said, "I have not attended because of my family. My family after church, we go out to eat. (However,) it is easier for my brother; all my nieces and nephews (that) do not speak Spanish. He brings them to the third service" Yet, the other female, second-generation emerging adult remarked, "I have not, but I want to. I serve; I have not had the opportunity. I think it is really cool. But I am used to the bilingual and Spanish. I do want to check it out."

A male, first-generation, intermarried adult explained that although he attended the monolingual English service, he felt better in the bilingual service. He said, "We are used to it. It is our preference. I like singing in Spanish and English."

The unity and overall worship experience of the 9 a.m. bilingual service due to the migration from the 11 a.m. bilingual service created an unexpected appeal, especially for intermarried couples. Four of the intermarried participants in the first post-focus group made similar striking statements explaining that they indeed attended the monolingual English service but enjoyed the new, unexpected experience of the bilingual service. These adherents seemed to prefer the feeling of the full house in the bilingual service. It is something they had not experienced before.

Question 6: The question of recruitment. When asked whether the implementation of a monolingual English service facilitated or impeded the inviting of friends and family to church most agreed that the English service made it easier to invite family and friends.

A male, second-generation emerging adult explained that in the past, he has attempted to invite his friends, but they did not understand the bilingual aspect. However, he noted, "The English service makes it easier to bring in the younger generation." He further stated, "There are a lot of people like me who grew up in a Spanish household but preferred English. Moving forward is going to help bring people my age or people that grew up like me. And for people to stay."

Additionally, a female, second-generation emerging adult shared that the monolingual English service facilitated the invitation of family members. She said, "We invited our cousin; her husband only speaks English ... they attended the English service, and they liked it. They would not come to a Spanish or bilingual. It was for them."

Refreshingly, a male, white, intermarried adult argued that even a non-Latino population would be drawn to the implemented English service. He elucidated, "I have been more inclined to invite my family, and they have attended a couple of times. I think that inviting Caucasian people would not affect them ... I do not think they would be turned off if they fall in love with the word."

It would appear that the question of relevancy became a stumbling block for some to invite others to the monolingual English service. A female, white, intermarried adult fairly admitted, "It has not impacted my desire to invite people. We have not if it would be different, I would."

Question 7: Changing demographics. When asked to reflect on the changing demographics among Latinos in America (i.e., language, inter-marriage, culture) after experiencing the monolingual English service, all agreed that there are definite differences between generations and that the implementation of the English service was vital to recruitment and retention of emerging adults and intermarried couples.

An articulate response from a male, second-generation emerging adult seemed to encapsulate this concept:

What defined the first-generation was their struggles. Coming from a different country and assimilating to somewhere where they do not know anybody or the culture. And we as a human being are defined by our culture. But now the struggles of the second-generation are not like the struggles of the first-generation. They have different perspectives. They (second-generation) have heard the stories of their immigrant parents and how they struggled back then and how they struggled to change here. But it is not their story. They have different stories. What will define them is trying to find their place in a country that they are a part of but not completely because of their heritage. That is what I see; they have a different outlook on life ... Second-generation did not experience having anything to moving to a different place. That affects their theology and what they expect from God and the church. Probably, the first-generation, they saw God as a provider and refuge, no matter what, God and the church will always be there. But for the second-generation is a different thing ... what does God have to do with my life? They were not exposed to the (same) struggles; they grew up in a different country. A different experience. That is what I see among Hispanics (second-generation) ... (they are) losing their background in a sense. They are part of them, but they are more defined by (the) here and the values and the morals of here, not their parents. That is the chasm between the first and second-generation.

Research Findings IV:
Questionnaire of Teachers of Children and Youth

Sixteen questionnaires were completed by teachers of children and youth at Faro Church (see Appendix F). These teachers dealt directly with students who were part of the primary focus of the research purpose and provided pertinent data for the research at hand. The questionnaires were done on February 17, 2019, the mid-point of the implementation of a monolingual English service at Faro Church. The only prerequisite for this questionnaire was to be part of the volunteer teaching staff of Faro Church. However, participants were selected for research as randomly as possible from within the volunteering teaching group of the church and the parameters of this survey to eliminate bias and prohibit the research findings from being inadvertently associated with a particular group of humans.

The questionnaires provided measurable data concerning the primary language used among teachers and students during teaching time and the primary language used when engaging the parents before and after class. This research provided a clear quantitative picture of the centrality of the issue as the evidence yielded hands-on proof about the changing demographics among Latinos especially linguistically, their effect on successful class engagement, and the need for monolingual church services and classes for the retention of second- and third-plus-generations and intermarried couples with children.

The questionnaires revealed that 69 percent of the teachers of children and youth conduct their classes in English, 25 percent bilingual (either separate or simultaneous interpreting), and only 6 percent in Spanish (Table 14).

	#	%
English dominant	11	69%
Spanish dominant	1	6%
Bilingual (Separate Services – separate English and Spanish services)	3	19%
Bilingual (Consecutive Interpreting – side by side live on-stage)	0	0%
Bilingual (Simultaneous Interpreting – using an in-ear device)	1	6%
Total	16	

Figure 34. Table 14—*Teacher's Primary Language Use When Teaching*

Conversely, the questionnaire revealed that 88 percent of the students preferred English as their primary learning language (Table 15). Only one student was identified as preferring Spanish and one preferring bilingual as the primary learning language (Table 35).

	#	%
English dominant	14	88%
Spanish dominant	1	6%
Bilingual (Separate Services – separate English and Spanish services)	1	6%
Bilingual (Consecutive Interpreting – side by side live on-stage)	0	0%
Bilingual (Simultaneous Interpreting – using an in-ear device)	0	0%
Total	16	

Figure 35. Table 35—*Student's Primary Language Preference When Learning*

Furthermore, the questionnaire revealed that the primary language used by teachers when speaking with parents before and after class was mainly bilingual and Spanish. Fifty-one percent of the teachers communicated bilingually (either separate or side by side), 38 percent in Spanish, and 13 percent in English (Table 16).

	#	%
English dominant	2	13%
Spanish dominant	6	38%
Bilingual (Separate Services – separate English and Spanish services)	6	38%
Bilingual (Consecutive Interpreting – side by side live on-stage)	2	13%
Bilingual (Simultaneous Interpreting – using an in-ear device)	0	0%
Total	16	

Figure 36. Table 16—*Teacher's Primary Language Use with Parents*

Conversely, the questionnaire revealed that the parents' preferred language when speaking with teachers was Spanish. Sixty-three percent of parents communicated with the teachers at Faro Church in Spanish, 31 percent bilingual (separately), and 6 percent in English (Table 17).

	#	%
English dominant	1	6%
Spanish dominant	10	63%
Bilingual (Separate Services – separate English and Spanish services)	5	31%
Bilingual (Consecutive Interpreting – side by side live on-stage)	0	0%
Bilingual (Simultaneous Interpreting – using an in-ear device)	0	0%
Total	16	

Figure 37. Table 17—*Parent's Primary Language Use When Speaking with Teachers*

Furthermore, when teachers were asked what language they thought parents would prefer for their children to worship in, 88 percent responded bilingual whereas 13 percent responded English with 0 responses for Spanish (Table 18).

	#	%
Monolingual Spanish service	0	0%
Bilingual service	14	88%
Monolingual English service	2	13%
Total	16	

Figure 38. Table 18—*Teacher's Opinion on Parent's Language Preference for Their Children*

Conversely, when teachers were asked what language they thought their students would prefer to worship in, 88 percent responded English whereas 13 percent responded bilingual with 0 responses for Spanish (Table 19).

	#	%
Monolingual Spanish service	0	0%
Bilingual service	2	13%
Monolingual English service	14	88%
Total	16	

Figure 39. Table 19—*Teacher's Opinion on Student's Language Preference*

Research Findings V:
Survey of Emerging Latino Adults at "Latino Bible College"
("Latino Bible College" is used to protect
the survey participants' privacy)

A Latino church congregation can be comprised of multiple generations, and the cultural differences and ministry needs of these groups result in a variety of challenges that must be addressed. A central problem in the retention of second- and third-plus-generation Latinos is the question of language preference and cultural identity (Guglani, 2016, p. 345). Therefore, a survey was administered to gauge the views of emerging first-, second-, and third-plus-generation Latinos from Latino Bible College, on the challenges of retention and recruitment in first-generation monolingual Spanish ministry models (see Appendix G). Latino Bible College is a Christian college that attracts mostly students who come from first-generation Latino churches similar to Faro Church. Latino Bible College students come from and attend Latino churches across Southern California.

Twenty-eight surveys were returned after the implementation of a monolingual English service at Faro Church on January 6, 2019, and before the fifteen weeks ending on April 21, 2019, exceeding forecasts. The two prerequisites for this survey were age and being a current student of Latino Bible College. The age parameter was eighteen to twenty-four years old in order to meet the emerging adult demographic central to the research. The participants were selected for research as randomly as possible within the parameters of this survey to eliminate bias and prohibit the research findings from being inadvertently associated with a particular group of humans.

Survey question 1. Research question one asked respondents to indicate the importance of challenges for emerging adults (18–25 years) in Latino churches through the use of a four-item three-point Likert scale (Extremely Important—3, Moderately Important—2, Mildly Important—1, and Not Important at All—0). Respondents were asked to rate the following possible items: lack of personal commitment, moral issues (i.e. drug, alcohol abuse, sex, etc.), the lack of spiritual development (discipleship), shortage of positive role models, problems related to immigration, English worship services, contemporary church services (worship and music), sermon format and content, small groups or ministries, and connectivity (friends at church, hospitality).

Overall, the surveys demonstrated that lack of personal commitment is extremely vital for emerging adults in Latino churches, averaging almost a perfect score with 2.9 points (Figure 40). Also reported as extremely vital were moral issues (i.e., drug, alcohol abuse, sex, etc.), ranking second and averaging 2.8 points; connectivity (friends at church, hospitality), averaging 2.7 points; lack of personal commitment, averaging 2.7; and the shortage of positive role models, averaging 2.7 points (Figure 40). Dipping slightly in rank but keeping moderate vitality was sermon format and content, averaging 2.6 points (Figure 40). Perhaps surprisingly, given the first-generation church background of the students and categorized as moderately vital was problems related to immigration averaging 2.3 points (Figure 40). As it relates to the research, the Latino Bible College students ranked the need for monolingual English services as tied for last with contemporary church services (worship music) with both factors averaging 2.2 points but keeping a moderate vitality (Figure 40).

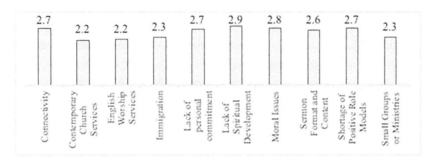

Figure 40. Latino Bible College average response to survey question 1

Survey question 2. Research question two asked respondents to indicate the most significant ministry model challenge that Latino churches have in retaining and discipling second- and third-plus-generation Latinos through the use of a four-item, three-point Likert scale (Extremely Important—3, Moderately Important—2, Mildly Important—1, and Not Important at All—0). Respondents were asked to rate the following possible items: refusal to accommodate to linguistic needs of emerging adults, the lack of spiritual development (discipleship), contemporary church services (worship and music), relativity (friends at church, hospitality), a belief that the church exists to maintain the Latino culture, a belief that Latino churches exist to provide ministry to Spanish speakers, fear in the first-generation to share or expand leadership roles, cultural anxieties and capabilities to reach English speakers (relevance), not recognizing the growth of Latino intermarriage, and an inability to answer difficult theological questions.

When asked to indicate the most significant ministry model challenge that Latino churches have in retaining and discipling second- and third-plus-generation Latinos, the emergent adults of Latino Bible College ranked the lack of spiritual development (discipleship) as the most important factor with extreme vitality, averaging 2.9 points (Figure 41). Relativity (friends at church, hospitality) ranked closely as second, averaging 2.8 points. Conversely, two options ranked the lowest with two-point averages but kept a moderate vitality. They were the belief that the church exists to maintain the Latino culture and the fear in the first-generation to share or expand leadership roles (Figure 41). The students of Latino Bible College indicated that the need for a monolingual English service was moderately vital, averaging 2.2, as a challenge for emerging adults in Latino churches (Figure 41). However, as it relates to the most significant ministry challenge and the key to the research at hand, the refusal to accommodate to linguistic needs of emerging adults ranked as extremely vital with an average of 2.6 points (Figure 41). This data seems to generalize the idea that although emerging adults moderately seem to view the monolingual English service as a personal need, they do think it is extremely vital for the church to accommodate to the changing linguistic demographics of Latinos at large. This could be an essential distinction.

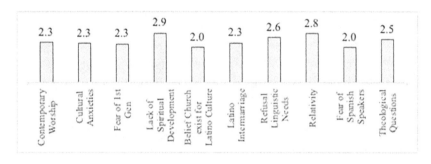

Figure 41. Latino Bible College average response to survey question 2

Survey question 3. The third pre-survey question asked respondents to indicate, in their opinion, why many Latino emerging adults are uninterested in church, including youth or young adult activities, by checking all the issues that applied. Respondents were asked to rate the following possible items: lack of personal commitment, moral issues (i.e. drug, alcohol abuse, sex, etc.), the lack of spiritual development (discipleship), shortage of positive role models, no Spanish worship services, no English worship services, contemporary church services (worship music), sermon format and content, small groups or ministries, and connectivity (friends at church, hospitality).

Concerning the pre-survey question gauging the reason why emerging adults are uninterested in church, including youth or young adult activities, the emerging adults of Latino Bible College responded that the lack of personal commitment, connectivity (friends at church, hospitality), and moral issues (i.e., drug, alcohol abuse, sex, etc.) are the primary reasons for disinterest, tallying 24 points each of the possible 28 survey points (Figure 42). Subsequently, the lack of spiritual development (discipleship) ranked as fourth by tallying 21 points (Figure 42). Key to the research at hand, the need for monolingual English services tallied 17 points and ranked fifth in importance as the reason for disinterest in the church among emerging adults (Figure 42). This data seems to generalize the idea that although emerging adults seem to view the lack of monolingual English services as a primary reason for disinterest, it is not the main driver, especially as it relates to personal responsibility and morality.

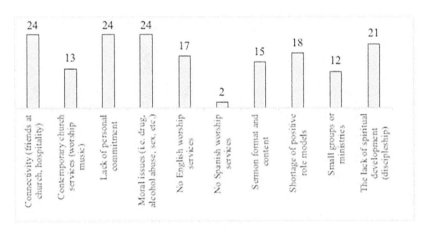

Figure 42. Latino Bible College total response to pre-survey question 3

Survey question 4. The fourth survey question asked respondents to indicate, in their opinion, why some emerging adults are leaving the Latino church (many after attending church for most of their lives) by checking all the issues that applied. Respondents were asked to rate the following possible items: lack of personal commitment, moral issues (i.e., drug, alcohol abuse, sex, etc.), the lack of spiritual development (discipleship), shortage of positive role models, no Spanish worship services, no English worship services, contemporary church services (worship and music), sermon format and content, small groups or ministries, and connectivity (friends at church, hospitality).

Concerning the survey question asking why emerging adults are leaving the Latino church (many after attending church for most of their lives), the emerging adults of Latino Bible College ranked connectivity (friends at church, hospitality) as the most serious, tallying 25 of the possible 28 points (Figure 43). The lack of spiritual development (discipleship) and moral issues (i.e., drug, alcohol abuse, sex, etc.) ranked as tied for second in importance with each scoring a total of 21 points (Figure 43). Ranking as the least important reason was the lack of monolingual Spanish services, tallying a single point (Figure 43). Central to the research at hand, the lack of monolingual English services ranked tied for fourth with lack of personal commitment, tallying 18 points each (Figure 43). Again, this data, as in research question 3, seems to generalize the idea that although emerging adults seem to view the lack monolingual English services as a primary reason for disinterest, it is not the main driver, especially as it relates to personal responsibility and morality.

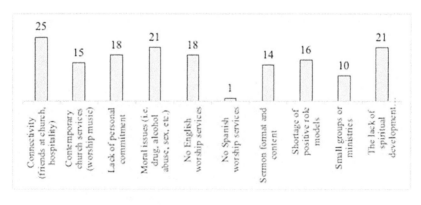

Figure 43. Latino Bible College total response to pre-survey question 4

Ultimately, the survey data gathered from the Latino Bible College emerging adults suggested that the implementation of the monolingual English service was moderately important to the retention and evangelizing of emerging adults, yielding an average score of 2.43 points in the four-item, three-point Likert scale (Extremely Important—3, Moderately Important—2, Mildly Important—1, and Not Important at All—0).

This survey confirmed the varying views of first-, second-, and third-generation Latino adults on the challenges of retention and recruitment at Faro Church and the role of language preference. The data gathered seems to contribute to the idea that although emerging adults view the lack of monolingual English services as one of the primary reasons for disinterest and desertion with the Latino church, it is not the primary driver, especially when contrasted to personal responsibility and morality, which appear to be the principal proponents.

Research Findings VI:
Focus Group of Pastoral and Ministry Leaders

Faro Church reflects a unique Latino demographic and is one of a handful of Latino churches that provides weekly services that are given entirely bilingual interchangeably between Spanish and English (Jelden, 2015). Everything spoken, printed, sung, or produced during a worship service is translated consecutively or with subtitles (for videos).

Therefore, pre- and post-focus groups of Faro Church's twelve pastors and ministry leaders was conducted to evaluate the church's readiness and identify unforeseen challenges in order to gain qualitative evidence for changing demographics and need for bilingual and monolingual services in Latino churches, all while documenting differences in outlook about the implementation of a monolingual English service at Faro Church.

Also considered were the intervening variables on the implementation of a monolingual English service at Faro Church and several factors affecting or limiting the implementation of the monolingual English service.

A third-party surveyor conducted the focus groups before the implementation of a monolingual English service at Faro Church on January 5, 2019, and after the fifteen-week research period ending on April 21, 2019. The surveyor was evaluating changing perspectives and outlooks about the changing demographics among Latinos and the implementation of a monolingual English service. The focus groups were audio- and video-recorded for analysis. The focus groups took place at Faro Church. The only prerequisite for this focus group was to be a pastor or ministry leader of Faro Church. Participants were asked to participate voluntarily and confidentially within the parameters of this focus group to eliminate bias and prohibit the research findings from being inadvertently associated with a particular group of humans.

Findings from the Pre-Focus Group

The pre-focus group provided an optimistic outlook about the implementation of the monolingual English service and reflected positive anticipation toward the church's ability to attract emerging adults and intermarried couples.

Question 1: The initial response. When asked to express their primary response to the initial discussion about the implementation of a monolingual English service at Faro Church, the pastors and ministry leaders responded with feelings of surprise and nervousness mixed with an optimistic outlook.

One of the pastors, a male, second-generation Latino, stated that he was "shocked" when the initial discussion of implementation began. One focus group participant, a second-generation, intermarried female explained her intrigue and anticipation about the monolingual English service. She said that upon the initial discussion, she was excited and wondered "what it would look like" and if it would make the church more multicultural.

One focus-group participant, a first-generation Latino, spoke scrupulously about the initial discussions about the monolingual English service. He said, "It was a necessity, it had to be done... but I felt nervous because I knew I had to do it." He added, "I feel insecure about my accent... but I have been practicing." He added, "I think that this is Spirit-led, and the dissertation research is just allowing for documentation of the process. That is why I do not feel anxious or nervous."

One focus group participant, a second-generation Latino, expressed feelings of anticipation and optimism. He explained, "I felt open to the idea ... I grew up in a church that was all Spanish; I attended a bilingual church (Faro Church) ... To now be part of a church moving to an English service was something I wanted to be a part of." Additionally, he added that being part of the implementation was something he wanted to be a part of.

The principal concern was for the effect on the first-generation Spanish speakers of the church. One focus-group participant, a first-generation, intermarried, non-Latino, expressed some reluctance until the reasons for implementation were explained during the silent exodus sermon series. He explained, "At first, I was reserved because our identity is bilingual ... Until we heard the 'why.'" Another focus group participant agreed, "until it was explained that we were not getting rid of the bilingual service ... then I was excited." Similarly, a male, second-generation ministry leader expressed curiosity about the effect of the implementation of the English service on the Spanish-speaking ministries and the first-generation adherents of the church. Another focus-group participant agreed, "The first-generation was my biggest concern ... would they feel that we are moving in a different direction? We are a bilingual church first ... now there is shift." He explained that the monolingual English service was "a demarcation in the history of the church ... so we have to be cautious."

Additionally, one focus-group participant explained her trepidation about how the first-generation adherent would respond. She said she worried they would feel left out until the silent exodus sermon series.

She said, "The explanation was huge ... it makes sense ... the church is growing; we have a different population than when we first started ... we are reaching different people than when we first started." She continued:

They explained ... that we have kids that are growing up that only speak English; they are Latinos who feel that they are not fitting in anywhere ... that is so true. I felt that when I went to an American English only church. I did not fit in; even my college was predominately white, and I felt I did not fit in in chapel services either. It is different ... that why it makes sense.

Question 2: The Question of preparation. When asked to categorize how they thought they would need to prepare differently, the pastors and ministry leaders of Faro Church provided practical responses focused on the church's readiness to face unforeseen challenges with a commitment to the already-established worship experience. The introduction of the monolingual English service would not mean a change in direction or experience. It was intended to be a parallel experience, a way of inviting people into an already-established experience.

The children's pastor explained her meticulous preparations. She said, I am making sure that we had people who speak both languages for first service (9 a.m., bilingual), so I had to use our younger third and fourth graders, they are assistants, and move them around to make sure we had translators into Spanish or English as needed.

She added:

For kids' worship, Pastor Araceli is using tracks ... this allows us to have the lyrics ready, bilingual for the first service, and only English for the second service ... so, we are preparing two songs of the same song ... This is a new implementation, not something we did before.

The senior pastor explained how his weekly planning and preparation would change. He explained, "(Before) I had to prepare my sermon in Spanish; that is what I did ... because the translator would translate it into English ... but now I have to write my sermon in English to preach in English." He clarified, "I was tabulating ... because I have been practicing for the last four weeks ... it has added twelve hours of sermon prep per week."

The discussion seemed to explain that the introduction of the monolingual English service did not mean change of culture and experience. The senior pastor explained how the preparation and planning must be done, ensuring that "nothing changes." This was a mantra or mechanism that was to be used to ensure that the worship experience at Faro Church in both services would be the same but not the language. That is to say, the preparation may be different, but the services should feel the same. It would essentially be the same service in different languages. The children's pastor echoed and captured the pastor's sentiment. She said, "There is no priority between the bilingual and English service."

The church pastors wanted to make sure that the change in language was not a change in direction or experience. It is a parallel experience. It is a way of inviting people into an already-established experience. Furthermore, the senior pastor explained:

We do not want to create division by creating a different experience ... we started the church bilingual to create unity ... so, if people start saying, "In that service the Spirit moves more ..." or "They are singing differently ..." or "The Word was different ..." I do not want to do that.

He appropriately warned, "We can create division by creating a different experience ... we are not trying to start a different ministry or church ... if we were sure! But, at least for now, that is not the initial intention."

A third-generation Latina ministry leader explained some of the preparations that the worship team would need to make. She explained, "With worship, it doubles the work ... You have to create a bilingual track (soundtrack is linked to projected lyrics), and then an all-English track."

Part of the preparation would also include conversations with first-generation leaders affected by the implementation of the monolingual English service. The senior pastor explained, "For example, we have Brother Aurelio. He is a pastor and elder of the church. He used to lead communion ... and did child dedications. So, he asked, 'How am I going to do child dedications in the English service?' He does not speak English." Similarly, the children's pastor added, "I have had some first-generation teachers who are concerned ... how is that going to look? I am okay with the change, but how will it look for me?"

Some of the pastors and ministry leaders explained that in addition to the necessary conversations, staff adjustments would need to be made to accommodate first-generation volunteers. Also, a measure of encouragement would be needed with some of the first-generation volunteer staff who would feel intimidated by having to engage in ministry only in English. The children's pastor explained, "It is kind of like Josh's (senior pastor) fear, (that English) it is not my first language ... But I was clear with the teachers when we announced it to them ... we want you to keep serving; we do not want them to stop." She explained her conversation with some of the teachers. She told them, "If you are nervous or scared or anything, we do not want you to stop serving but continue ... if it ever it arises where you feel it is too hard, let me know, and we will partner you up with somebody else."

Question 3: The Question of change. When asked how they explained the change to those who had not heard the announcement of the implementation of the monolingual English service or those who questioned the decision, the pastors and ministry leaders responded by providing a strategic contextual awareness. This was done by reiterating the message that nothing is changing culturally except the adding of a service due to some emerging adults getting lost in translation, which was leading to the silent exodus. In addition, church members were also encouraged to review the silent exodus sermon series given at Faro Church to explain the need for the monolingual English service. This two-week series given on August 26, 2018, and September 2, 2018, served as the primary driving mechanism by which the implementation of the English service was announced and explained to the church at large (See the series at https://www.youtube.com/watch?v=kocu8va07ag and https://www.youtube.com/watch?v=OBuCcxVDrzo).

Some of the questions that the pastors and leaders received revolved around the natural fear of change: "What is going to happen?" and "Is this changing us?" What was helpful in those conversations was explaining the purpose of retention and recruitment among Latino emerging adults. The senior pastor explained, "What is changing is that we (now) have an English only service ... the only difference (in that service) is that now there is no Spanish associated to it ... no translation, but nothing else changes." The senior pastor further explained that he tells inquirers that "we are doing this to have the ability to reach the people we are not reaching." Similarly, a male, first-generation ministry leader explained the change by "trying to relieve some of the pressure and nervousness by addressing that not much is changing and that they are getting the same thing they would in the first (9 a.m. bilingual) service."

A female, third-generation pastor described how she explained the implementation of the monolingual English service to her close friends and family. She said, "They thought that it was weird that we were having an English-only service because they thought ... 'you (Faro Church) are bilingual.'" However, she explained, "We are losing some of our second and third generation, who speak English first. Some of them were really excited because, for them, the bilingual or the translation is a lot for them."

Others questioned whether the monolingual English service would be changed enough. To this, the senior pastor responded, "What I have heard from English-only-speaking people that come to church is that they get lost in the translation ... that bothers them. They love the church, but they cannot handle that. That is why the change is important ... to retain those people."

There were also concerns revolving around the church's digital presence. Some, upon coming across the online announcement, asked if the church was "splitting up." In response, a female, third-generation pastor explained, "We are not a (planting) a different church in English." Additionally, although the announcement on social media was well received and understood by most, it was necessary to provide additional references. The ministry leader explained, "On Facebook and Instagram, they were referred to Pastor Steve's YouTube sermon as the answer and for more detail ... the silent exodus series."

The common understanding among the leaders and adherents of Faro Church was that the silent exodus series existed as the fundamental driving mechanism by which the implementation of the English service was announced and explained. The children's ministry pastor explained, "I let my teachers know on the newsletter, if you missed Pastor Steve's two sermons, please go on YouTube and watch it." A female third-generation pastor ministry leader agreed, "I have sent the links to people who have asked." A male first-generation ministry leader clarified, "I feel that if unless they missed both of them, then they would not have been able to tell because it was very explicit."

Question 5: Comments from Adherents. When asked to share any comments they had heard about the decision to implement a monolingual English service, the pastors and leaders of Faro Church responded candidly, some expressing words of approval and support, while others expressed words of doubt and concern. A female third-generation pastor shared what she heard: "That is awesome, so good, great, excited to see what will happen with this change." A typical comment heard by the pastors can be summarized by the comment of a male, first-generation pastor who heard, "When is the Spanish-only service coming?" The ministries pastor agreed, "Very similar ... Spanish only comes up a lot."

The children's pastor provided some comic relief as she explained, "The only one I can think about was, 'Why did the bilingual service have to be the first one at 9 a.m. instead of 11 a.m.?' They are interested in sleeping in. She loves the idea, but why did it have to be the first service? Similarly, the ministries pastor heard people comment, "I have to wake up earlier now (to attend the bilingual)." He further provided some helpful detail:

We get a good group that comes to the second service that is bilingual but predominately Spanish. However, in the past month, this group is training themselves to wake up earlier. This group is a group that is predominately Spanish speaking but more acclimated to the United States, yet they hold on to that identity. This group includes a Vietnam war vet and an entrepreneur. Their roots are here but have not let go of their culture. Different to a person that came just a few years ago and still cannot speak the language. The church is part of the culture and identity that they are holding onto. But his group is on board with the change. They are not fighting it. They are just joking about waking up earlier to attend the bilingual service. It is not a question of being against it but what it means to their personal convenience.

In addition to the initial purpose of retention and recruitment, the younger demographic of Faro Church seemed to express to the pastors of the church that one of the desired potential outcomes was further worship engagement and discipleship. They felt that the removal of the bilingual impediment would allow for such engagement. Consequently, among the younger demographic, the male, second-generation youth pastor explained, "With us, the discussion has been whether we are going to go. This could be an opportunity for us to do something with them because it will attract a lot of English-only youth and families...."

Refreshingly, a female, third-generation pastor provided some context. She said that she heard some adherents say that they

> "appreciate that the pastors are aware of the change and how they communicate it to the church... they have been so intentional. Every time there is a change, they are not freaking out, but they explain it and what it produces and what it serves. So, I think a lot of these members now trust and are ok and continue to be faithful."

Findings from the Post-Focus Group

The post-focus group demonstrated affirming attitudes toward the benefits of a monolingual English service. It provided optimistic stories and testimonies of new and returning emerging adults and intermarried couples who attend Faro Church as a result of the implemented mono-lingual English service.

Question 1: The Question of feelings about the implementation. When asked to express their conclusive feelings about the implemented monolingual English service at Faro Church, the pastors and ministry leaders described evidence of recruitment and retention of Latino emerging adults, acknowledged the unintended impact on the bilingual (9 a.m.) service, and expressed words of approval and further interest.

A male, first-generation Latino ministry leader spoke of the visual evidence on recruitment. He stated, "I see more people coming who speak only English, and that is good." Similarly, a female, second-generation ministry leader commented, "I know that initially, we thought we were going to get more third-generation ... but now we see a different type of demographic, so that has been really interesting to see." She explained, "I have seen an Asian family, just different kinds. Not neces-sarily what we were expecting. We are casting a wider net. I do see that different people are coming.

One focus group participant commented, "One of the things, I thought we were going to see was more Caucasian, English, but what we have been seeing is more multicultural people. There is a big differ-ence between the two." A male, first-generation, Latino pastor shared a similar sentiment describing a different draw. He said, "I see people I did not expect to see ... I thought they were more predominantly Spanish speaking; I actually see them only to the English service."

The male, second-generation, Latino worship pastor shared how the transition affected him and his team. He said, "From the worship per-spective, it was a lot smoother than I thought it would be." A female, second-generation, Latina ministry leader introduced the unintended and unexpected impact on the 9 a.m. bilingual service upon the imple-mentation of the monolingual English service. From a children's min-istry perspective, she shared, "it helped our numbers in our first service (bilingual); there are less kids in the English service, but it helps us to teach better. One focus group participant agreed, "The same for the sanctuary; I feel it has filled all the room in the 9 a.m. service." Further, a female, second-generation, Latina ministry leader added that from a logistics perspective "our bilingual service is our most-attended service ... we have to put out some extra chairs. The senior pastor explained, "People who would go to the 11 a.m. bilingual service started coming to the 9 a.m. (after the implementation of the monolingual English service); that is why it got filled."

The focus group discussed that perhaps the bilingual factor and not the time was the driver for this unintended increase in attendance to the bilingual 9 a.m. service. A female, second-generation, Latina ministry leader explained, "I think that we see most of the families at the bilingual service because there is that language preference between parents and their kids." In contrast, she continued, "Our English service is attracting more couples and young families, not the older concept (Latino) families that come to our bilingual service." Another female, second-generation, Latina ministry leader summarized the draw of the monolingual English service, saying that it is drawing primarily "young adults."

A welcomed added benefit of the monolingual English service was the more profound worship engagement and discipleship. A male, second-generation ministry leader explained:

I have heard from some young adults that were in the only English (service) ... that it has enabled them to understand Pastor Josh's message better, and they feel they do not get lost in the translation ... one of them said, "I understand the message better now that it is just in one language."

As it relates to the appeal of the monolingual English service among the intermarried couples, one focus-group participant provided evidence of attraction. He stated, "I heard of a specific couple where the husband would attend our church and the wife would attend another church ... but since we started the monolingual English, they are now both coming here." One focus group participant added, "Yeah, that is what I have noticed, besides young adults, it is the interracial couples ...

the wives may know both languages, but the husband speaks English or vice versa ... they are coming to the service (monolingual English service) too."

Upon discussing how feelings may have changed since the implementation of the monolingual English service, the pastors and leaders of Faro Church expressed further excitement and expectancy. A male, first-generation ministry leader explained, "I am more excited because at first, I had said, I was expectant ... but now I am looking forward to it." Another second-generation ministry leader added, "I was not too sure how it was going to ... bring in and retain the second-and third-generation ... but it has been cool hearing them say I am going to go because it is English only."

Question 2: The actualization of initial concerns. When asked about the actualization of initial questions or concerns, the pastors and ministry leaders of Faro Church expressed that the ability of the senior pastor to preach in English, the acclimation to the new service, the separation of church culture, and the first-generation feeling they were left behind were the primary factors related to their concerns.

A female, second-generation Latina ministry leader explained, "I had that fear but ... I have seen people who tried it out (the monolingual English service) and ended up liking it. So, I think that I see it progressing."

The senior pastor reminded the focus group, "The concern for me was preaching in English ... that was a big one ... yeah, it has been actualized." He explained, "The first three weeks were very rough for me ... it created a lot more work for me as a speaker because I have to basically prepare two sermons."

As it relates to children's ministry worship, a female, third-generation, Latina explained, "The work was actualized in all parts ... for kids' worship, we do slides; I have to have bilingual and English-only slides." She added, "The kids who sing with me ... a couple of them speak primarily in Spanish, so I have to work on the English pronunciation with them and those who speak predominantly English work with the Spanish pronunciation with them." However, she explained:

I would say it is a burden, for them, it is great because they are learning that second language and especially for the Spanish speakers because they get to practice their English and vice versa. And it allows us to build a relationship with the singers, but they have gotten more familiar with the songs and, they have become comfortable singing it too.

As it related to the worship team, the worship pastor stated:

At the beginning, I was scared, that I was still going to speak Spanish (in the monolingual English service), and it was actualized for me. I am so used to translating for myself (in the bilingual service); I do not have a translator during worship; I do it bilingual myself ... we were just so used to the groove of it; it has been a challenge.

The senior pastor related, "In one of the sermons (during the monolingual English service), I started speaking Spanish ... and five seconds into it, I was like wait, rewind, rewind."

There was an actualized concern that revolved around the idea of creating two separate cultural atmospheres. One focus-group participant said, "There are two different feelings ... the bilingual (service) is more vibrant; people say 'amen' back to you; they are more involved ...." In contrast, he said, "The English service is more ... and I hate to say what I am going to say, but it does represent the people we want to reach ... they are there with their cup of coffee ... (thinking) 'so good, so good.'" Another focus group participant agreed, "They are more relaxed." Comically, one focus-group participant commented, "I go to the (monolingual English) service ... and I think ... 'that was good.'"

Another concern was first-generation Latinos feeling ostracized by the implementation of the monolingual English service; however, unexpectedly, some are actually drawn to the English service rather than the bilingual. One focus-group participant, a second-generation male Latino said, "I identified several members of our church that I thought would attend the bilingual service, but they are coming to the English. I would have never thought that family or group coming to the English service. I thought they would be at the bilingual service." In agreement, one focus group participant observed, "You think ... 'they are in the English service' I would have never thought these people would attend the English service—a different demographic within the church."

Question 3: The Question of change. When asked to share how the implementation of the monolingual service changed the church, the pastors and leaders of Faro Church provided several reactions, including unexpected camaraderie, an increase in intergenerational interaction and attendance, increased evangelistic appeal, ministry opportunities, enhanced worship engagement, and interchange between logical processing and emotional engagement.

The implementation of the monolingual English service allowed Faro Church to follow through in the recognition of the need to implement a monolingual Spanish service due to space restriction in the main sanctuary. One focus group participant explained, "It allowed us to see the need for the Spanish-only service." Another focus group participant added, "We had already been discussing the Spanish service as a third option but decided we absolutely needed to have a Spanish service."

The unexpected but welcomed camaraderie created by the filled sanctuary during the 9 a.m. bilingual service, upon the implementation of the monolingual English service, created an appealing environment to many adherents. One focus group participant said, "More people [are] mingling because they are not coming to a different service, or because of the overlap." Another focus group participant added, "People are sticking around longer than before. Before people would disperse a lot faster; now they are hanging out more."

The implementation of the monolingual English service also delivered an increase in intergenerational interaction and attendance. One focus group participant guessed, "I think that our attendance has increased. It feels like there is an increase. I think an average of about forty to fifty people more. Right?" One focus group participant provided an example:

Josh mentioned the couple that attended different churches; I do know of a family that started coming and only show up to the English service and are brand new from the moment we started the English service, and that is a family of four. So, that is an example of a family that is coming only because we started the English service. I have never seen that family attend any of our other services. They were brand new when we made the change.

A female, third-generation Latina ministry leader explained the intergenerational interaction. She said, "I see more young people interacting and engaging with (older) people, not just among themselves, but around other adults. I do not know if that has to do with feeling more noticed."

A male, first-generation Latino ministry leader spoke about a new evangelistic appeal. About the provision of the three services, he said, "I think it sounds better ... when you invite people, you can tell them that there are three services to choose from. It makes the invitation stronger."

Pastor and ministry leaders also commented on new ministry opportunities created by the monolingual English service. The children's pastor provided one example:

There have been more opportunities (for) the assistants (teachers) to actually teach ... relying on them a lot more and using them more, no matter what their age has been. If they want to do it, from the kid that is nine years old to older kids, they have that opportunity to serve.

The monolingual English service has also provided deeper worship engagement. The worship pastor explained, "Because of the bilingual service, we were only able to sing one verse because the second verse was the same verse in the other language ... It felt like we would repeat the song so much ... now, we can sing the normal song."

Finally, the monolingual English service has helped pastors and leaders acknowledge that there will be varying worship interactions with some generations leaning toward logical processing and others toward emotional engagement. A female, third-generation Latina ministry leader explained, "It is just a different response because of the type of people that are in each service. First service (9 a.m. bilingual) they may be ... responsive in terms of energy ... (during) the sermon they may be the ones shouting Amen and Halleluiah." She continued and contrasted, "For the English service ... when they are receiving the Word, they are taking it in, and afterward the way they want to respond ... (is) to have this conversation about how it affected me."

Question 4: The Question of retention and recruitment. When asked about the vitality of the implementation of the monolingual English service to the retention and evangelizing of emerging adults, the pastors and ministry leaders of Faro Church answered by sharing encouraging eyewitness accounts of its effectiveness with added unexpected engagement.

The senior pastor explained the success in recruitment of the emerging adult Latinos of Faro Church by stating, "For sure, it is reaching that target audience." He further explained, "If you come to our English service, that is what you see, emerging adults ... you only see a few older couples; everyone else is young adults." In agreement, the children's pastor noted, "That is true because we notice the drop in attendance in the kid's classes ... and we think ... well, look who's in there (the sanctuary) ... they do not have kids yet ... they are young couples." As it relates to retention, a Latina, female, second-generation ministry leader said, "I have seen people that maybe have not been here in a while ... and maybe its curiosity or they just want to try it again ... try a different service ... I have noticed people who have not been here in a while."

The monolingual English service has also helped not only in recruitment and retention, but it has also added an element of deeper engagement. The senior pastor explained, "When we had our bilingual services, I would hear [feedback about the sermon] from older people ... but now with the English service, to hear it from younger people is weird because before, I would never hear it. He continued, "So, people tell me, thank you for this series, those were things I would hear before from first-generation not emerging adults." The youth pastor provided further explanation. He said, "In my opinion that has been one of the biggest effects that the monolingual service has had ... I speak both languages fluently, [but] I understand more in the English-only service ... I am more engaged in the Word...." He summarized, "So, more than just evangelizing and retaining, getting them to engage deeper with the Word is probably going to be a bigger effect ... we will not be able to measure it, to be able to put it on a graph."

Question 5: Commentaries. When asked about unforeseen challenges or changes because of the implementation of the monolingual English service naturally, the pastors and ministry leaders of Faro Church answered by pointing directly to the implementation of the monolingual Spanish service. As explained earlier in this chapter, due to the increased attendance to the 9 a.m. bilingual service, logistically, the elders and pastors of Faro Church had to create a sense of reprieve as the meeting space was straining at capacity. Therefore, the first option of relief was the resolution to implement a monolingual Spanish service to start on April 21, 2019, after the fifteen-week research period of the monolingual English service. This was decided, early in February, based on the opportunity to serve the monolingual Spanish-speaking adherents of the church community while keeping the desired focus on retaining and recruiting emerging Latino adults through the monolingual English service. Consequently, since Easter Sunday, April 21, 2019, Faro Church has provided three services: an 8 a.m. monolingual Spanish service, a 9:30 a.m. bilingual (English and Spanish) service, and an 11 a.m. monolingual English service.

In addition, the pastors and ministry leaders of the church spoke about the effect on the discipleship ministry of the church. A first-generation, male Latino said, "One of the challenges is that we are getting more people that speak only English ... so how do we transition to offer the discipleship (courses) in English only ... how do we connect them more into the culture of the church ... into the ministries of the church."

Furthermore, the monolingual English service seemed to provide a different worship expression from its adherents. One focus group participant explained, "I did not expect that ... [it] was super hard, honestly, [it was] like two different churches [in terms of personality]." Another focus-group participant jested, "like going from a Pentecostal church to a Baptist church." However, some anticipated the difference in response. One focus group participant explained, "We did kind of know that was going to happen ... we expected that ... maybe it was just me." A female, Latina, first-generation ministry leader reminded the focus group, "The majority of the people who attend the third service are kind of new ... they are trying to figure out how the church environment is."

The monolingual English service seems to be providing a layering of cultures, among them, a generational culture, a church culture, and an institutional culture. The challenge is teasing out what is Faro culture and what is not. One focus-group participant explained, "It is more indicative of what American culture is like and the third-generation being more assimilated than first-generation." He continued:

First-generation bring in more of the traditional church shouts more open to spirit Pentecostal fire–preaching type ... where second and third are more mellow, and I think it has to do with higher education ... second-and third-generation are used to sitting in class, listening to the teacher whereas most first-generation Hispanics probably would not have that experience.

Ultimately, the monolingual English service has provided the unexpected challenge of synergy and camaraderie. However, the pastors and ministry leaders of Faro Church agreed that, as stated by one focus-group participant, "Church culture is set by the message, not the method." Therefore, the focus groups demonstrated that Faro Church was mostly prepared and ready to face the challenges and changes during and after the implementation of a monolingual English service. Consequently, the focus groups provided vital qualitative data concerning the changing demographics and ministry preferences of second- and third-plus-generation Latinos, including intermarried Latinos in the church at large.

Summary of Findings

This study analyzed the data in three main sections to answer the primary areas of research. The first section analyzed the diverse sample of qualitative sources collected from a sample of first-, second-, and third-plus-generation Latinos. The second section provided a quantitative analysis of a broader scope of observations and data that contribute to the primary area of research. The third section considered a mixture of extraneous or intervening variables for the research.

Ultimately, this research provided data surveying the impact of monolingual English church services on the reduction of the silent exodus of second- and third-plus-generation Latinos, including intermarried Latinos, at Faro Church. The results demonstrated that acknowledging and meeting expectations of specific lingual, generational, and cultural ideologies among Latino Americans are incredibly vital to the existential realities of first-generation monolingual Spanish churches.

Conclusions and Applications

Given the considerable and changing differences in population, sociological factors, fluency in English, and religious attitudes between foreign-born Latinos and native-born Latinos, there are profound implications for many realms of the mission of Latino churches in America and indeed for anyone seeking to understand the nature of changing demographics in multicultural, yet monoethnic churches, in the United States.

Ministry trends and outreach need to acknowledge and change toward shifts in population, sociological factors, and the growth of English-dominant Latinos. Hence, this study explored the implementation of a monolingual English service at Faro Church and its ability to target and retain second- and third-plus-generation Latinos, including intermarried couples.

Applications

The research explored and challenged the reluctance of Spanish speaking dominant churches to accommodate to changing demographics and found that a commitment by first-generation Latino church leaders to evangelize and disciple second- and third-plus-generation Latinos, including intermarried Latinos, primarily through a monolingual English church service is a successful model in their retention.

Changes in the general composition of the Latino population have severe consequences for first-generation Latino churches hoping to retain second- and third-generation Latinos. Such was the challenge and opportunity for Faro Church, a bilingual, multicultural, and mostly monoethnic church in Southern California.

As explained in this book, part of the research purpose was to implement a monolingual English service as a conscientious effort to combat the plateau in the "life cycle" of Faro Church (Malphurs, 2013, p. 9). This research encompassed the implementation of monolingual English church services in order to reduce the silent exodus of second- and third-plus-generation Latinos, including intermarried Latinos, by removing the bilingual and Spanish-language barrier. These competing lingual ideologies threatened the church's existence and created missional challenges.

Research Questions Addressed

Two hypotheses provided a framework for the research design. First, this study theorized that the implementation of a monolingual English service might provoke a response from the second- and third-plus-generation Latino of a desire to maintain a connection with Faro Church and to continue to worship at the monolingual service.

The surveys of emerging adults of Faro Church seem to agree with this premise. In the surveys, the need for monolingual English services demonstrated a moderate vitality rating as a challenge for emerging adults (Figure 36). Similarly, the refusal to accommodate linguistic needs was identified as a significant ministry challenge in the retention and recruitment of emerging adults as indicated by an average of 2.4 survey points, a moderate ranking (Figure 37).

Similarly, the focus groups reported pleasant anticipation upon hearing news of the implementation of a monolingual English service, and when asked to speak on the vitality of the implementation of a monolingual English service to the retention and evangelizing of emerging adults, the focus group expressed an established agreement on its significance.

When asked whether they would attend the monolingual English service, most emerging adults responded affirmatively; only some said they would not attend due to familial ties and scheduling hindrances. The emerging adults also agreed that the monolingual English service would provide an added benefit to the evangelistic efforts of Faro Church. Additionally, the pastors and ministry leaders of Faro Church shared encouraging eyewitness accounts of the effectiveness of the retention and evangelizing of the emerging adults of Faro Church and spoke of an added unexpected worship engagement.

Similarly, the questionnaire of teachers of children and youth at Faro Church provided a clear quantitative picture of the centrality of the issue as the evidence yielded proof for the need of monolingual English church services and classes for the retention of second- and third-plus-generations and intermarried couples with children. The questionnaires revealed that 69 percent of the teachers of children and youth conduct their classes in English, 25 percent bilingual (either separate or simultaneous interpreting), and only 6 percent in Spanish (Table 14). Additionally, the questionnaire revealed that 88 percent of the students preferred English as their primary learning language (Table 15). Only one student was identified as preferring Spanish and one preferring bilingual as the primary learning language (Table 15).

The data seem to indicate that a monolingual English service initiated a trend to steadily and solidly reduce the silent exodus of second- and third-plus-generations of Latinos. The service allows emerging adults of

Faro Church to worship with their native congregation without having to seek other monolingual English alternatives or stop church attendance altogether. Subsequently, in keeping with the church's mission, the retention will aid the incremental quantitative growth of church attendance by the drawing disengaged, disillusioned, and disconnected emerging adults into the community.

Second, this study postulated that the implementation of a monolingual English worship service at Faro Church would provide worship space for intermarried Latinos to worship alongside spouses who may find a bilingual service linguistically challenging to adjust to but who still appreciate the multicultural atmosphere that draws their Latino spouse.

Both the qualitative and quantitative data demonstrated an equal appeal to the bilingual and monolingual English services as a way of retention and recruitment among intermarried Latinos. When asked to express opinions on the most significant benefits of attending a bilingual church, most respondents expressed linguistic enrichment, familial unification, intermarital benefit, and generational linkage as the primary driving factors (Research Findings II). Some respondents perceived this gained advantage either from the bilingual service or the English service.

Thus, the implementation allowed for more second- and third-plus-generation intermarried Latinos to worship at Faro Church without having to seek other monolingual English alternatives or stop church attendance altogether. Subsequently, in keeping with the church's mission, the retention will aid the incremental quantitative growth of church attendance by drawing disengaged, disillusioned, and disconnected intermarried Latinos into the church.

Application I:
Confirming Changing Demographics

The research data seem to confirm the changing demographics stated and outlined in Chapters 1 and 2 as they relate to changing linguistic patterns across generations, educational attainment for Latinos, and the need for varied linguistic ministry opportunities.

For example, the research found that linguistic preferences from the emerging adults of Faro Church and Latino Bible College confirmed "the three-generational pattern" (Ortman & Stevens, 2008, p. 3) of an overwhelming changing language preference toward bilingualism (Spanish and English) and monolingual English among second- and third-generation Latinos as revealed in the literature.

The pre- and post-surveys of emerging adults of Faro Church revealed that although all emerging adult respondents identified their ethnic origin as Latino, none elected the Spanish language as their primary language preference. When comparing both the pre- and post-preferences, this statistic was proven right even among the first-generation Latino respondents with six electing the bilingual language preference and three electing the English preference. Likewise, among second-generation Latino respondents, ten elected the bilingual language preference, and twenty-four elected the English language preference. As expected, the lone third-generation Latino respondent elected the English language preference.

Similarly, although all twenty-eight Latino Bible College partici-pants identified their ethnic origin as Latino, of the nine first-genera-tion surveys, six elected bilingual (English and Spanish) as their primary speaking language preference, one selected the English-only preference, and only one elected the Spanish-only preference. The lone third-gen-eration participant elected English as their primary speaking language, whereas twelve of the eighteen second-generation respondents elected bilingual and six elected English as their primary speaking language.

Also, confirming some of the growing educational attainment among Latinos, the emerging adults and intermarried couples of Faro Church seemed to confirm this data by demonstrating high rates of col-lege enrollment and degree attainment. Both the pre- and post-surveys of emerging adults of Faro Church revealed that more than half of the emerging adult respondents reported their highest level of education as having some college at 45 percent in the pre- and post-surveys, an associate's degree at 14 percent in the pre-survey, or a bachelor's degree at 18 percent in the pre-survey and 23 percent in the post-survey. Additionally, both the pre- and post-surveys revealed that intermarried adult respondents reported high levels of postgraduate degrees. The data appear to confirm the research reported in Part 1 stating that US-born Latinos have distinctly higher levels of education than their first-generation parents.

Furthermore, the number of surveys returned by each generation confirmed the apparent inability of both Faro Church and Latino Bible College to attract third-generation Latinos due to changing demographical needs and preferences. The emerging adults pre-survey only generated four surveys from the first-generation, seventeen from the second generation, and one from the third generation. Although the same number of surveys were returned for post-surveys, the only range was a +1 variable in a first-generation return and −1 variable in a third-generation return, confirming the discrepancy both before and after the fifteen-week research period and again reflecting the apparent inability to attract third-generation Latinos due to changing demographical needs and preferences.

The surveys of emerging adults of Latino Bible College generated nine from the first-generation, eighteen from the second-generation, and only one from the third-generation. This discrepancy demonstrated the apparent inability of Latino Bible College and Faro Church to attract third-generation Latino due to changing demographical needs and preferences.

On the other hand, the surveys seem to confirm the sustainable attraction of the second-generation bilingual appeal central to the mission of Faro Church and Latino Bible College. Consequently, the research findings may inspire church leaders to stimulate further ministry changes to better suit the demographics in their communities by providing both bilingual and monolingual services, not just one or the other, similar to the implementation researched here.

It is essential in understanding the silent exodus to recognize the unique general factors impacting Latino churches in America. Therefore, this research may serve as a catalyst to teach and train Latino leaders to better serve their communities by an awareness of the changing differences in population, sociological factors, fluency in English, and religious attitudes between foreign-born Latinos and native-born Latinos.

Application II:
Faro Church as a Model of Change

As stated in Chapter 2, the available evidence seems to suggest that the Latino population, which was 42 million in 2005, will rise to 128 million in 2050, tripling in size (Passel & Cohn, 2008, p. 1). On these grounds, it can be argued that the Latino church in America must create linguistic models that fit a ministry vision focused on the retention and recruitment of the growing population of Latinos in the United States.

A close look at the qualitative and quantitative findings of this research demonstrated that the implementation of the monolingual English service at Faro Church could serve as a template for Latino churches and organizations that minister to second- and third-plus-generation Latinos, including intermarried Latinos. Latino churches and organizations seeking to reach Latino emerging adults and intermarried couples must recognize the relevance of the implementation of a monolingual English service and its potential to reduce the silent exodus of second -and third-plus-generation Latinos, including intermarried Latinos. This is evidenced primarily by the quantitative growth of 29 people since the implementation of the monolingual English service as compared to the prior year church attendance average.

As outlined in Chapter 2, the implementation of the monolingual English service seemed to confirm Rodriguez's (2009) idea that traditionally White, English-dominant churches have failed to attract the growing number of second- and third-plus-generation Latinos due to cultural variances (p. 113). Underlining the importance of linguistic options and as evidenced by the qualitative data in this research, although many Latino emerging adults base their church attendance preference on community and atmosphere, most independent Latino emerging adults prefer to attend a monolingual English service with a Latino cultural component.

According to this research, younger Latino emerging adults seem to attend the bilingual service based on familial ties; however, as these emerging adults gain independence, they tend to show a preference toward a monolingual English service with a Latino cultural expression. That is to say, Latino emerging adults prefer a monolingual English service at a Latino church; however, if they demonstrate close first-generation familial ties, they are likely to attend a bilingual service to pander to the family.

Furthermore, as a result of the research, Faro Church gained a better understanding of the nature of the changing demographics among Latinos and the significant impact it has on the retention of emerging adults and intermarried couples. This process helped many adherents realize the changing demographics among second- and third-plus-generation Latinos, including intermarried Latinos, and the need to meet their needs.

Additionally, the implementation of the monolingual English service provides Latino servicing churches, ministries, and organizations a model to better prepare and engage second- and third-plus-generation Latinos, including intermarried Latinos by creating options relevant to linguistic needs. As an extension, many leaders within the scope of influence of Faro Church have witnessed and been encouraged by the evangelistic and discipleship efforts to retain and recruit second- and third-plus-generation Latinos, including intermarried Latinos. As a result, the researcher has been invited to share on the research findings among others at district leadership training for the Southern Pacific Youth Ministries of the Assemblies of God and the SoCal Network of the Assemblies of God. Additionally, the leadership of Faro Church has been invited to engage and mentor several churches in the transition and translation of ministry DNA to first-generation monolingual Spanish ministries in their attempt to meet changing demographical needs.

Application III:
Reaping the Benefits of the Monolingual English Service

As a result of the implementation and research behind the implementation of a monolingual English service, Faro Church will continue to reap the growing benefits of linguistic variety and appeal. Both qualitative and quantitative evidence demonstrated evidence of growth and clarified focus on the ministry goals among second- and third-plus-generation Latinos, including intermarried Latinos.

Faro Church saw considerable growth in numbers as it provided a worship space, through the monolingual English service, for the growing and changing Latino demographics of Lake Forest and Orange County. This study hypothesized that the implementation of a monolingual English service might provoke a response from the second- and third-plus-generation Latino of a desire to maintain a connection with Faro Church and to continue to worship at the monolingual service. This was evidenced by the quantitative evidence demonstrated in the fifteen-week average attendance of ninety-four people (Table 1). On Easter Sunday (April 21, 2019), the Sunday following the fifteen-week research period, the monolingual English service recorded an attendance of 120 people. This perhaps is pointing toward the potential growth outlook of the monolingual English service as in the past several years, Easter Sunday attendance numbers have helped Faro Church predict annual potential numerical likelihood.

The ministry saw an emerging sense of enthusiasm as second- and third-generation emerging adults at Faro Church felt that the church was meeting their needs and providing a place where they can invite their friends and family. Consequently, on logical grounds, the monolingual service has initiated a trend to steadily and solidly reduce the silent exodus of second- and third-plus-generations of Latinos. It allows for emerging adults of Faro Church to worship with their native congregation without having to seek other monolingual English alternatives or stop church attendance altogether. Subsequently, in keeping with the church's mission, the retention will aid the incremental quantitative growth of church attendance by the drawing disengaged, disillusioned, and disconnected emerging adults into the church community.

The church developed an enhanced evangelistic outreach that was limited by a bilingual model but significantly improved by a monolingual English service. When asked about their thoughts about the implementation of the monolingual English service with regard to the retention and evangelizing of emerging adults, most emerging adults of Faro Church responded with positive feedback optimistic outlook.

Application IV:
Navigating Two Worlds

As noted in this book, Justo Gonzalez noted that even though 60 percent of all Latinos are American citizens by birth, native-born Latinos—second- and third-plus-generation Latinos—are still "made to feel as if they are newcomers" due to cultural and ecclesiastical negligence (as cited in Smith-Christopher, 1996, p. 93). Latino churches must recognize, as outlined in the case studies in this book, the success of multilingual and multigenerational churches.

Case studies seem to be confirmed by the data findings of the research at hand dealing with the implementation of a monolingual English service at Faro Church. Therefore, leaders must embrace a more contextually appropriate ministry model for English-dominant Latinos who feel out of place or even unwelcome in churches that are exclusively Spanish speaking.

However, although Latino churches must realize that the Spanish monolingual model is generally not successful in retaining second- and third-plus-generation Latinos, they must acknowledge the foundational transgenerational linkage as it relates to worship needs. As stated above and evidenced by the qualitative data in this research, although many Latino emerging adults base their church attendance preference on community and atmosphere, most independent Latino emerging adults prefer to attend a monolingual English service. That is to say, most emerging Latino adults pick their worship preference primarily based on a relationship, and linguistic preferences are secondary when making a decision.

The monolingual English service provides a layering of cultures, among them, a generational culture, a church culture, and an institutional culture. Therefore, churches like Faro Church who offer services in monolingual Spanish, bilingual, and monolingual English are attempting to navigate and service two worlds that require greater diversity and generational awareness. Leaders in such churches are not either/or but are both/and, bilingual and bicultural, and, therefore, can navigate and serve in two worlds.

Therefore, the silent exodus of second- and third-plus-generation Latinos is addressed and reduced by the use of a monolingual English service as a primary tool for retention and recruitment. However, due to generational ties, it is not the only necessary tool. The monolingual English service must be tightly bound to a monolingual Spanish or bilingual service, creating space for the foundational element for a transition.

This challenge can be an opportunity to be a church of a healthy contextual ministry, a people with a healthy balance of both Spanish and English outreach that consequently mends linguistic and generational schisms by accepting a wholesome and healthy ministry approach to first-, second-, and third-generation Latinos.

For Further Research

Many challenges and opportunities still lie ahead for Faro Church. Although the bilingual model and the monolingual English service has served as a tool to retain and recruit second- and third-generation

Latinos, this addresses only one major challenge in the question of evangelization and discipleship among emerging adults.

Beyond the questions of culture and language, there are several more issues at hand to research as they relate to the evangelization and discipleship of emerging adults. This is reflected primarily through the data findings from the emerging adults of Faro Church and Latino Bible College. Consequently, the researcher identified five significant areas for further research related to reaching second- and third-plus-generation Latinos in Latino churches.

Does a Monolingual Language Allow for Deeper Engagement?

First, one of the primary peripheral benefits of the monolingual service was that it not only helped in recruitment and retention, but it has also added an element of deeper engagement. Those who attended said they understand the message more deeply due to the change of language. Perhaps, Mullin's three-stage model of immigrant ethnic churches can help church leaders understand how to better disciple second- and third-generation Latinos. This speaks of the challenge and question of worship and fellowship at a deeper level.

Does Sermon Relevance Trump Language Preference?

Second, perhaps one of the primary findings is the fact that, according to the research, the implementation of the monolingual English service goes beyond the meeting of a linguistic need. It is apparent that among the emerging adults and intermarried couples of Faro Church, the monolingual English service must meet specific contextual requirements. For example, for some, the subject matter of the sermon mattered more than the language preference. They desired more relatable topics as opposed to complicated, in-depth theological sermons. This speaks of the challenge and question of discipleship at a more relatable level.

The monolingual English service was beneficial in the retention of some of the emerging adults that grew up in Faro Church due to the familiarity to the senior pastor and the culture of Faro Church. However, in terms of recruitment and growth, there are challenges. Many respondents suggested a focus on changing sermon style because younger English-speaking millennials "want sermons that speak about the things they are going through."

Does Accent Have a Negative Connotation?

Third, further research is needed on the impact of cultural awareness and relativity as it relates to the recruitment and retainment of second- and third-plus-generation Latinos. Although at first glance it would appear that the speaker on any given Sunday did not seem to affect the attendance to the monolingual English service, the speaker did affect some of the potential to grow beyond the scope of Faro Church adherents. The implementation of the monolingual English service was met with enthusiastic expectations and evangelistic hopefulness; however, some members of the church also expressed a reserved fear about the senior pastor's ability to preach in English and his ability to appeal to a population outside the Faro Church realm of influence.

The emerging adults and intermarried couples of Faro Church explained that they understand the heart and conviction behind "having the same services and message" for all services, but they feel this can still be done with different speakers and subject matters. Further research in the field of cultural relevancy and its effect on the evangelization and discipleship of second- and third-plus-generation Latinos is needed. This is particularly important as it is not addressed in Mullins' "Three-Stage Model of Immigrant Churches" or Goette's Six-Stage Transformational Model for Immigrant Churches.

Lack of Personal Responsibility and Immorality as Primary Drivers of Disinterest and Desertion

Fourth, the data gathered seems to contribute to the idea that although emerging adults view the lack of monolingual English services as one of the primary reasons for disinterest with and desertion of the Latino church, it is not the primary driver, especially when contrasted to personal responsibility and morality, which appear to be the principal factors. For example, concerning the question dealing with the challenges of emerging adults in Latino churches, the most significant responses in both the surveys of emerging adults of Faro Church was connectivity (friends at church, hospitality), the lack of spiritual development (discipleship), and moral issues (i.e., drug, alcohol abuse, sex, etc.), all ranking as extremely vital. The emerging adults of Latino Bible College ranked the same three factors as extremely vital.

Relativity and Discipleship as Primary Challenges of Retention and Recruitment

Similarly, when asked about the most significant challenge in the retention and recruitment of emerging adult in Latino churches, the emerging adults of Faro Church ranked relativity (friends at church, hospitality), the lack of spiritual development (discipleship), and the inability to answer difficult theological questions all as extremely vital. The emerging adults of Latino Bible College ranked the same top two as extremely vital.

Chapter Summary

The implementation of a monolingual English service at Faro Church to target and retain second- and third-plus-generation Latinos, including intermarried couples, explored and challenged the reluctance of Spanish-speaking-dominant churches to accommodate changing demographics. The research found that a commitment by first-generation Latino church leaders to evangelize and disciple second- and third-plus-generation Latinos, including intermarried Latinos, primarily through a monolingual English church service is a successful model in their retention. However, due to generational ties, it is not the only necessary tool. The monolingual English service must be tightly bound to a monolingual Spanish or bilingual service, creating space for the foundational element for a transition.

The implementation of the monolingual English service steadily and solidly reduced the silent exodus by allowing the emerging adults and intermarried couples of Faro Church to worship with their native congregation without having to seek other monolingual English alternatives or stop church attendance altogether.

Additionally, the research confirmed the changing demographics as they relate to changing linguistic patterns across generations, educational attainment for Latinos, and the need for varied linguistic ministry opportunities. Furthermore, as a result of the research, the population of Faro Church gained a better understanding of the nature of the changing demographics among Latinos and the significant impact they have on the retention of emerging adults and intermarried couples.

Ultimately, the implementation of a monolingual English service provided space to be a church of a healthy contextual ministry, a people with a healthy balance of both Spanish and English outreach that can consequently mend linguistic and generational schisms by accepting a wholesome and healthy ministry approach to first-, second-, and third-generation Latinos.

As a result, Faro Church will continue to reap the growing benefits of linguistic variety and appeal. Both qualitative and quantitative evidence demonstrated evidence of growth and clarified focus on the ministry goals among second- and third-plus-generation Latinos, including intermarried Latinos. Faro Church saw considerable growth in numbers as it provided a worship space, through the monolingual English service, for the growing and changing Latino demographics of Lake Forest and Orange County.

REFERENCES

Alford, H. D. D. (1868). *The New Testament for English readers and a critical and explanatory commentary.* London, England: Deighton, Bell, and Co.

Allender, D. B. (2009). *Sabbath.* Nashville: Thomas Nelson.

Arce, C. (1981). A Reconsideration of Chicano culture and identity. *Daedalus, 110*(2), 177–191. https://www.jstor.org/stable/20024728

Arnett, J. J. (2000). Emerging adulthood: A theory of development from the late teens through the twenties. *American Psychologist, 55*(5), 469–480. https://doi.org/10.1037//0003-066x.55.5.469

Banks, R. (1993). *Redeeming the Routines: Bringing Theology to Life.* Wheaton: Victor Books/SP publications, Inc.

Bañuelas, A. J. (1995). *Mestizo Christianity: Theology from the Latino perspective.* Maryknoll, NY: Orbis Books.

Barna Group. (2019, December 4). 18-35-Year-Olds Rate the Church's Reputation for Justice. Retrieved from http: https://www.barna.com/research/churchs-reputation-for-justice/

Barna Group and Impact 360 Institute. (2018). *Gen Z: The Culture, Beliefs, and Motivations Shaping the Next Generation.*

Barnett, Larry. (2015). A General Introduction to the Next Generation Project: Understanding and Reversing Christianity's Recent Decline in the US. Retrieved from www.projectnextgen.org.

Baym, N. K. (2015). *Personal Connections in the Digital Age.* Malden, MA: Polity Press.

Brooks, David. (2015) *The Road of Character.* Random House, NY.

Calvillo, J. E., & Bailey, S. R. (2015). Latino religious affiliation and ethnic identity.

Journal for the Scientific Study of Religion, 54(1), 57–78. Retrieved from https://doi.org/10.1111/jssr.12164

Carroll, Jackson. (2006). *God's Potters: Pastoral Leadership and the Shaping of Congregations.* W.B. Eerdmans Publishing Co.

Carr, N. (2011). *The Shallows: What the Internet is Doing to our Brains.* New York: W. W. Norton & Company, Inc.

Chai, K. J. (1998). Competing for the second generation: English-language ministry at a Korean Protestant church. In R. S. Warner & J. G. Wittner (Eds.), *Gatherings in diaspora: Religious communities and the new immigration* (pp. 295–331). Philadelphia, PA: Temple University Press.

Choi, C. W., & Berhó, D. (2016). Ethnic identity maintenance within the Latino-

American church: A structuration perspective. *Journal of Intercultural Communication Research, 45*(2), 91–107. https://doi.org/10.1080/174 75759.2015.1086811

City of Lake Forest. (2017). *City of Lake Forest 2017 profile.* Retrieved from http://www.lakeforestca.gov/DocumentCenter/View/1227/ Lake-Forest-Demographic-Profile-Spring-2017-PDF?bidId=

Cohen, S. (Director). (2013). *The Innovation of Loneliness* [Motion Picture].

Conn, Harvie M. (1994). *The American City and the Evangelical Church: A Historical Overview.* Michigan: Baker Publishing Group.

Couchman, David. Facing the Challenge of Our Times. Equipping Christians to Respond

Biblically and Effectively to Postmodernism. *Evangel* 20.3 (Autumn 2002): 74–78.

Crane, K. R. (2003). *Latino churches: Faith, family, and ethnicity in the second generation.* New York, NY: LFB Scholarly.

Ebaugh, H. R., & Chafetz, J. S. (2000). Dilemmas of language in immigrant congregations: The tie that binds or the tower of Babel? *Review of Religious Research, 41*(4), 432–452. https://doi.org/10.2307/3512314

Ellisen, S. A. (2009) Everyone's question. In R. D. Winter & S. C. Hawthorne (Eds.), *Perspectives on the world Christian movement: A reader* (4th ed.). Pasadena, CA: William Carey Library.

Ennis, S. R., Rios-Vargas, M., & Albert, N. G. (2011, May). *The Hispanic population: 2010.* Retrieved from https://www.census.gov/prod/cen2010/ briefs/c2010br-04.pdf

Faro Church (2015) *Vision, mission, and objectives.* Retrieved December 17, 2018, from http://www.farochurch.com/vision.htm

Flores, A. (2017, September 18). *How the US Hispanic population is changing.* Retrieved from http://www.pewresearch.org/fact-tank/2017/09/18/how-the-u-s-hispanic-population-is-changing/

Galvan Estrada, R., III. (2015). Is a contextualized hermeneutic the future of Pentecostal readings? *Pneuma, 37*(3), 341–355. https://doi.org/10.1163/15700747–03703004

Galvan Estrada, R., III. (2018). Renewing theological education: Developing networks of Latino/a ethnocultural inclusion. *PentecoStudies: An Interdisciplinary Journal for Research on the Pentecostal and Charismatic Movements, 17*(2), 134–157. https://doi.org/10.1558/pent.36243

George, C. F., & Bird, W. (1993). *How to break growth barriers: Capturing overlooked opportunities for church growth.* Grand Rapids, MI: Baker Book House.

Goleman, Boyatzis, & McKee. (2013). *Primal Leadership: Unleashing the Power of Emotional Intelligence.* Harvard Business Press.

Goodstein, L. (2011, May 10). *Presbyterians Approve Ordination of Gay People.* Retrieved from The New York Times: http://www.nytimes.com/2011/05/11/us/11presbyterian.html

Greer, P., Horst, C., & Haggard, A. (2014). *Mission Drift: The Unspoken Crisis Facing Leaders, Charities, and Churches.* Grand Rapids: Baker Publishing Group.

Groothuis, D. (2000). *Truth Decay.* Downers Grove: IVP Books.

Guglani, L. (2016). American, Hispanic, Spanish-Speaking? Hispanic immigrants and the question of identity. *Journal of Language, Identity, and Education, 15*(6), 344–360. https://doi.org/10.1080/15348458.2016.1217161

Guinness, O., & Wells, D. (2012). *Christ Our Reconciler: Gospel, Church, World.* Downers Grove: InterVarsity Press.

Hernández, E., & Davis, K. G., III (2003*) Reconstructing the sacred tower: Challenge and promise of Latino/a theological education.* Scranton, PA: University of Scranton Press.

Howard, J. (2008, Sept/Oct 1). *Surviving the Subculture.* Relevant Magazine.

Hunter, J. D. (2010). *To Change the World: The Irony, Tragedy, and Possibility of Christianity in the Late Modern World.* Oxford: Oxford University Press.

Jelden, I. (2015, June 24). *Faro Church reflects community.* Retrieved from https://www.ocregister.com/2015/06/24/jelden-faro-church-reflects-community/

Kaiser, W. C. (2009) Israel's missionary call. In R. D. Winter & S. C. Hawthorne (Eds.), *Perspectives on the world Christian movement: A reader* (4th ed.). Pasadena, CA: William Carey Library.

Kinnaman, D. (2011). *You Lost Me: Why Young Christians Are Leaving Church . . . and Rethinking Faith.* Grand Rapids: Baker Books.

Krogstad, J. M. (2016, April 20a). *English proficiency's rise among Hispanics driven by young.* Retrieved from http://www.pewresearch.org/fact-tank/2016/04/20/rise-in-english-proficiency-among-u-s-hispanics-is-driven-by-the-young/

Krogstad, J. M. (2016, July 28b). *5 facts about Latinos and education.* Retrieved from http://www.pewresearch.org/fact-tank/2016/07/28/5-facts-about-latinos-and-education/

Krogstad, J. M. (2017, August 3). US Hispanic population growth has leveled off.

Retrieved from http://www.pewresearch.org/fact-tank/2017/08/03/u-s-hispanic-population-growth-has-leveled-off/

Krogstad, J. M., & Lopez, M. H. (2017, October 31). Spanish speaking declines for Hispanics in US metro areas. Retrieved from http://www.pewresearch.org/fact-tank/2017/10/31/use-of-spanish-declines-among-latinos-in-major-u-s-metros/

Kwon, H-Y., Kim, K. C., & Warner, R. S. (2001). *Korean Americans and their religions: Pilgrims and missionaries from a different shore.* University Park, PA: Pennsylvania State University Press.

Ledbetter, Banks, & Greenhalgh. (2016) *Reviewing Leadership: A Christian Evaluation of Current Approaches.* Baker Academic.

Lopez, M. H., Gonzalez-Barrera, A., & López, G. (2017, December 20). Hispanic identity fades across generations as immigrant connections fall away. Retrieved from http://www.pewhispanic.org/2017/12/20/hispanic-identity-fades-across-generations-as-immigrant-connections-fall-away/

Malphurs, A. (2013). *Advanced strategic planning: A 21st-century model for church and ministry leaders.* Grand Rapids, MI: Baker Books.

Martínez, A. E. (2011). US Hispanic/Latino biblical interpretation: a critique from within. *Theology Today, 68*(2), 134–148. https://doi.org/10.1177/0040573611405881

Martî, G. (2015). Latino Protestants and their congregations: Establishing an agenda for sociological research. *Sociology of Religion, 76*(2), 145–154. Retrieved from https://doi.org/10.1093/socrel/srv016

Mission Ebenezer Family Church. (2017) *About the mission.* Retrieved December 17, 2018, from http://www.missionebenezer.org/about

Moreau, S., Corwin, G. R., & McGee, G. B. (2004) *Introducing world missions: A biblical, historical, and practical survey.* Grand Rapids, MI: Baker Academic.

Mullins, M. (1987). The life-cycle of ethnic churches in sociological perspective. *Japanese Journal of Religious Studies, 14*(4), 321–334. https://doi.org/10.18874/jjrs.14.4.1987.321–334

Myers, B. L. (2017). *Engaging Globalization.* Grand Rapids: Baker Academic.

New King James Version. (1982). HarperCollins Publishers.

Ortiz, M. (1993). *The Hispanic challenge: Opportunities confronting the church.* Downers Grove, IL: InterVarsity Press.

Ortman, J. M., & Stevens, G. (2008, February 16). *Shift happens, but when? Inter- and intra-generational language shift among Hispanic Americans.* Paper presented at the Population Association of America 2008 Meeting, New Orleans, LA. Retrieved from http://paa2008.princeton.edu/papers/80685

Passel, J. S., & Cohn, D. (2008, February 11). *US population projections: 2005–2050.* Retrieved from http://www.pewhispanic.org/2008/02/11/us-population-projections-2005–2050/

Passel, J. S., Cohn, D., & Lopez, M. H. (2011, March 24). *Hispanics account for more than half of nation's growth in past decade.* Retrieved from http://www.pewhispanic.org/2011/03/24/hispanics-account-for-more-than-half-of-nations-growth-in-past-decade/

Pew Research Center. (2013, February 7). *Second-Generation Americans, A portrait of the adult children of immigrants.* Retrieved from http://www.pewsocialtrends.org/2013/02/07/second-generation-americans/

Pew Research Center. (2015, September 23). Sources of immigration to the US, by era. Retrieved from http://www.pewhispanic.org/2015/09/28/modern-immigration-wave-brings-59-million-to-u-s-driving-population-growth-and-change-through-2065/ph_2015-09-28_immigration-through-2065-06/

Presmanes, J. L. 2007. Bilingual liturgy: A US Latino perspective. *Liturgical Ministry, 16*(4), 139–46.

Rodríguez, D. A. (2008). Becoming all things to all Latinos: Case studies in contextualization from the barrio. *Stone-Campbell Journal, 11*(2), 199–211.

Rodríguez, D. A. (2009). Hispanic ministry where language is no barrier: church growth among US-born English-dominant Latinos. *Apuntes, 29*(3), 103–119.

Roxburgh, A. J. (1997). *The Missionary Congregation, Leadership, & Liminality.* Harrisburg, PA: Trinity Press International.

Sánchez, D. R. (2010). *Hispanic realities impacting America: Implications for evangelism & missions.* Fort Worth, TX: Church Starting Network.

Santa Biblia: Reina-Valera. (1995). Miami, FL: Sociedades Bíblicas Unidas.

Scazzero, P. (2015). *The emotionally healthy leader: How transforming your inner life will deeply transform your church, team, and the world.* Grand Rapids, MI: Zondervan.

Smith, Christian and Denton, M.L. (2005). *The Religious and Spiritual Lives of American Teenagers.* Oxford University Press Inc.: New York, NY.

Smith-Christopher, D. L. (1998). Review of Justo L. Gonzalez, Santa Biblia: The Bible through Hispanic eyes. *The Journal of Hispanic/Latino Theology, 5*(3), 52–56. Retrieved from https://digitalcommons.lmu.edu/cgi/viewcontent.cgi?referer=&httpsredir=1&article=1323&context=theo_fac

Spurgeon, C. H. (1879, July 20). Our Motto Sermon #1484. *Metropolitan Tabernacle Pulpit.*

Spurgeon, C. H. (2016). *The Soul Winner.* Kansas City: Gideon House Books.

Stevens, W. D., (2004). Spreading the Word: Religious beliefs and the evolution of immigrant congregations. *Sociology of Religion, 65*(2), 121. https://doi.org/10.2307/3712402

Suro, R., & Passel, J. S. (2003, October 2003). *The rise of the second generation: changing patterns in Hispanic population growth.* Retrieved from https://files.eric.ed.gov/fulltext/ED481813.pdf

Templo Calvario. (2018). *Our story.* Retrieved from http://templocalvarioenglish.com/about-us/our-history/

Thayer, J. H. (1995). *Thayer's Greek-English lexicon of the New Testament.* Peabody, MA: Hendrickson.

The Holy Bible, NIV. (1984). Grand Rapids: Zondervan Publishing House.

Turkle, S. (February 2012). Connected, But Alone? Retrieved from https://www.ted.com/talks/sherry_turkle_connected_but_alone?language=en

Van Veen, D. (2017, December 05). *A man with a mission: Pastor Danny de León.* Retrieved from https://news.ag.org/features/a-man-with-a-mission-pastor-danny-de-leon

Yang, F., & Enbaugh, H. R. (2001). Religion and ethnicity among new immigrants: The impact of majority/minority status in home and host countries. *Journal for the Scientific Study of Religion, 40*(3), 367–368. https://doi.org/10.1111/0021-8294.00063

ABOUT THE AUTHOR

D r. Steve Pinto serves as the Associate Pastor of Faro Church, a multicultural and bilingual fellowship he and his brother planted in the heart of Orange County, CA. His knowledge of God's Word and love for people, mixed with his high energy and sense of humor, has been a powerful tool in God's hands as a keynote speaker at various youth events, camps, and conventions. Additionally, he functions as an adjunct professor at Vanguard University and LABI College. His primary teaching areas are Christian Worldview, Youth Ministry, Effective Leadership, Discipleship Making, and Expository Preaching. He and his wife, Diane, live in Southern California with their children, Alexi and Nathan.

CPSIA information can be obtained
at www.ICGtesting.com
Printed in the USA
BVHW061355040321
601715BV00007B/463

9 781662 805004